FREE SPACES

FREE
SPACES

THE SOURCES OF DEMOCRATIC
CHANGE IN AMERICA

Sara M. Evans and Harry C. Boyte

HARPER & ROW, PUBLISHERS, *New York*
Cambridge, Philadelphia, San Francisco, London,
Mexico City, São Paulo, Singapore, Sydney

1817

For Craig and Rachel

FIRST EDITION

Designer: Sidney Feinberg

Library of Congress Cataloging-in-Publication Data

Evans, Sara M. (Sara Margaret), 1943–
  Free spaces.

  Includes index.
  1. Social movements—United States—History.
2. Democracy. I. Boyte, Harry Chatten, 1945–
II. Title.
HN57.E9   1986   303.4'84   85-45191
ISBN 0-06-015509-4

86 87 88 89 90 HC 10 9 8 7 6 5 4 3 2 1

CONTENTS

PREFACE AND ACKNOWLEDGMENTS

"Free spaces" is a term that evokes complex, sometimes contra-
dictory thoughts and images for those with whom we have
discussed our ideas about the subject over the years. Women
active in the early years of the modern feminist movement
often associate it with the exhilarating and intense small group
discussions through which women discover that their personal
experiences were shared.* Those involved in the earlier civil
rights days in the Deep South remember the "free pulpit" of
the black church, in many communities the only public platform that had seriously and honestly addressed the contradictions and shame of southern culture. For students of the Third
World, free spaces suggest the "liberated zones" created by the
struggles of independence movements. In contrast, skeptics
customarily raise the specter of right-wing groups like the Ku
Klux Klan, arguing that what we describe could just as easily
apply to them. Along a rather different axis, one friend with a
background in the physical sciences says the idea inevitably
conveys space travel.

The diverse resonances and ambiguities make a central point:
free spaces are not a single "thing"; their boundaries are not

*Indeed, Pamela Allen described the early women's liberation groups in a
pamphlet entitled *Free Space: A Perspective on the Small Groups in Women's
Liberation* (New York: Times Change, 1970).

neat or quantifiable. Indeed, the nature of the criticism of the idea itself reflects certain fundamental issues that the concept seeks to address. The idea of free spaces, and the lived realities behind the idea, highlight limitations in the very language and terms of much of social science. Democratic values, human dignity, or the themes of citizenship and a vision of the common good are not reducible to the "resource mobilization" approach of most contemporary social movement theory, nor the charts and graphs used by Marxists to define the "class location" or "objective determinants of oppression" of various social group-ings, nor the voting behavior profiles of which modern political science is enamored.

We know that there is a well-established school of thought that disputes any significant analytical differences in the inter-nal dynamics of democratic movements, on the one hand, and right-wing, authoritarian movements, on the other. Yet we be-lieve that free spaces, complex and inevitably ambiguous, not only are real enough—their existence, we have found, is attested to eagerly by people who have actually experienced movements like civil rights and early feminism, or by those who have seriously and sympathetically explored past movements with a democratic cast. An understanding of their nature and function is also indispensable to an adequate understanding of the processes of social change. The participatory, egalitarian, and open character of public life at the heart of democratic movements is qualitatively unlike protests with a defensive and parochial cast like the Ku Klux Klan, where "public" has a much thinner and more static meaning (these themes are explored especially in our chapter on Populism, Chapter 5). And the very nature of public life in free spaces conveys older, richer mean-ings of the term "public,"pertaining to the community as a whole in its diversity, and notions of human dignity that mod-ern thought neglects to its considerable impoverishment. Thus we hope the arguments that *Free Spaces* helps to generate will focus in part on the relevance of these underlying themes—the nature of public life, the importance of community, the substance and meaning of democratic values—and on the features of conventional wisdom that have rendered such themes largely invisible.

Whatever the debate, we expect it will be useful and lively, as it has been over the years of our intellectual collaboration, common engagement in social movements and personal partnership. Indeed, for more than fifteen years, this concept of free spaces has formed an ongoing, continuous thread. We have also, in the course of discussing and developing the idea, benefited from an evolving intellectual community that, uncomfortably, is much too large to acknowledge properly. There are several, however, whose participation, feedback, encouragement, and creative engagement with these themes deserves thanks, expressly.

We talked in the Sixties about the "free environments" we perceived in civil rights, feminist activities, and particular sorts of community organizing (especially those that brought poor southern whites together with the black community in a new way). But we first wrote about the importance of "independent cultural institutions" in 1969 in an article challenging dominant directions in the student and antiwar movements called "The Blue Paper," which we coauthored with several others. Heather Booth, Paul Booth, and Steve Max, partners of ours in that first project, have continued to be colleagues over the years, in ways for which we are deeply grateful.

For more than a decade we explored aspects of the idea in our separate writings, only gradually developing a more general theory. Our work was considerably enriched by our discovery of E. P. Thompson's monumental treatment of the origins of the English working class. For instance, Harry Boyte's study of the history of protest in the southern textile industry highlighted the relative absence of autonomous institutions in southern mill villages. He contrasted the villages to the dense networks of local voluntary institutions that were the foundations of protest in early-nineteenth-century England, which E. P. Thompson described as "the people's own." There, "in the 'unsteepled' places of worship there was room for free intellectual life and for democratic experiments."*

Sara Evans' research on the origins of contemporary feminism centered on the problem of insurgent group consciousness. She used the term "social space" to highlight the experiential and communal rather than geographic dimensions of the idea. Conversations with Lawrence Goodwyn about early drafts of his book *Democratic Promise* reinforced ideas about the importance of "movement culture" with its autonomy, ideological effervescence, and intense community. Through the Seventies and into the Eighties new studies by others, many of them inspired by E. P. Thompson, explored diverse forms of independent social spaces and the oppositional subcultures that formed around them. In particular, the discovery of a female subculture in Victorian America was a major achievement of feminist historiography. Labor historians, led by Herbert Gutman, traced the critical links between labor militance and local communities. Similarly, black historiography in the same time revealed the importance of familial and religious institutions in the creation and maintenance of black culture and black resistance under slavery.

Harry Boyte's studies of community and citizen organizations in the 1970s showed that attentiveness to "free social spaces" led to a substantively different social mapping of the 1970s than conventional interpretations. Increasingly aware of the broader implications of the concept, we explored with Eugene Genovese the idea for an article arguing that "free social space" presents a fundamental challenge to Marxist political and social theory. That piece later appeared in *democracy.* The critical responses of Genovese and *democracy* editor Sheldon Wolin proved very helpful. Debates through these years with figures like Michael Harrington and Irving Howe, as well as the symposia that *Socialist Review* organized around Harry Boyte's

*E. P. Thompson, *The Making of the English Working Class* (New York: Vintage Books, 1963), p. 156.

articles, furnished useful feedback from democratic socialist points of view.

In 1981, Colin Greer insisted, with unrelenting determination, that we write a major piece on our concept of free social spaces for a book he planned to edit. The book was never published, it turned out, but we were left with a 90-page treatment of the idea, and a momentum that led to this work. As in other projects, Colin Greer's help was invaluable. In this book we have decided to use the term "free space" rather than "free social space," largely because the latter tends to be cumbersome and too reminiscent of social scientific jargon.

We want to thank a number of people whose feedback, ideas, and contributions have gone into this work over the years: Ron Aminzade, David Bensman, Craig Calhoun, William Chafe, Tom Dewar, Mary Dietz, Steven Foldes, Lawrence Goodwyn, Dorothy Healey, Richard Healey, Allen Isaacman, John Judis, Si Kahn, Amy Kaminsky, Manning Marable, Elaine May, Larry May, Mary Jo Maynes, Deborah Meier, Mike Miller, S. M. Miller, Elizabeth Minnich, Gianna Pomata, Riv-Ellen Prell, Peter Rachleff, Cheri Register, Frank Riessman, Emily Rosenberg, and Norman Rosenberg. Their help has been wonderful, when we have agreed with their thoughts and when we have disagreed, alike. We want to thank Janet Ferguson for her helpful proofreading. And we want especially to express our appreciation to our editors at Harper & Row, Hugh Van Dusen and Janet Goldstein, for their unflagging pressures on us to produce a manuscript that has some degree of readability.

Finally, we want to express our hope that the democratic legacy and aspirations described in these pages transform the world of our children, Craig and Rachel. It is to them that our work is dedicated, and for their future that it is written.

The genius of the United States is not best or most in its executives or legislatures, nor in its ambassadors or authors or colleges or churches or parlors, nor even in its newspapers or inventors . . . but always most in the common people . . . their good temper and openhandedness—the terrible significance of their elections—the President's taking off his hat to them not they to him—these too are unrhymed poetry. . . . The largeness of nature or the nation were monstrous without a corresponding largeness and generosity of the spirit of the citizen.

—WALT WHITMAN, *Leaves of*
Grass, 1855, Preface

CHAPTER 1

"THE PEOPLE SHALL RULE"

On June 28, 1822, Denmark Vesey stood before a Charleston, South Carolina, court for sentencing. The white judge addressed the silent black man with incredulity: "It is difficult to imagine what infatuation could have prompted you to attempt an enterprise so wild and visionary. You were a free man; were comparatively wealthy; and enjoyed every comfort compatible with your situation."[1]

Vesey embodied white southerners' deepest fears. An investigation of rumored plots among the slaves had uncovered a vast, well-planned conspiracy across hundreds of square miles. Vesey, a free carpenter and devout Christian, a man with apparently everything to lose and little to gain, was a key leader.

Vesey remained quiet before the bewildered judge, obedient to the injunction of his compatriot, Peter Royas, who said, "Do not open your lips! Die silent, as you shall see me do." He and thirty-six others were sentenced to death. Forty-three were forced into exile. Forty-eight more were whipped before being released for lack of evidence. Most were silent to the end.[2]

White Charlestonians constantly feared an eruption of murderous rage from their slaves. But they did not comprehend the complex realities of a man like Vesey, whose passionate religious convictions and leadership in a long struggle to maintain black churches' independence from white control had led directly to his leadership of the plot. Though southern whites worried about what went on in black worship services and periodically sought to control them, they had convinced themselves that Christianity pacified the black population. Black religion was thought to be "childlike" and otherworldly. Indeed, Christian conversion had been a mode of "root[ing] out all living connection with the [African] homeland," as black historian Vincent Harding has observed.

The paradox is that, far from succeeding, Christianity furnished the basic language of freedom for black Americans. And the places where it was practiced, from hidden services at the margins of plantations to black churches struggling to survive in southern cities, proved the staging areas for action. "The religion of white America," said Harding, "was insistently, continually wrested from the white mediators by black hands and minds and transformed into an instrument of struggle." Put simply, blacks, like the first Christians themselves, forged a religion of and by the slaves and the dispossessed. They found in the insights, language, and communion of religion a transformative source of self-affirmation. In doing so, they turned questions like those of the incredulous judge back on themselves, and challenged the very values that he equated with contentment and happiness.[3]

How is such radical transformation of value and culture possible? Where do ordinary people, steeped in lifelong experiences of humiliation, barred from acquisition of basic skills of citizenship—from running meetings to speaking in public—gain the courage, the self-confidence, and above all the hope to take action in their own behalf? What are the structures of support, the resources, and the experiences that generate the capacity and the inspiration to challenge "the way things are" and imagine a different world? To ask such questions is to challenge the fundamentals of conventional wisdom—and to pose in new ways the meaning and possibility of democracy in the modern world.

Democracy: "The People Shall Rule"

In 1975, a writer for *Business Week* magazine sounded a theme heard often in the business press during the decade. What previously people had accepted with gratitude, the man complained, now were assumed to be rights. The Sixties' social unrest had made the American public all too demanding and self-assertive about concerns that ranged from taxes to the environment. But the problem was not new. Current unruliness brought to the surface "a conflict as old as the American republic: the conflict between a political democracy and a capitalist economy."[4]

To say a fundamental conflict exists between capitalism and democracy sounds odd. The two are entwined in most people's minds, supposedly inseparable. But in fact up until the late nineteenth century, "democracy" was seen as a disturbing, even as a subversive, idea in polite society. The source of unease was obvious enough. From antiquity, democracy—simply, the notion that "the people shall rule"—had been associated with a constellation of ideas that accompanied wide-ranging efforts at social change.

Indeed, both subject and verb of the formulation that "the people shall rule" held unsettling implications. In the first instance, the meaning of "the people" denoted the idea of *popular power:* locating control over the institutions of society and government in the majority of the population, the common people. As Aristotle defined it, "a democracy is a state where the freemen and the poor, being in the majority, are invested with the power of the state." According to Plato, Socrates predicted that violence would inevitably accompany the transition to such government: "Democracy comes into being after the poor have conquered their opponents, slaughtering some and banishing others, while to the remainder they give an equal share of freedom and power."[5]

The insurgent content of the term, with its implications of a "world turned upside down," asserted itself repeatedly in democratic popular uprisings. One can imagine the terror which John Ball, leader of a fourteenth-century English peasant revolt, struck in the hearts of the powerful when he orated: "Things cannot go well in England, nor ever will, until all goods are held in common and until there will be neither serfs nor gentlemen, and we shall be equal." For subsequent democratic rebels in English history, the vision of a far-reaching "commonwealth" proved a recurring pattern. Thus Gerrard Winstanley, theoretician of a radical faction of the seventeenth-century English Civil War, which had in fact established what was called "The Commonwealth," took the term with a shocking literalness: "The whole earth shall be a common treasury," Winstanley wrote. "For the earth is the Lord's. . . . There shall be no lords over others, but everyone shall be a lord of himself, subject to the law of righteousness, reason and equity."[6]

If the concept of "the people" embodied in democracy was troubling, the prospect of direct "rule" was at least as bothersome for those who believed society was best governed by a few. Again dating from ancient Greece, the concept of direct rule involved the idea of free and active participation (albeit a limited franchise) by those defined as citizens. As G. Lowes Dickinson has described the Greek polis, "to be a citizen of a state did not merely imply the payment of taxes and the possession of a vote; it implied a direct and active cooperation in all the functions of civil and military life. A citizen was normally a soldier, a judge, and a member of the governing assembly; and all his public duties he performed not by deputy, but in person." Even in the Middle Ages, when feudal relationships characterized political life, an occasional political theorist ruminated upon the benefits that direct participation might produce. Thus, for example, Marsiglio of Padua wrote in the early fourteenth century that "a law made by the hearing or consent of the whole multitude, even though it were less useful, would be readily observed and endured by every one of the citizens, because then each would seem to have set the law upon himself and hence would have no protest against it, but would rather tolerate it with equanimity."[7]

With the settlement of the New World, a laboratory existed for putting such ideas into practice. Thus, the first political constitution to use the term democracy—Rhode Island's in 1641—meant "popular government; that is to say it is the power of the body of freemen orderly assembled, or major part of them, to make or constitute just Lawes, by which they will be regulated."[8]

Finally, the notion of democracy entailed not only rights to participate, but the responsibilities of citizenship. The concept of "the citizen" suggested one who was able to put aside at times immediate and personal interests and focus on public affairs. Such a trait amounted to civic virtue, suggested by Walt Whitman's observation in 1855 that a nation the size and extent of America "were monstrous" without a citizenry of correspondingly large and generous spirit. The values associated with citizenship included a concern for the common good, the welfare of the community as a whole, willingness to honor the same rights for others that one possesses, tolerance of diverse religious, political, and social beliefs, acceptance of the primacy of the community's decisions over one's own private inclinations, and a recognition of one's obligations to defend and serve the public.*[9]

*Citizenship, in an active sense, emerges out of face-to-face encounter over time. As Robert Bellah and his colleagues observe in *Habits of the Heart,* this understanding of citizenship, in American folklore and practice, is grounded in community, associated with the widespread belief in "getting involved" and "making a contribution." Thus, it can be contrasted with definitions of citizenship as a politics of interest-group bargaining, normally conducted by professionals; or a politics of the nation, expressing generalized visions of common purpose uniting disparate groups. In democratic movements, all three meanings of citizenship are held in tension and balance, but it is a central argument of this book that without rich opportunities for a "politics of community," democracy becomes a hollow and ritualized formality. Others have made the point in more general terms. As G. D. H. Cole put it many decades ago, "Over the vast mechanism of modern politics the individual has no control, not because the state is too big, but because he is given no chance of learning the rudiments of self-government within a smaller unit." Bellah et al., *Habits of the Heart: Individualism and Commitment in American Life* (Berkeley: University

Democratic Heritage of the American Revolution

America's founders were divided about these ideas. For most, drawing on biblical and republican traditions, the concepts of participation and civic virtue were central—though very few indeed imagined "citizens" as including women, slaves, or the very poor. Private property, for instance, was rarely seen as an end in itself. Even our archetypical entrepreneur, Benjamin Franklin, held that "property" is simply "the creature of Society . . . subject to the calls of that Society." The independence which small amounts of property—small farms, for example, or small stores or artisanal skills—allowed was important in this view, in fact, because it thereby freed citizens to participate in the public life of the self-governing community, or commonwealth.[10]

Such participation was seen as the foundation of a free society —indeed, the only way in which skills of active public life, values of communal responsibility, and consciousness of the broader common good or commonwealth could be renewed and sustained. Thus, Thomas Jefferson contrasted the Europeans, who he claimed "have divided their nations into two classes, wolves and sheep," with the Indians. Groups like the Iroquois, he believed, furnished a model for self-government because of their reliance on the moral force of community opinion instead of government action to control crime and other social problems: "Controls are their manners and the moral sense of right and wrong." From such perspectives, great extremes of wealth or speculative sale of property, like the squandering of the means of one's independence, were seen in the most unfavorable light because of the clear danger that the community might be eroded or disrupted. The values prized included service to the community, frugality, hard work, inde-

of California Press, 1985), especially pp. 200–213; Cole in Carole Pateman, *Participation and Democratic Theory* (London: Cambridge University Press, 1970), p. 38.

pendence, and self-restraint. Their opposites—extravagance, self-indulgence, idleness, and so forth—had no place in a virtuous and just republic.[11]

Tied to the principles of this republican political tradition, which can be traced back to classic Greek and Roman thought, Americans repeatedly turned to apocalyptic themes, largely inherited from the Bible, to describe their mission in a "new world" and to reinforce their sense of communal obligation. For settlers naming communities Salem or Shiloh, Canaan, Jerusalem, Nazareth, Bethlehem, Eden, and Paradise, the new continent represented the "promised land," a chance to create a Kingdom of God on earth. Immigrants readily identified themselves as being like the Hebrew children, fleeing corrupt and unjust societies in the Old World, beginning again as "chosen people" in the new. "The Lord will be our God and delight to dwell among us, as His own people, and . . . command a blessing upon us in all our ways," said John Winthrop aboard the *Arbella* in 1630. Biblically oriented interweaving of religious and political themes has, especially, been characteristic of populist and democratic endeavors. The preachers and pamphleteers of the 1740s and 1750s decried "selfishness and avarice" and called for a "vital communion of kindred spirits" against the new "Lords of Mammon." And their populist sentiments laid powerful groundwork for the democratic spirit of the Revolutionary period.[12]

For all the potency of American democratic traditions, certain flaws are unmistakable and they weakened the very movements those traditions nourished. At times, such flaws also furnished material for subsequent democratic protest, as groups excluded or marginalized by the original terms of citizenship and democracy came to point out the chasm between myth and reality.

America's Puritan settlers had a strongly communal sense, but in many ways it was narrow and static. Puritans saw themselves as a "saving remnant," which would redeem a wicked Europe, and feared the "chaos" outside their communities. In doctrines permeated with Calvinism, human depravity could only be checked by the strictest of controls. And the notion that human sinfulness must be checked by external law and rigid enforcements has continued throughout the American experience, shaping a long tradition of local censorship and legislation about private moral issues.[13]

The republican tradition itself, though prizing service to the community, became fused with an eighteenth-century individual rights philosophy that emphasized the liberation of the individual from constricting traditions and communal ties.* Indeed, in many ways the hallmark of American democracy became the stress upon individualism. Thus, though visions of republican community, nourished by small-town and rural experience, provided potent contrasts to large-scale, centralized institutions, the language of American republicanism took community for granted. Women were charged with tending to the sustenance and replenishment of community life in ways that simultaneously excluded such activities from conventional definitions of "public," and barred women themselves from most "public" affairs. Those who protested a spreading spirit of avarice and growing concentrations of economic and political power throughout the nineteenth century often spoke in a language of "equal rights," and "manliness" that could be co-opted by a dominant, acquisitive culture stressing individual success. Ralph Waldo Emerson might observe, in despair, the system of selfishness which he feared would destroy democracy: "We eat and drink and wear perjury and fraud in a hundred commodities." But his emphatic focus on the democratic *individual* held no room for acknowledgment of human interconnection. "Take

---

*The concerns with individual dignity that emerge from the Enlightenment have also formed a crucial dimension of modern democracy, infusing many of the movements we examine with a restless, experimental, and liberatory spirit. The problem has come here, as with other supposed oppositions (the clash between tradition and rationality, for instance, or between organic ties and freedom), in political and social languages and conceptions that suppose individual identity and communal ties to be opposed, rather than interdependent. The erosion of communal ties, in reality, erodes the very possibilities of a rich individualism. Such themes are explored especially in Chapters 3 and 6.

away from me the feeling that I must depend upon myself, give me the least hint that I have good friends & backers there in reserve who will gladly help me, and instantly I relax my diligence and obey the first impulse of generosity that is to cost me nothing and a certain slackness will creep over my conduct of affairs."[14]

The notions of a "chosen people" were all too likely to serve as justifications for campaigns against the Indians, blindness to gross injustices like the slave system, and military adventures abroad as the new nation developed. And those who were counted as legitimate "citizens"—full participants in the affairs of the commonwealth—remained sharply limited. Women, blacks, American Indians, and the very poor and propertyless were not included as full members of John Winthrop's "city on the hill," the powerful symbol of America's mission. Similarly, through the nineteenth and twentieth centuries, subsequent waves of immigrants found it difficult to be accepted as full members of the "American commonwealth."

If the democratic traditions in America contained weaknesses and flaws, however, the more conservative wing of the American Revolution had a somewhat different, but clear enough, view of democracy: They didn't like the idea. Elite perspectives instead stressed themes of radical individualism and rule by the most wealthy. For Alexander Hamilton, the nation's first treasury secretary, "Every man ought to be supposed a knave; and to have no other end in all his actions, but private interests . . . insatiable avarice and ambition." Hamilton advocated the rapid growth of a manufacturing system as the arrangement most appropriate for "sorting out" those most fit to lead. And in his view—expressed with uncommon candor in a nation which has always celebrated egalitarian manners and speech—those natural leaders were never in doubt. "All communities divide themselves into the few and the many," wrote Hamilton. "The first are rich and well-born, the other the mass of the people. The people are turbulent and changing; they seldom judge or determine right. Give, therefore, to the first class a distinct, permanent share in government." Such views led Hamilton to distinguish carefully between democracy, "where the deliberative or judicial powers are vested wholly or partly in the collective body of the people," and "representative" government, which he much preferred, "where the right of election is well-secured and regulated, and the exercise of the legislative, executive and judicial authorities is vested in select persons."[15]

Though elite control and the ideologies which accompany and reinforce such control have undergone constant and dynamic change throughout American history, Hamiltonian perspectives, more or less overtly, have centrally informed the views of American elites ever since. Hamilton's words resonate unmistakably with those of John Calhoun, for example, the great apologist for the slave South, who argued (in remarkably direct challenge to the Declaration of Independence) that "it is a great and dangerous error to suppose that all people are equally entitled to liberty. It is a reward to be earned, not a blessing to be gratuitously lavished on all alike." In turn, such views find contemporary expression in the positions of those such as the *Business Week* editorialist, or the current political philosopher George Gilder, who argues capitalism's great virtue is that it "exalts the few extraordinary men who can produce wealth over the democratic masses who consume it."[16]

Directly to the point, throughout the nineteenth and twentieth centuries, these tamed, elite versions of democracy increasingly prevailed in the mainstream, as Americans came to think of an active, participatory democracy as simply a nostalgic echo from the past. The eroding faith in democratic possibility, in turn, grew from the changes that were reshaping the nation in fundamental ways.

Throughout the nineteenth century, America remained largely a "nation of villagers," in Walter Lippmann's apt phrase. Small towns and the rural landscape, organized around families, friends, churches, mutual aid societies, farm organizations and the like, provided the matrix for most peoples' lives from birth to death. Moreover, the explosive growth in voluntary organizations, both male and female, contributed significantly to a broadening definition of "citizenship" and public affairs. In rural settings (with some dramatic exceptions, like slave-holding areas of the South), wealth, if not evenly distributed, did not normally produce the enormous social cleavages into rich and poor that would later characterize urban life. Neighbors knew each other, visited regularly, and helped each other out in a variety of ways—from barn raisings to quilting bees and voluntary fire departments. And an understanding of democracy that emphasized the active, continuing involvement of citizens made sense.

"Democracy" suggested New England town meetings, or more informally, decision-making in religious congregations or the discussion of local affairs in voluntary groups. Government was seen, in these terms, not as the primary arena of democracy but, more authentically, as the instrument of citizens joined together. Even for popular protest movements, political engagement was seen as an expression of the values and activities of community life, not as an end in itself. Thus, for instance, the nineteenth-century Knights of Labor, a movement of laboring men and women protesting the rise of giant trusts and cartels and their threat to artisan traditions, "looked to self-organized society—not to the individual and not to the state—as the redeemer of their American dream," as labor historian Leon Fink put it. "Neither ultimate antagonist nor source of salvation, the state represented a mediator in the conflict between the civil forces of democracy and its enemies."[17]

But the developments of the late nineteenth and early twentieth centuries—technological change, urbanization, industrialization, waves of immigration, the growth of new professions and scientific knowledge applied to social life—radically changed the very texture of life in America. In enormous cities, one could scarcely know one's neighbors, much less those down the street or on the other side of the tracks. Waves of immigrants brought new customs, traditions, and languages. Communications technologies like the railroad, telegraph, and mass newspaper began to shatter the boundaries of the local community; technologies at work and in professions sharply eroded older patterns of craft and community tradition. Civic involvement in town meetings and voluntary groups became less and less the model of "democracy." In its place emerged corrupt big-city political machines and the manipulation of a mass electorate by techniques of public relations and sloganeering. Modernity, as Lippmann observed, "had upset the old life on the prairies, made new demands upon democracy, introduced specialization and science, had destroyed village loyalties . . . and created the impersonal relationships of the modern world."[18]

Middle-class reformers, meanwhile, adapted to the changes with alacrity—but in ways that further eclipsed any notion of small-scale, participatory, and community-based democracy. According to the Progressive thinkers like Lippmann, *New Republic* editor Herbert Croly, Theodore Roosevelt, and others in the early twentieth century, the erosion of local community ties and a sense of civic responsibility was more than compensated for by possibilities for broader involvement. Local community life had had positive features, sustaining values like participation, egalitarianism, and a sense of civic involvement. But the new changes had great potential, in the view of such observers, to bring in the place of small communities a far better great community that would dissolve all differences of nationality, ethnicity, religion, and region into a "melting pot." Thus, Herbert Croly argued that "the responsibility and loyalty which the citizens of a democratic nation must feel one towards another is comprehensive and unmitigable." The communal feeling of small-town life would be re-created by the "loyal realization of a comprehensive democratic social ideal." And the new techniques of science and the professions could be applied to solve age-old problems and social ills. As Frederick Taylor, pioneer in scientific management techniques in the world of business, put it: "The same principles can be applied with equal force to all social activities."[19]

Progressives—and those who followed in their tradition, like many liberal reformers of the New Deal—continued to advocate direct involvement of citizens in decision-making processes. But the locus of civic involvement shifted from voluntary association and community activity to government itself. Through various public agencies and electoral reforms—regulatory commissions, civil service reform, nonpartisan local elections, direct election of senators, referenda and initiative, and the like—citizens would shape the "great community" of the country. Women's suffrage, in this understanding, would be democracy's greatest realization. And democracy itself, in Croly's words, no longer meant that citizens "assemble after the manner of a New England town-meeting" since there existed "abundant opportunities of communications and consultation without any meeting. . . . The active citizenship of the country meets every morning and evening and discusses the affairs of the nation with the newspaper as an impersonal interlocuter."[20]

But the reality proved to be radically different. Aside from the new, rising middle class of professionals and white-collar workers in large private and public bureaucracies, most Americans continued to identify with their locales, their traditions, their heritages and cultures. But their worlds seemed increasingly shaped by distant forces over which they had no control whatsoever. Corner grocers gave way to chain stores; local decisions over education were removed to state or national bureaucracies; ways of doing things—from childrearing to family home remedies—that had been passed down for generations were replaced by "expert advice" from professionals who claimed specialized knowledge.

By mid-twentieth century, political theorists celebrated the relative noninvolvement of most citizens in public life as a source of stability and order. Indeed, the *International Encyclopedia of the Social Sciences,* the seventeen-volume summary of social sciences containing 900-odd articles, offered nothing at all on the theme of "citizenship," a concept at the heart of active and participatory democracy. What C. B. Macpherson calls "equilibrium democracy" had largely replaced classic understandings of the word. In equilibrium democracy, a mainly passive citizenry—composed of individuals pulled in different directions by competing interests—chooses among representatives based on the attractiveness of their "consumer promises." The political system resembles a marketplace. And the point of society is not participation but "possessive individualism," where each has the right to compete, on roughly equal footing, for acquisition of material goods, status, and power.[21]

It is this background of pessimism about the very possibility of active, participatory democracy which shapes the ways Americans talk about change, protest, and social movement. Neoconservatives such as Peter Berger share with left-wing theorists such as Frances Fox Piven and Richard Cloward the view that the shape and contours of modern society are largely fixed. "If the lower classes do not ordinarily have great disruptive power, it is the only power they do have," argued Piven and Cloward in their book *Poor People's Movements: Why They Succeed, How They Fail.* Those who study movements use a language—terms like "movement entrepreneurs," "the free rider problem," "rational self-interest," and so forth—which neglects the issues of democratic values or democratic goals entirely. To the extent that questions of value, tradition, and voluntary association are considered, they are called "mobilizable resources," in the manner of financial deposits and access to meeting halls.[22] Despite the explosion of studies comparing popular social movements across time and space, little work has been done to examine the specific features characterizing movements that can be called broadly "democratic," or the processes that generate Whitman's generous and large-spirited citizenry.*

*Major changes have occurred over time in the treatment given to democracy in the theoretical literature about social movements. A generation ago, traces of concern with the distinguishing features of democratic movements could still be found; this question formed a theme, for instance, in Lewis M.

Thus, on the face of it, the emergence of democratic movements is a puzzle—and, undoubtedly, the exception. Popular
movements, it has now been widely enough documented, normally arise in defense of rights or ways of life that a changing
world threatens to destroy. Examples of defensive and limited
protests abound, from the nativist movements of the nineteenth century to the Ku Klux Klan and the White Citizens
Council of the 1960s, from the National Union for Social Justice
of the 1930s to fights against "dangerous books" in the present.
Backward-looking in their central construction, such protests
are in a basic sense survival efforts, aimed at returning things
to "the way they were" at best, and at the least retaining whatever elements of identity, culture, and place can be salvaged.

Whatever the diminished sense of possibility afflicting modern thought, however, ordinary men and women have also

---

Killian's "Social Movements: A Review of the Field," written in 1964. Yet by
the late 1960s or early 1970s, theorists dismissed the issue entirely. Thus, Anthony Oberschall argued that it was counterproductive to seek to distinguish
fascist from democratic movements. Any such effort "treats mass movement
and its cousin, extremist, totalitarian and antidemocratic movements, as a distinct phenomenon, with mobilizing processes different from movements that
have nonextremist or prodemocratic goals," a distinction he saw as unjustified.
(Oberschall based his argument on Seymour Martin Lipset's work on the farmers' movement in Saskatchewan, *Agrarian Socialism* [Berkeley: University of
California Press, 1950]. But he managed to ignore Lipset's basic point that
unusually widespread participation in the Saskatchewan movement was the
key to its democratic character.) Oberschall's perspective was characteristic of
the resource-mobilization approach of the 1970s. Recently, however, themes of
democracy have reemerged in the literature. Thus, Wini Breines has pointed
out that conventional criticisms of the Sixties' student movement for its resistance to "instrumental values" miss the movement's central point. The New
Left, according to Breines, "took form as a revulsion against large-scale centralized and inhuman institutions; its most acute concern was to avoid duplication
of the hierarchical and manipulative relationships characteristic of society."
Though unsuccessful in its broadest aims, its structuring theme was "the unresolved tension between the grassroots social movement committed to participatory democracy and the intention (necessitating organization) of achiev-
ing power or radical structural change." Lewis Killian, "Social Movements: A
Review of the Field," in Robert Evans, ed., *Social Movements: A Reader and
Source Book* (Chicago: Rand McNally, 1973), pp. 9–53; Anthony Oberschall,
Social Conflict and Social Movements (Englewood Cliffs, N.J.: Prentice-Hall,
1973), pp. 112–13; Wini Breines, "The New Left and Michel's 'Iron Law,'"
Social Problems 45 (April 1980): 419–30, quote p. 421.

found the courage and spirit again and again to imagine the possibility of an active, participatory democracy—to seek something radically *different,* rather than simply a "bigger piece of the pie" or a return to the way things were. From nineteenth-century farmers' populist struggles and women's fight for citizenship and suffrage to modern movements like the rise of the CIO in the 1930s, the southern civil rights struggle and the youth movement in the 1960s, and the neighborhood and citizen movements in the 1970s and 1980s, Americans have again and again articulated a broad and inclusive vision of direct participation and civic virtue that renews and enriches earlier conceptions of democracy. With varying degrees of success they have fashioned the practical skills and organizational means to seek to realize their aspirations.

The most radical challenges to conventional American politics have drawn their vocabulary and power from core issues remembered from the past. Thus, Sarah Grimké replied to a group of ministers who questioned her right as a woman to speak publicly against slavery in the 1830s, "How monstrous, how anti-Christian is the doctrine that woman is to be dependent on man! Where in all the sacred Scriptures is this taught? This doctrine of dependence upon man is utterly at variance with the doctrine of the Bible." Black Americans, for whom the notion of America as the promised land contained no small irony, inverted the imagery: in black song and religion, America was like Egypt, the land of bondage, if also like Canaan-in-potential—someday to be the land of milk and honey. Similarly, Eugene Debs, visionary spokesman for the American Socialist Party in its halcyon days of the early twentieth century, built his denunciations of corporate greed and business concentration on "the eighteenth century Revolutionary heritage," according to his biographer, Nicholas Salvatore, "the concept that the government will rest upon the intelligence and virtue of the people." Martin Luther King, Jr., described the civil rights movement as "bringing the entire nation back to the great wells of democracy that were dug deep by the founding fathers."[23]

We argue that there is little mysterious or unknowable about democratic movements for change. In their failure to examine the particular features that produce such endeavors, contemporary writers miss the forest for the trees.

The drama and passion in the histories which follow revolve, in no small measure, around the ways in which the dispossessed and powerless have again and again sought simultaneously to revive and remember older notions of democratic participation, on the one hand, and on the other given them new and deeper meanings and applications. Democracy, in these terms, then, means more than changing structures so as to make democracy possible. It means, also, schooling citizens in "citizenship"—that is, in the varied skills and values which are essential to sustaining effective participation. Democratic social movements, efforts whose goal is an enlarged democracy, are themselves vehicles for such schooling.

Free Spaces

To understand the inner life of democratic movements, one must rethink such traditional categories as "politics," "private life," "public activity," "reaction," and "progress." Only then can we hope to fathom how people draw upon their past for strength, create out of traditions—which may seem on their face simply to reinforce the status quo—new visions of the future, gain out of the experiences of their daily lives new public skills and a broader sense of hope and possibility.

The central argument of this book is that particular sorts of public places in the community, what we call free spaces, are the environments in which people are able to learn a new self-respect, a deeper and more assertive group identity, public skills, and values of cooperation and civic virtue. Put simply, free spaces are settings between private lives and large-scale institutions where ordinary citizens can act with dignity, independence, and vision. These are, in the main, voluntary forms of association with a relatively open and participatory character

—many religious organizations, clubs, self-help and mutual aid societies, reform groups, neighborhood, civic, and ethnic groups, and a host of other associations grounded in the fabric of community life. The sustained public vitality and egalitarianism of free spaces are strikingly unlike the "public" face of reactionary or backward-looking protests. Democratic action depends upon these free spaces, where people experience a schooling in citizenship and learn a vision of the common good in the course of struggling for change.*

*In more theoretical terms, a focus on the free spaces at the heart of democratic movements aids in the resolution of polarities that have long and bitterly divided modern observers and critics—expressive individualism versus ties of community; modernity versus tradition; public and private values, and so forth —by highlighting the living environments where people draw upon both "oppositions" to create new experiments. See especially Chapters 3, 4, and 6 for a discussion of these issues. For earlier discussions of the concept of free space, see Harry C. Boyte, "The Textile Industry: Keel of Southern Industrialization," *Radical America* (March–April 1972); Sara M. Evans, *Personal Politics: The Roots of Women's Liberation in the Civil Rights Movement and the New Left* (New York: Knopf, 1979); Harry C. Boyte, "Populism and the Left," *democracy* 1 (April 1981): 53–66. and Sara M. Evans and Harry C. Boyte, "Schools for Action: Radical Uses of Social Space," *democracy* 2 (fall 1982): 55–65. Though we have developed the concept in our explorations of American social movements, it clearly has application to other cultural and social settings. For interesting applications of the idea to other societies, see, for instance, Craig Calhoun, "Class, Place and Industrial Revolution," in N. Thrift and P. Williams, eds., *The Making of Urban Society: Historical Essays on Class Formation and Place* (London: Routledge & Kegan Paul, 1985); Allen Isaacman et al., " 'Cotton Is the Mother of Poverty': Peasant Resistance to Forced Cotton Production in Mozambique, 1938–1961," *The International Journal of African Historical Studies* 13 (1980); Allen Isaacman and Barbara Isaacman, *Mozambique: From Colonialism to Revolution, 1900–1982* (Hampshire, England: Gower, 1983); Ronald Aminzade, *Class, Politics and Early Industrial Capitalism: A Study of Mid-Nineteenth-Century Toulouse, France* (Albany: State University of New York Press, 1981).

We have used the terms "space" and "social space" to suggest the lived, daily character of those networks and relationships that form the primary base of social movements. The concept of social space grows from traditions of social geography, ethnology, and phenomenology. It suggests strongly an "objective," physical dimension—the ways in which places are organized and connected, fragmented, and so forth; and a subjective dimension, space as understood, perceived, and lived—what seems customary, familiar, part of daily experience. For discussions of the "socially constructed" nature of physical reality, see for instance Edward Hall, *The Hidden Dimension* (New York: Doubleday, 1966), and Anne Buttimer, "Social Space in Interdisciplinary Perspective," in John Gabree, ed., *Surviving the City* (New York: Ballantine Books, 1973). We stress,

Free spaces are never a pure phenomenon. In the real world, they are always complex, shifting, and dynamic—partial in their freedom and democratic participation, marked by parochialism of class, gender, race, and other biases of the groups which maintain them. There are no easy or simple ways to sustain experiences of democratic participation and values of civic virtue in the heart of broader environments that undermine them and demand, at least on the face of it, very different sorts of values. Democratic movements have had varying degrees of success in sustaining themselves, in spreading their values, symbols, and ideas to larger audiences, in changing the world. They have in different ways and with different outcomes addressed issues such as the bureaucratic state, the problem of size in organization, the role of experts, the power of conventional media. They have sought to hold leaders accountable through a variety of measures—from direct election and recall to frequent turnover in top leadership, and widespread dissemination of information—or they have failed to develop such measures. And they have drawn upon and transformed threads in peoples' cultures and traditions, weaving ideas into new sets of values, beliefs and interpretations of the world, codes of behavior, and visions of the future. Together, these new elements make up, in democratic movements, basic alternatives to the conventional ways of the world, what might be called "movement cultures," that suggest a different way of living.

Free spaces are the foundations for such movement counter-

in addition to the communal nature of free space, the importance of voluntary organizational forms through which people can learn public skills and values and take sustained action over time. But it should be noted that informal, local relations themselves normally have an important element of independence from centers of power that can sustain brief forms of resistance. As Anthony Leeds put it, "The amorphousness, multiplicity and kaleidoscopic quality of the organization of localities . . . are virtually impossible to legislate for (or against) or to control by uniform sets of sanctions. . . . In this independence and its social and ecological bases is found a locus of power for cooperation with—but especially for resistance against the encroachments of—the supralocal institutions." "Locality Power in Relation to Supralocal Institutions," in Aidan Southall, ed., *Urban Anthropology: Crosscultural Studies of Urbanization* (New York: Oxford University Press, 1973), pp. 15–42.

cultures. And for all their variations, free spaces have certain common features, observable in movements varying widely in time, aims, composition, and social environment. They are defined by their roots in community, the dense, rich networks of daily life; by their autonomy; and by their public or quasi-public character as participatory environments which nurture values associated with citizenship and a vision of the common good. In a full way, the spirit, dynamics, and character of free spaces can only be understood in the concreteness of particular stories, where people gain new skills, a new sense of possibility, and a broadened understanding of whom "the people" include.

Imagine a large assembly hall, festooned with symbols and signs, in Hamilton, Ontario, early October 1885. Several hundred delegates to the ninth annual convention of the Noble Order of the Knights of Labor assembled from Arkansas, New York, Missouri, Maryland, Illinois, Louisiana, Pennsylvania, Connecticut, Virginia, and a dozen other states. Old-timers from Union battles of the late 1860s mingled with young immigrant men and women, part of that vast wave of five million people who came to America from cities like Glasgow, Liverpool, Vienna, and Minsk during the 1880s. Confederate veterans gave the secret sign of recognition. Former soldiers of the Union Army responded in kind. Signaling with hand across forehead, they showed that they, too, worked by "the sweat of our brow."

They were full of rising confidence. The growing movement had generated hopes that the overwhelming power of the new economic cartels and monopolies in America might be broken. Strikes and boycotts, spreading across the country, had achieved significant victories against the new breed of industrialists like Jay Gould, the railroad magnate who boasted that he could "hire one half of the working class to kill the other half." In keeping with the mood of the occasion, Master Workman William Mullen, Knights leader from Richmond, Virginia, convened the meeting.

"I have here a gavel to present this General Assembly," Mullen began, with modest disclaimers. "It is as plain a gavel as I have ever seen, in fitful keeping with the plain but beautiful workings of our honored Order." As he described how his District Assembly of white working men and women had put it together, the audience listened, transfixed.

"The handle of this gavel is made from a piece of the sounding board that stood in old St. John's Church at the time that Patrick Henry made his famous speech. [It is] therefore a piece of the instrument that echoed and re-echoed the patriotic words, 'give me liberty or give me death!' The handle of this gavel is, as you can see, topped with a piece of wood of a different kind, cut at Yorktown, Virginia, as near as possible to the scene of the surrender of Cornwallis to Washington, and therefore represents the close of the first Revolution." Thus Mullen drew on the legacy which northerners and southerners shared. As he described the ball, he turned to the issue which had torn the nation apart. "It is," he explained, "from one of the pillars of the old Libby prison that the ball of this gavel is made. This building has been made historic by the part it played in the second Revolution. In this house of ancient architectural design were confined true and patriotic sons of our common country as prisoners of war for being engaged in a struggle to liberate a race of people from the galling yoke of slavery."

Finally, with the evangelical fervor that ignited audiences in Richmond time after time, Mullen turned to the future. "There still remains a battle to be fought for the establishment of universal freedom. Can those who are now the slaves of monopoly and oppression be liberated as easily as was the African race in America?" He answered himself as he passed the gavel to Grandmaster Workman Terence Powderly, leader of the national movement. "Yea, even more easily! To accomplish the second requires only organization, education and cooperation. To you, sir," he concluded, "as the representative of that grand army that is to work the third Revolution in which all the nations of the earth are to be liberated, I present you with this gavel, clothed with so much of our past history. God grant that this gavel may, in your hands, preside over in the future many happy gatherings of the noble-hearted sons of toil to celebrate the holiday of the establishment of these grand principles—a fair day's pay for a fair day's work, and an injury to one is the concern of all!'"[24]

Mullen's enthusiasm reflected the excitement of the convention. But it also grew from changes in towns like Richmond. An interracial movement had rapidly emerged in the city, addressing not only specific issues of wages and jobs but also the most revolutionary of cultural issues in that former capital of the Confederacy. As historian Peter Rachleff described, "a new movement culture [developed], centered on the Knights, which not only supported a revitalized labor movement but also promoted a biracial popular movement which threatened to turn Southern society upside down." The ultimate purpose of the Knights was expressed in the solemnly intoned hope that "the day will come when men of all the nations of the earth shall govern themselves." Every initiate into the Order heard the words as they joined.[25]

The experiment in interracial cooperation and workers' self-organization ultimately failed in Richmond in the 1880s. And the day when people "of all the nations of the earth shall govern themselves" remains yet a distant goal. But both their achievement and their sentiments reach across time and space. For decades afterwards, in Richmond and across the South, white youngsters growing up with games of "Johnny Reb" and songs of Dixie's faded glory would fail to understand the common ties binding North and South together which those doughty laboring men and women had symbolized with their careful handicraft. And it would be generations before black and white workers would again make common cause in the old Confederacy's capital on such a scale.

When listened to attentively, the members of the Richmond Knights of Labor have a contemporary impact with peculiar parallel to their challenge to the culture of the Old South. Put simply, their endeavors turn our modern, up-to-date, and sophisticated ways of thinking about things like democracy and self-government upside down, as well.

The Richmond Knights' achievements were a testimony to hard work and spirited leadership, but they were possible because of the particular features of the voluntary associations and community roots from which the Knights emerged, and the nature of the institution itself as it flourished and expanded. The Knights drew their power from religious and democratic traditions deeply embedded in both white and black communities of Richmond. A reinterpretation of such traditions in ways that furthered working people's self-assertion and even common action between black and white communities was possible because the Knights' assemblies were autonomous institutions—that is, they were voluntary organizations that working people controlled themselves, relatively free of outside sanction. Finally, for a time, the Knights created a remarkable "public" environment where workers from different communities—and most amazingly, even different races—could come together, forge relationships that had never been imagined, and develop regular communications with other communities of working people in northern states once simply stereotyped as "damn Yankees." Such new relationships, emerging from particular community histories, created simultaneously an enlarged vision of community, a sense of the common good that had never before existed in the South in this way.

In sum, the free spaces at the heart of the Richmond Knights of Labor were schools for citizenship that made "democracy" come alive with a powerful, heady sense of possibility. Such schooling in citizenship has proven indispensable for democratic movements in widely varying times and places. In turn, a more detailed understanding of the ways in which free spaces are crucial to the revitalization and sustenance of democratic vision and activity requires a look at different democratic movements.

This study will explore the major democratic movements in United States history, movements for the rights, dignity, and voice of blacks, women, workers, and farmers. In each case, we trace the ebb and flow of social protest across time, noting the characteristics of the free spaces that nourished them and the influence of broader historical and social settings.

A broadly comparative approach demonstrates the common elements which make these movements democratic. It also clarifies the limitations of particular movements' vision. Despite dramatic differences, in each case we find the common characteristics of free spaces which we have identified: communal roots, autonomy, and public character. At the same time, the specific features of different movements allow us to explore how free spaces shape the structure, leadership, and ideology of each.

For example, under slavery, the very possibility of thinking and speaking in ways that opposed the dominant culture depended upon the creation of autonomous institutions— churches—about which white slaveowners had little knowledge and over which they had little control. The charismatic leadership of black ministers, in turn, shaped a leadership style which persists to the present. Thus the black church is an especially clear illustration of free space. Chapter 2 treats three particular historical moments when its role was highlighted.

One could make a similar argument about the importance of autonomous institutions such as churches, clubs, and saloons for the emergence of working-class culture. But for a highly mobile and culturally uprooted American work force, the issue of autonomy has been inseparably connected with the question of community. Indeed, in the case of American workers' movements, the possibility of group action has depended crucially upon the survival, sustenance, and sometimes the retrieval of historical memories and the re-creation of voluntary associations that bridge segmented worlds of work and community. An exploration of the theme of community, in turn, leads to some thoughts about the need to reevaluate widely used concepts such as "class consciousness."

The chapter on the history of feminism shifts the primary

focus to the public aspects of free spaces. For women to claim their citizenship rights, they required environments in which they could develop public identities and skills, simultaneously drawing upon and changing traditions that defined women in terms of family and personal worlds. In the process, women redefined the meaning of "public" and "common good." Yet the fact that those environments were also shaped by the realities of class and race ultimately limited both the claim to female citizenship and the constituency that could be mobilized in its name. Finally, populist movements rooted in rural America illustrate the powerful and complex role of traditional ideologies. And they highlight in particular the importance of democratic participation that teaches values of citizenship, racial tolerance, and the common good to any inclusive vision of "the people."

Free spaces, then, are the places in which the pieties we learn in school or hear in Fourth of July speeches take on living substance and meaning. A deeper understanding of them recasts the role of voluntary associations—considered, for example, in current neoconservative thought to be the main barrier against an all-encompassing modern state—from that of defensive refuge to active source of change. And it suggests, finally, the need to rethink our contemporary approaches to public life and politics, social change, and democracy itself.

CHAPTER 2

CROSSING THE JORDAN

> And what was Meridian, who had always thought of the
> black church as mainly a reactionary power, to make of this?
> . . . Perhaps it was, after all, the only place left for black
> people to congregate, where the problems of life were not
> discussed fraudulently and the approach to the future was
> considered communally, and moral questions were taken
> seriously.
>
> —Alice Walker, *Meridian*

FOLLOWING the War of 1812, blacks along the South Carolina
coast heard rumors of an imminent British invasion and
planned a rebellion to take advantage of the opportunity it
might present. In the course of their meetings, they composed
a song:

> Hail! all Hail! ye Afric clan
> Hail! ye oppressed, ye Afric band,
> Who toil and sweat in Slavery Bound;
> And when your health & strength are gone,
> Are left to hunger & to mourn,
> Let Independence be your aim,
> Ever mindful what 'tis worth.
> Pledge your bodies for the prize,
> Pile them even to the skies!
> Firm, united let us be,
> Resolved on death or liberty
> As a band of Patriots joined
> Peace and Plenty we shall find.

The concluding lines of the song called blacks to insurrection, drawing on biblical imagery and America's unfulfilled promises:

> Arise! Arise! Shake off your chains
> Your cause is just so heaven ordains
> To you shall Freedom be proclaimed
> Raise your arms & bare your breasts,
> Almighty God will do the rest.
> Blow the clarion! a warlike blast!
> Call every Negro from his task!
> Wrest the scourge from Buckra's hand,
> And drive each tyrant from the land.[1]

The song is remarkable on a number of counts. The radicalism and militancy are vivid and unmistakable—undisguised by otherworldly references which often wove through spirituals to confound white audiences. There is a call for revolutionary transformation of America, by force of arms if necessary. The ideological themes that fuse together in the lyrics are the main currents of early-nineteenth-century American political philosophy: religion and the republican natural rights beliefs of the American Revolution. But the meaning of such ideas has been radically changed. Moreover, the song clearly envisions a homeland in America. Despite the horrors of slavery, the Sea Island black community had come to claim America as their home. And they had developed a determination to fight, in order to realize such a claim, for a vision of America that was distinctively, unmistakably, their own.

In the history of black America, like the history of other dispossessed and powerless peoples, the question of dignity and moral worth is at the heart of movements for freedom. And black history demonstrates with particular power the way in which oppressed and powerless people can discover and use subversive themes hidden in dominant ideas as resources for self-affirmation, resistance, and struggle. For such alternative cultures to emerge and survive, people need community places that they own themselves, voluntary associations where they can think and talk and socialize, removed from the scrutiny and control of those who hold power over their lives.

The black church especially has played this crucial role as a free space in black history. Its function has changed in different times and settings—from an underground, semisecret meeting place under slavery, for instance, to a central reference point for cultural survival and renewal after emancipation, when pressures to assimilate into the dominant white world became more acute. Throughout black history, the insights and spirit of black religion have remained at the center of what might be called a culture of resistance that formed an alternative to the values and humiliations of dominant white culture. Moreover, within this culture of resistance germinated elements of democratic aspiration and vision that suggested not only survival but wide-ranging transformation of the broader society. At moments—for example, when the civil rights movement of the 1950s and 1960s developed into a powerful democratic challenge to basic American values of racial prejudice and radical individualism—the language and vision of black culture and black religion have had enormous meaning and relevance for the whole society.

Classic interpretations of the black experience under slavery stressed the fashion in which white institutions and culture had atomized and uprooted the African peoples forcibly brought to this continent. Values, traditions, customs, family ties—all were seen as stripped away. As Abram Kardiner and Lionel Ovesey put it, the black American, at the time of emancipation, "had no culture, and he was quite green in his semi-acculturated state in the new one. He did not know his way about and had no intrapsychic defenses—no pride, no group solidarity, no tradition." For the slave, dependency on the dominant American culture supposedly was absolute. "Where was he to look for new standards, new cues?" asked Stanley Elkins. "He could look to none but his master, the one man to whom the system had committed his entire being."[2]

Such a view of slavery renders the spirited, militant words of the coastal black community simply incomprehensible. It offers no suggestion of experiences or language that might nurture a distinctive and dissenting black interpretation of American values and culture. But a more recent generation of historians has provided tools for explaining what earlier views could not, stressing the ways in which slaves were "actors in their own right who not only responded to their situation, but often affected it in crucial ways." As Herbert Gutman described, for example, in his pioneering work *The Black Family in Slavery and Freedom,* in "social space" left in plantation life between owners and slaves, the black community was able to develop distinctive Afro-American culture forms and institutions that "shielded them . . . from the cultural dominance . . . of the planter class."[3]

Family ties, drawing on African traditions and evolving to meet the harsh new challenges, provided the key to survival of tradition and identity. Despite the savagery of a system that regularly separated families—parents from children, husbands from wives—couples showed a fierce commitment to each other and to their offspring. Moreover, family ties became the model for other relationships, teaching a respect for the wisdom and experiences of the old, and binding unrelated adults to one another. As Gutman described, "making children address all adult blacks as either 'aunt' or 'uncle' socialized them into the enlarged slave community and also invested nonkin slave relationships with symbolic meanings and functions."[4]

Yet the very strengths of kinship patterns in socializing children and creating means through which folklore, music, and values could be transmitted also provided owners with a leverage that dampened protest. The threat of punishment of kin or sale to a distant plantation was a curb on insurgency. In such a context, the existence of places in the slave community beyond the immediate ties of family proved essential for the articulation and development of a language of freedom. Such settings, in the slave environment, were preeminently religious.[5]

Christianity was originally taught to the slave population in part as a "program for pacification," an effort to adapt the rebellious captives to the discipline of a dehumanizing labor system by destroying native beliefs and traditions. Yet from the beginning, slaves recast what they learned in radical ways, drawing on the African past. They also turned the white versions of Christianity on their head, finding, within scripture, rich resources for an alternative interpretation of the world and, within the places of worship, crucial free spaces for voicing rebellious and sometimes insurrectionary ideas.

At times, whites realized the dangerous possibilities of black religion and sought to take preventive action. South Carolina's Whitemarsh Seabrook, pointing out the need to prevent slave literacy, suggested that anyone who wanted blacks to read the entire Bible should be consigned to an insane asylum. Laws banning black worship services in the South appeared before the American Revolution. And in the later antebellum period, slave owners often employed their own white preachers to conduct services and required their slaves to attend.[6]

Yet slaves met regularly by themselves in services and other religious events like funerals. There was general leniency about such meetings: owners found that overly restrictive regulations of slaves in "off hours"—from sundown to sunup, on holidays and the Sabbath—markedly undermined plantation morale and productivity. Even where bans on slave worship were enforced, slaves often found ways to meet secretly. Songs like "Steal Away to Jesus" at work would signal later meetings. Services were regularly held in secret, well-hidden areas called "hush harbors." During the services, a pot would be overturned to "catch the sound." As Joseph Carrol described the pattern in Virginia in 1722, "Sunday was a favorite day on which the slaves often planned outbreaks, because it was easy to get together. . . . The slaves were given a deal of liberty in assembling for religious worship."[7]

A number of factors screened black religious services and the rebellious themes woven through religious language and music.

Little was known about slave preachings when whites were not there. Blacks themselves were scarcely likely to reveal what went on. From the elliptical references in slave spirituals, to the apparently "innocent" excitability of black services, indeed, blacks wove elaborate covers that hid plans and meetings from outside view. "Subterfuge, sabotage, fraud, trickery, footdragging and other behavior patterns of resistance were insinuated into the daily intercourse as a tactic of simple survival," Gayraud Wilmore has noted. Although slaves certainly found solace and hope in religion, the core of black Christianity was not quiet resignation. Rather, reflecting a pervasive spirituality which had roots in African religious practices and beliefs, their religion sought to release the human spirit "from every power . . . that would seek to exercise tyranny over it."[8]

Few whites had any regular contact at all with the depths of black religion. Those who did—such as white missionaries, motivated to report on their own successes to their supporters —had their own reasons for circumspection. The dominant notion that emerges from whites' discussions of black religiosity was its "childlike" and otherworldly character. But Frederick Law Olmsted's own accounts, generally reflecting white stereotypes, contain hints of invisible undercurrents. "The black people talk among themselves about this do they?" asks Olmsted, in an exchange with an elderly man. "They talk about being free a good deal, do they?" "Yes, sir," the man replies. "Dey— that is, dey say dey wish it was so; dat's all dey talk, master, dat's all, sir."[9]

In black Christianity, Jesus Christ appears, in the words of Julius Lester, as "someone who had suffered as they had suffered, someone who understood, someone who offered them rest from their sufferings." But there is little sense of the New Testament as the supercession of the Old. Blacks constantly rejected white attempts to make religion into an ethic of submissiveness. As one old black worshiper in the African Church of Richmond put it, after a white minister had counseled obedience, "He be d—d! God am not sich a fool!" And slaves were often highly selective in their use of the Bible. Howard Thurman remembered how his grandmother, years before, had refused to let him read from Paul. "When at length I asked the reason, she told me that during the days of slavery, the master on the plantation was always preaching from the Pauline letters —'Slaves, be obedient to your masters,' etc. 'I vowed to myself,' she said, 'that if freedom ever came and I learned to read, I would never read that part of the Bible!' "[10]

Indeed, the figures of Jesus and Moses were often blended in themes of deliverance and redemption. Black religion found strong resonance in the Hebraic stories. The words of the prophets, calling Israel to judgment, spoke directly to the experiences of blacks in America. The God of Israel who swept away the enemies of His people was a mighty source of hope and inspiration. And the story of Exodus itself, the Egyptian captivity and the people's deliverance from Pharaoh, became centrally interwoven with black aspirations, folkways, and music. Like the Hebrews in Egypt, blacks were captives in a strange and foreign land, brutalized and dehumanized by an all-pervasive system of oppression. Like the midwives, outwitting Pharaoh's officers when they ordered the slaughter of Hebrew babies, and like Miriam, hiding her brother in the Nile, black resistance depended on guile, cunning, and subterfuge. Finally, like Moses and Aaron, great leaders of the people arose, ordained by God, to lead the people from captivity, through the wilderness, across the Jordan, and into the promised land of freedom. Thus, America in black imagery and song became a dual symbol. It was simultaneously Egypt, the land of bondage, and potentially Canaan, the promised land of milk and honey.

Preachers assumed leadership in the community and contributed the distinctive style to the black freedom struggle. It was the preacher who articulated and gave expression to powerful religious feelings and hopes for freedom, drawing on African themes in a new context of oppression and reinterpreting and reworking Christian and biblical concepts in the process. During the eighteenth century, free black preachers enjoyed

wide recognition in the South. "Forbidden by law from functioning as preachers during the 19th Century," Eugene Genovese recounts, "they insinuated themselves into the confidence
of local whites as 'assistants' to white clergymen and went about
their own business." Even after laws passed in 1831 forbade
preaching by free blacks, a number continued to function
openly. And the figure of the preacher became the embodiment of articulate and skillful leadership. As W. E. B. Du Bois
put it, "The Preacher is the most unique personality developed
by the Negro on American soil. A leader, a politician, an orator,
a 'boss,' an intriguer, an idealist—all these he is, and ever too,
the center of a group of men, now twenty, now a thousand in
number." When trained free preachers were not available,
"drivers, craftsmen, exhorters or other prestigious slaves filled
in" for communal functions like funerals.[11]

Thus the preacher was the mediating figure between the
community and the white world. He fought for control over
spaces, finances, and the life of the service itself. He simultaneously hid its subversive dimensions from view and nurtured
hope and spirit among the congregation. Necessarily, then, the
preacher was part strategist, part tactician, part political organizer. He "bided his time" and looked for signs and opportunities. Such a role in an institution forged in underground adver-
sity necessarily entailed autocratic dimensions which continued
long after the abolition of slavery. But it also encouraged great
feats of daring and organizing.

In both North and South, blacks sought to create institution-
ally independent structures through which religious conviction
could find expression. During the Revolution, when the colo-
nists' natural-rights rhetoric opened a certain measure of cultural space, blacks took advantage of the situation to begin
petitioning for autonomous churches. An independent black
Baptist church appeared in Petersburg, Virginia, in 1776, the
Harrison Street Baptist Church. In 1785, the First Negro Baptist Church was established in Williamsburg. And in 1788, Andrew Bryan, a major figure in the church movement, created

the African Baptist church in Savannah, Georgia. After the Revolutionary war, the white community periodically sought to
close African Baptist, at one point whipping Bryan. But the
church survived and continued to function as the major center
of the black community.[12]

In the North, a protracted conflict with Methodist authorities
led Richard Allen, Absolem Jones, and other friends to an eventual break with the white denomination as a whole. Allen was
born into slavery in Philadelphia, and had been taken later to
Delaware. While an adolescent, he converted to Methodism,
believing in the low-church version which combined intense
spirituality with simplicity and an appeal to poor blacks. After
his conversion, Allen became a freedman and a powerful itiner-
ant preacher. He lived off hand labor and spread the gospel.

In 1786, he returned to Philadelphia. At first, church authorities gave him considerable support, hoping that he would increase membership among blacks. But they soon became wary
of his independence and sought to circumscribe his actions. In
1787, Allen and others formed the Free African Society, originally a quasi-religious association combining social services, mutual aid programs, and religious activities.[13]

The Free African Society spread rapidly to other cities, taking
on an abolitionist coloration as it did so. By 1790, the Society had
established a church which became the founding congregation
of the African Methodist Episcopal denomination, the religious
body that was to figure prominently in black history. Allen's
home church, Bethel, turned into a major station on the underground railroad, offering aid and support for slaves fleeing the
South. By 1818, AME had grown to 6,748 members, with other
congregations in many cities. Moreover, it formed a far-reaching base for underground activity and abolitionist organizing.
At various times, Frederick Douglass, Sojourner Truth, Harriet
Tubman, Catherine Harris, and many other prominent cham-
pions of black freedom had association with the denomination.[14]

Independent black churches were more difficult to organize

in the South. As early as 1800, South Carolina had passed laws forbidding any black religious meetings between sunset and sunrise. Yet even in the slave states, such legislation often proved difficult to enforce. Slaves often had religious gathering places in the forests or swamps where they would meet on Sundays to worship—and to keep dreams of emancipation alive. In cities, moreover, independent churches slowly multiplied.[15]

In Charleston, Methodism in particular won many converts among the black population. By the end of the War of 1812, black Methodists outnumbered whites in the city by ten to one. They maintained a quarterly conference of their own, with custody of their collections and control over church trials of members, though they still remained nominally part of the white denomination.

A clash was inevitable in the midst of the slave South. White authorities could not allow such an independent institutional network to indefinitely expand. In 1816, the *Times* of Charleston voiced growing worries:

> Almost every night there is a meeting of these noisy worshippers. . . . Midnight! Is that the season for religious convocation? . . . That the meeting of numerous black people to hear the scriptures expounded by an ignorant and (too frequently) vicious person of their own color can be of no benefit either to themselves or the community is certain.

White Methodists sought to reestablish control.[16]

Meanwhile, black church leaders had visited Philadelphia and had met with the founders of AME. Later in 1816, AME ordained two black ministers in Charleston for pastorates. The next year, an independent African Association was organized which soon attracted more than three-fourths of the 6,000 black Methodists in the city.

City political officials, aware of the dangers such an independent denomination might pose, constantly harassed the black churches. They broke up meetings. They made periodical arrests of leaders and members. Finally, in 1821, Charleston authorities closed the Hamstead Church, a center of the whole movement. Denmark Vesey, a leading figure in Hamstead, saw the closing of the church as both an outrage and an opportunity.

Vesey had spent many years traveling through the Caribbean, along the African coast, and elsewhere as a sailor. Finally, in his mid-thirties, he was able to purchase his freedom from the ship captain in 1800. Settling in Charleston, Vesey became well known as a prosperous member of the free black community. Tall, spare, he was a familiar figure on the streets, and a man who refused many customary conventions. For instance, he refused to bow to whites when he passed. According to a friend, Vesey believed "all men were born equal . . . he was surprised that anyone would degrade himself by such conduct."

When Hamstead closed, Vesey and other friends—Rolla Bennet, "Gullah Jack" Pritchard, Monday Gell, and Ned and Peter Royas—began to meet frequently in Vesey's home and also in the religious meeting places on nearby plantations. According to one conspirator, Vesey argued that "we were deprived of our rights and privileges by the white people and . . . our church was shut up so that we could not use it. . . . It was high time for us to seek for our rights, and conquer the whites."

Vesey and the others drew hope from the successful revolution in Haiti. Vesey had traveled to Santo Domingo and knew of the slave rebellion there at first hand. Gullah Jack's spiritual powers were also seen as a powerful asset—he was thought to be able to conjure aid from the African continent by magical means. In addition, Vesey knew of the growing national controversy over the question of slavery, and may have expected some aid from national authorities or northern abolitionists. Finally, the conspirators drew inspiration from the Bible and the story of the Exodus. At almost every meeting, remembered one man regularly present, Vesey or someone else would "read to us from the Bible, how the children of Israel were delivered out of Egypt from bondage."

The men developed an elaborate plan. They obtained horses

from butchers and draymen. Blacksmiths in the community made bayonets and other weapons. And they set a date, the second week of July 1822. Whites discovered the plan only at the last moment.[17]

Vesey's adaptation of biblical themes for insurrectionary ends formed a pattern that reappeared again and again in the years before the Civil War. In 1829, David Walker, a black abolitionist who was an active member of the black Methodist church in Boston, stunned white America with his explosive pamphlet "Walker's Appeal to the Colored Citizens of the World But in Particular and Very Expressly to Those of the United States of America." In fiery and eloquent language, "Walker's Appeal" called for a holy crusade, an armed rebellion against the slave system.

The southern states panicked. One group in Georgia offered $1,000 for Walker's death (he soon dropped dead on his doorstep mysteriously; the black community was convinced he had been poisoned). White abolitionists also reacted with horror at such incendiary rhetoric. But the evidence is strong that "Walker's Appeal" had an electrifying effect on black communities both North and South. Scores risked their lives to distribute the pamphlet in southern states. It may well have found its way to Nat Turner, an evangelical Christian who had been seeking a sign that the moment had arrived "when the first should be last and the last should be first."[18]

White fears of independent black religious activity spread throughout the country. The *Richmond Enquirer* made the common point: "The case of Nat Turner warns us. No black man ought to be permitted to turn a preacher throughout the country." Southern states passed a series of new laws forbidding slaves to read and write, to preach, to meet separately. In Mississippi, the legislature declared, "It is unlawful for any slave, free Negro or mulatto to preach the gospel upon pain of receiving thirty-nine lashes upon the naked back of the . . . preacher."[19]

Thus, at the heart of the slave system was a destructiveness that transcended physical suffering. The power structure of the white South assaulted the very foundations of black identity and independence.

But resistance continued, nonetheless. As historian Gary Nash has described, "despite the enactment of harsh slave codes, the plantation was never so efficient or rationally managed as to leave the slaves without considerable 'social space' in which to maneuver." Even in the most severe moments of repression, slave families continued to sustain and transmit oral traditions of cultural independence and black identity. In more open times, blacks not only sustained but acted upon aspirations for freedom. In the cities, there existed more free space still. And the currents of African-American Christianity drew too directly upon the dominant ideology of the white world to be suppressed entirely, whatever white fears. By the end of the 1830s, blacks had begun once again to reestablish the free churches and benevolent societies in cities such as Wilmington, Savannah and Richmond.[20]

At the close of the Civil War, black hopes flared. "The safety of this country depends on giving the Colored man all the rights of a white and especially the Rebel," said one former Mississippi slave who had fought for the Union. "Let him know that there is enough in the arm of the Government to give Justice to all her loyal citizens."[21] Demands like the widespread proposal of "forty acres and a mule" for freed slaves recalled directly the republican and biblical themes of the commonwealth which had undergirded the Revolutionary period itself. But in the black vision of America's future which was articulated during Reconstruction, the "community" in which all citizens participated, exercising virtue and equal rights, was to be reconstructed in a new, racially inclusive way.*

*Eric Foner has pointed out how widespread were republican notions among the slave population itself. "What is remarkable is how quickly blacks who were only recently released from bondage adopted precisely the same political language [as northern republican demands] to express their grievances and aspirations. From the protests over unequal pay to post–Civil War petitions for the right to vote, black soldiers couched their appeals in the language of republican-

Again, struggle for control over religious institutions proved a crucial element in strategy. Repeatedly in churches associated with white denominations, black congregations sought to gain autonomy. In Wilmington, North Carolina, the Front Street Church demanded that the Southern Methodists dismiss the white pastor and allow them to affiliate with AME. In Raleigh, the Wesley Chapel community argued that white control corrupted the Gospel: "We Desiar to despence [sic] with the Services of men whos fidelity to the government by us is doubted in order therefore that we may be able to worship God According to the dictates of our consciances."[22]

In areas where strong traditions of black church independence continued, the communities had "spokespersons who had been nurtured among the people and their indigenous institutions for decades and longer," as Vincent Harding described. When Sherman and Stanton led the northern armies into Savannah, they were met by a group of black ministers who traced their roles to the efforts of Andrew Bryan and the black Baptists of sixty-five years before. In Richmond, capital of the Confederacy itself, a strong and cohesive black population immediately set about pressing its claims for equal rights in the new era that was beginning.[23]

Events immediately after the war fed the black community's confidence. On April 3, 1866, first anniversary of the fall of Richmond to Union Army troops (a date the community preferred to celebrate as the "real" moment of emancipation, rather than January 1, date of the Presidential Proclamation), a parade and enormous rally at Capitol Square indicated the new mood.

"An immense cavalcade of black horsemen led the van,

ism; they insisted that racial discrimination violated the fundamental principles upon which the nation was founded. . . . Instead of emerging from slavery wholly estranged from the rest of the country, black soldiers, in their claims for rights at least, were quintessentially American." Eric Foner, "The Hidden History of Emancipation," *New York Review of Books,* March 1, 1984, p. 39.

preceded by a dusky son of Ham," read the report in the *Citizen*, which conveyed the festive spirit despite its condescending tone. "Then came a Patriarch with a stick, with a gourd on the top of it, all covered over with ribands; this individual was decorated in an apron of black and gold, and a gold stripe down his legs. . . . After the band there marched a long string of unsentimental, unbleached, some with aprons, some with rosettes, and some with sashes. . . . Finally [it] climaxed with a parcel of field hands, in jeans walking in squads, without commander, uniform or decorum."

Craft, benevolent, and religious societies of all sorts marched together alongside newly formed political organizations. One section of the crowd, "The humble Christian Benevolents of the Chesterfield Coal Pits," testified to an old occupation in the area; another, decked in broad black scarves with white tips, carried a banner proclaiming, "Union Liberties Protective Society, organized February 4, 1866—Peace and Goodwill Toward Men." Several thousand strong, the paraders converged on the buildings that once housed the Confederate government. There, the gathering swelled to 15,000 or more. A local white leader of the Republican Party, the Reverend Hunnicutt, called for racial equality and hard work. Several black speakers followed, voicing similar sentiments.[24]

The black community had faced acute problems immediately after the war, but had addressed them with cohesion and effectiveness. As in other southern towns, the war's conclusion brought formal freedom to slaves but little substantive change in the rigid patterns of segregated work and social life. White workers were concentrated in skilled trades, by and large. A prosperous, homogeneous white elite composed of merchants, manufacturers, bankers, and other affluent men continued to predominate in Richmond's political affairs. Blacks labored largely in tobacco production, iron, domestic service, and a variety of other industrial occupations—Richmond had the most diversified economy of any southern city before the war; and through the 1850s, factory employment had grown 581 percent. Though informal interracial social contact existed—among childhood playmates, for example, or in illicit sexual encounters—social clubs, public facilities, and the like were sharply divided by race. And Richmond whites made apparent their strong determination to maintain the uncompromising caste system. Indeed, in some respects blacks found themselves more circumscribed than before: Federal military authorities joined with local employers and city officials to clamp restrictions on the movement of newly freed slaves and former freedmen alike. Noting the influx of former slaves from rural areas, one local officer wrote General Stanton: "There are thousands of colored people flocking into town and roaming throughout the country. They should be sent to work." Authorities required passes from all blacks who traveled in public.[25]

But the black community was in no mood to accept passively such humiliations. Work life had long entailed an important measure of freedom for both slave and free men and women. Even in the larger factories, management had learned that "industrial slave workers responded better to incentives than punishments," as historian Peter Rachleff observed, and thus the system "still had far more space within it than that of the rural agricultural world." In other occupations, like the teamsters, boatmen, stevedores, carpenters, and plasterers, slaves had a degree of autonomy as well. And income from such work had further sustained a variety of independent black businesses —boardinghouses, barbers, tailors, seamstresses, shoemakers, and many others. Off the job, there was even more free space. Many slaves were given allowances for housing, food, and other necessities, and had intermingled freely with the nonslave black population.[26]

The two central institutions of church and family had especially encouraged independence. Family patterns were close-knit, involving not only husbands, wives, and children but also extended networks of grandparents, aunts, uncles, cousins, sisters and brothers, and fictive kin. When freedom came in 1865, thousands of former slaves evidenced the depth of their relationships by immediately seeking legal sanction for their marriages and families.

In the antebellum years, whites had retained formal control over the black churches, but in practice, boards of black deacons ran daily church businesses. Churches were schools of a sort, in which many community leaders learned a variety of civic skills such as how to run meetings, keep records, and plan events. Churches like the First African Baptist Church had long been symbols of the whole community's pride and relative autonomy. More than four and a half thousand blacks belonged to the three African Baptist churches in the city alone. Finally, on the foundation of the church, family, trade, and other relationships, the beginnings of what was to prove an enormous interlocking network of "secret societies" (so named because the membership lists were kept confidential) had begun to emerge in the years before the war. Such societies were organized for religious, recreational, and mutual aid functions. They provided resources to care for orphans, widows, widowers, the indigent, and the disabled.

With such a history and such extensive networks, black Richmond had long enjoyed a noteworthy reputation. "No one southern city furnished a larger number of brave, wide-awake, and likely looking Underground Railroad passengers," said William Still, a key figure in the underground operations. In keeping with these traditions, a group of men drew up a petition two months after the Union Army reached Richmond that expressed the community's grievances. They addressed it to Andrew Johnson, the new President.

"We represent a population of more than 20,000 colored people," read the document. "More than 6,000 of our people are members in good standing of Christian churches, and nearly our whole population constantly attend divine services." It mentioned the fact that many had modest means, and a few owned property valued from $5,000 to $20,000. It stressed the frugality and independence prized by the community. "None of our people are in the alms house, and when we were slaves the aged and infirm who were turned away from the homes of hard masters, who had been enriched by their toil, our benevolent societies supported while they lived and buried when they died." Despite the fact that reading and writing were illegal for blacks under slavery, the petition highlighted the strong value placed upon education. "Three thousand of us can read," it maintained, "and at least 2,000 can read and write, and a large number of us are engaged in useful and profitable employment on our own account."[27]

The petition asked that the pass system restricting black mobility be abolished, that the "rebel controlled" local government be removed, and that the black congregations secure legal title to their own churches. The pass system was a special humiliation. "The present treatment is worse than we ever suffered before," complained former freemen who had come and gone with relative ease. Now, they were "required to get some white person to give us passes to attend to our daily occupation, without which we are marched off to the old Rebel Hospital, now called the Negro bull pen."

When Union forces and local police arrested 800 men, women, and children in early June of that year for pass violations, the tensions had come to a head. At a mass meeting, June 10, 1865, a large number of people met to plan what to do. They decided to send a delegation of seven to visit President Johnson directly, and set about raising funds for the trip through the black churches. The protest proved successful. Governor Pierpont removed the mayor, Joseph Mayo, from office. President Johnson shifted the military officers in charge of the city. The new presiding general, Aldred Terry, quickly ended the pass system and offered to work cooperatively with Richmond blacks. That summer and fall, blacks had held a number of additional mass meetings to plan strategy and seek redress of their grievances.[28]

But after the early successes, other problems proved far more intractable. The black community suffered sometimes violent attack. Economic recession and a large influx of immigrants from outside the city strained the resources of the community. Supposed allies in the Republican Party evidenced no interest in racial equality after all; indeed, the black leaders of Jackson ward, the largely black political district in the city, fought a series of protracted battles with the local Republican "ring" for control of politics in the area. Thus, over the years, periods of quiescence alternated with periods of renewed activism. But by the late 1870s, the black community was once again hoping to make gains on long-standing issues of concern. As the movement expanded, it impacted on the internal life of institutions like the church itself.

A new generation of young black leadership had developed by the late 1870s, many in middle-class professions such as teaching, medicine, law, and small businesses not dependent on white largess in any fashion. Such leaders began to assert a new racial pride and interest in community self-improvement. They organized select secret societies like the Chatauqua Literary and Scientific Circle, the Palmetto Club, and the Knights of King Solomon. And they saw themselves as models, "representative men of the race." Thus, the Acme Literary Association defined its mission: "To consider questions of vital importance to our people, so that the masses of them may be drawn out to be entertained, enlightened and instructed thereby." The Association held lectures and discussions on topics like "the trades" and "the vexed problem: labor," and debated issues like temperance, dancing, and forms of self-help.[29]

These same years saw the growth of considerable independent political activity. Since the war, blacks in Richmond had periodically sought to gain some independence from the Republican Party, whose profession of interest in the black vote was not matched by action on issues like black education or desegregation of public facilities. But there had been little alternative. Almost no connection existed between white workers in Richmond and the black community. Indeed, the schism was glaringly obvious in divisions which occurred along racial lines at moments of work-place conflict. When black coopers struck against the Richmond barrel shops in September 1877, for instance, protesting the use of convict labor which threatened their jobs, white workers voiced no opposition to a massive use of police power against the strikers, which soon crushed the walkout.[30]

But the late 1870s saw the first stirrings of a popular movement among white small farmers, businessmen, and workers, in Richmond and throughout the state of Virginia, coming together in a movement called the "Readjusters" that demanded readjustment of the state debt. After considerable discussion, an alliance was worked out with Readjusters in the state legislature in 1879. And for the first time, state government began to give serious attention to a number of black concerns. Blacks gained appointment to juries. The poll tax was repealed. Blacks as well as whites received patronage jobs. And a number of new schools were built for black children—the enrollment of children increased from 36,000 in 1879 to 91,000 in 1883.[31]

Such victories electrified the black community. Seniors and staff of the Richmond Normal School voted to hold graduation ceremonies in one of the school's small classrooms, rather than the spacious—but segregated—Richmond Theater. Workers evidenced a new spirit. In May 1881, black brickmakers struck, winning major gains against their employers. Paperboys also caught the mood. When conservative Democratic interests sought to inflame racial antagonism to destroy the Readjuster–black political coalition, blacks refused to sell the local Democratic paper and pressured their white counterparts to do likewise. "Now for the first time," one young man told a reporter for a northern newspaper, "colored men begin to feel they are men."

In such a heady environment, controversy emerged within First African Baptist Church. Henry Buford, a lay preacher who worked in a tobacco factory and had taught himself to read and write, led a protest of several hundred male and female church members—many of them young and middle class—against the "unChristianlike" conduct of the minister, the Reverend James

Holmes, toward female members of the congregation. When the deacons met to consider the issue, Susan Washington, leader of a secret society, advocate of black cooperation with the populist Readjusters, created pandemonium. She presented a petition signed by 200 female members of the congregation demanding the right to vote in the proceedings. Holmes barely survived the challenge, and the deacons called the police. African Baptist expelled forty-seven leaders of the "rebel faction," including the editor of the leading black newspaper and a representative of the community to the state political convention in 1879 which had led to the alliance with the Readjusters. To the consternation of the established leadership who sided with Holmes, the ousted group formed the Fifth Street Baptist Church, which soon attracted a large congregation of its own.[32]

Despite gains on specific issues and the buoyant mood of the community, the black movement continued to be plagued by its lack of a vehicle for expressing and sustaining the interests, values, and power of the community as a whole. Indeed, the very successes in political terms weakened black leadership in an ironic way: R. A. Paul, once a key figure in organizing the community, was appointed to the new governor's staff as personal messenger and given a seat on the school board as well. There, he continued to champion black needs and concerns, but his role as independent catalyst and organizer of black protest was ended. In a similar way, Lewis Lindsay, long a visible and articulate spokesman for the community, received a patronage job in the post office in the expectation he would "do good service" for the Readjusters. But the culmination of such patronage appointments turned out to be the progressive distancing of many strong leaders from the black community base which had been responsible for their appointments. As key black activists became integrated into the Readjuster Party, as Peter Rachleff described the process, "they became free from their earlier dependence on the black popular movement" itself.[33]

Meanwhile, electoral activity alone did little to address the deeper imperatives of organizing in the community. Thus, though whites and blacks had formed an alliance for convenience in the Readjusters, few substantive ties developed between white and black communities. White workers, originally attracted to the Readjuster banner by issues like the state debt and education—also a concern of major importance to blacks—dropped away when conservative Democrats raised the issue of the "color line." Indeed, in the election of 1883, a concerted campaign by powerful business interests successfully depicted the Readjusters as advocates of "social equality," spinning visions of "savages and despots, lechers, polygamists, cannibals, worshippers of snakes and devils." As the political coalition fell apart, divisions along class lines also surfaced in the black community. "Many persons seem to think that because a person happens to dress respectably and draws a reasonable salary, that they look with contempt upon those in lower walks of life," wrote the *Richmond Planet,* defensively, in February 1885.[34] From the point of view of those in "lower walks of life," meanwhile, the established black leadership evidenced little concern with their situation. A deep recession threatened their livelihoods. And new technology in tobacco, barrel-making, and other industries threatened permanent displacement of many workers. The popular movement in Richmond looked for a new organizational vessel that could move beyond the rivalries and factionalism of electoral politics and also begin to make inroads into the rigid segmentation imposed by southern racial prejudice. For a time in the mid-1880s, the Knights of Labor proved to be just such an instrument—a story taken up in Chapter 4.

Following the Knights of Labor, black aspirations for dignity, "manhood," and equal participation in an American commonwealth did not disappear. They surfaced again in movements like the populist revolt among small farmers in the southern states during the 1880s and 1890s; in the Garveyite movement of the 1920s and in trade union struggles in the twentieth century; and in distinctive black-defined institutions like the Brotherhood of Sleeping Car Porters, headed by A. Philip Randolph,

and the National Association for the Advancement of Colored
People. Less visibly, moreover, black traditions of resistance
and the continuity and integrity of black culture itself were
nourished and sustained by women's activities in home and
church organizations and in particular contexts like the black
YWCAs that multiplied across the South. "Ever since slavery
times it's been the Negro woman in the South who has had to
shoulder the burden of strength and dignity in the colored
family," explained Mahalia Jackson. "Down in the South the
white man has never given the Negro man a job he could be
very proud of. He has always called him 'Boy' or by some nick-
name. . . . it was usually the Negro mother who had to keep a
certain dignity in the family to offset the inferiority the white
man inflicted on her husband. She held her head up high and
she showed the way to her children."[35]

In the post–Civil War years, the black community faced
threats to its identity and culture other than white prejudice
and repression. With formal freedom came an end to the cultural isolation which generated a separate, vital culture as a
simple matter of survival. Blacks, with a greater range of op-
tions and choices, faced pressures to assimilate that generations
of immigrants have encountered in America. Moreover, such
pressures were augmented by an aggressive campaign from the
North to "reeducate" the newly freed slaves in dominant
American culture. Five thousand teachers arrived during the
war and Reconstruction, for example, with much the same sentiments as Lucy Chase. "At one of their prayer-meetings, which
we attended last night, we saw a painful exhibition of their
barbarism," wrote Chase to her New England family about her
first experiences in Craney Island, Virginia. "Tonight I have
been to a 'shout,' which seems to me certainly the remains of
some old idol worship," explained another woman, Laura
Towne, about a service she witnessed on St. Helena's Island.

Northerners brought with them a perspective basically different from white southerners. "Where southern whites generally
were perfectly content to allow the blacks to stew in their own

cultural juices," as historian Lawrence Levine put it, "the northerners pined to wipe them clean and participate as midwives at a rebirth." As one teacher said, "our work is just as much a missionary work as if we were in India or China." White teachers and missionaries brought with them the tools of a literate, powerful culture, but also different values like radical individualism. "Young black children who were inducted into the mysteries of *McGuffey's Eclectic Reader* and similar textbooks were ushered into a world in which no one had to be poor," as Levine explained, if they were sufficiently motivated as individuals to "make it" on their own. Literacy—avidly taken up by freed blacks who had for decades been barred from reading—meant a change in the very relation of past and present. Stories handed down orally conveyed a personal immediacy; sense of ancestors' *presence* becomes lost in the more abstract and detached medium of the written word.[36]

Blacks adjusted to such pressures by learning to speak in two worlds. "In the classroom we all learned past participles, but in the streets and in our homes the Blacks learned to drop s's from plurals and suffixes from past tense verbs," described Maya Angelou. "We learned to slide out of one language and into another without being conscious of the effort."[37]

Despite attenuations, independent black cultural forms survived formal "emancipation," as they had survived slavery. Once again, the autonomy of the church proved a bedrock for community cohesion and autonomy, and its religious resources furnished, in such an environment, the main wellsprings of cultural renewal. Black music, for instance, adapted and changed—the more polished gospel music replacing informal and spontaneous spirituals as the main form. But gospel itself, as developed by great singers like Thomas Dorsey and Mahalia Jackson, "took the people back to slavery times," as singer Robert Anderson put it, creating a medium for connecting past with present that broke beyond the confines of the dominant culture and sustained communal and participatory values. Thus, though gospel music was written and composed, in the black community it remained strongly improvisational and participatory. "A white chorus of one hundred voices will buy one hundred copies" of a gospel song, explained Dorsey. "A Negro chorus, two. . . . One for the director and one for the pianist." Everyone else learned it and changed it as the music unfolded.[38]

Not until the 1950s, however, did the independent cultural resources of the black community result in a movement for equality and full participation on the scale of the years after the Civil War. Once again, the religious spirit which had always sustained black hopes, the churches which had furnished free spaces for its animus, and the preachers who had long "looked for signs" and waited for the proper moment found both signs and opportunity. Black Christian traditions, intermingling with American democratic themes, exploded in a sweeping civil rights revolt which transformed the religious message from comfort, survival, and resistance to a positive call for the nation to live up to her values and promises.[39]

The civil rights movement of the 1950s and '60s grew out of a social and economic environment that was rapidly changing. In the 1940s, the overwhelming majority of southern blacks lived and worked in rural areas; less than 5 percent of the black population had professional occupations, and those who did were concentrated in jobs such as the ministry, medicine, and education. But economic shifts encouraged a migration from the countryside to cities such as Atlanta, Montgomery, Birmingham, Raleigh, and Richmond. In the 1950s, the adoption of tractors and mechanical cotton pickers on many southern farms combined with the reduction in cotton acreage to create widespread underemployment for many rural families. Relatively low unemployment rates in the cities, by way of contrast, seemed to offer expanding opportunities that were especially attractive to a generation whose young men had fought for "American democracy" in the Second World War and were impatient to gain some of its fruits at home.[40]

Cities offered an alternative to the closed system of much of the rural South in more intangible ways. In many rural areas, patterns of subordination reminiscent of slavery continued into the mid-twentieth century. Economic dependence, scattered patterns of residency, the relatively small and insecure black professional class, and the ever-present threat of white terror had all combined to make protest against segregation extraordinarily difficult. Black voter registration in most rural Black Belt counties was well below 15 percent; in some it was virtually nonexistent. In the cities, blacks had new forms of economic independence and new forms of power, such as their purchases of consumer goods. Free space was far more extensive. In urban work settings, blacks heard of the union traditions of self-organization and self-assertion pioneered by A. Philip Randolph and others. And in dense, black urban communities, a rich network of voluntary associations, centering on the black church, created opportunities for leadership to develop, and news and information to spread rapidly. Simply, urban life held greater promise of social freedom and independence. The Reverend Fred Shuttlesworth, leader in the Birmingham civil rights movement, spoke from an ancient tradition of urban black church independence when he replied to the local sheriff's attempt to prohibit ministers from encouraging their congregations to participate in a boycott: "Only God can tell me what to say in the pulpit."[41]

Yet life in any area of the South remained sharply circumscribed for blacks, and as the decade of the Fifties progressed, changes seemed painstakingly slow at best. A national preoccupation with the Red scare and McCarthyism had put protest and social change efforts of any kind dramatically on the defensive. In the years from 1949 to 1954, membership in the largest civil rights organization, the National Association for the Advancement of Colored People (NAACP) had declined from a wartime high of about 500,000 to 200,000.

The first developments after the landmark Supreme Court decision *Brown* v. *The Board of Education* in 1954, outlawing the principle of "separate but equal" education, seemed to threaten what measure of protection and freedom the black community enjoyed. According to a Southern Regional Council report published in 1956, southern white reaction to the court decision ranged from evasion to crude violence. Following networks of service clubs like the Lions and Kiwanis, whose membership was drawn from the "respectable" white middle class, White Citizens Councils sprang up all across the South with the explicit purpose of preventing any desegregation in the schools. Louis Lomax described the bitter mood of disillusionment that affected southern blacks: "We—particularly those of us who were Southern-born—had faith in a class of white people known to Negroes as 'good white people.' These were respectable white people who were pillars of the Southern community and who appeared to be the power structure of the community. It never occurred to us that professional white people would let poor white trash storm the town and take over." Yet here the "good white people" themselves were leading the reaction.[42]

The black community was subjected to mounting violence. Emmett Till, a fourteen-year-old from Chicago visiting his relatives in Greenwood, Mississippi, was rumored to have whistled at a white woman. He was found dead in the Tallahatchie River, a 70-pound cotton gin fan tied around his neck with barbed wire. Jeremiah Reeves, a high school drummer convicted in 1952 by an all-white court of raping a white woman, was killed after a series of unsuccessful appeals. His death formed a stark contrast to the regular rapes and deaths inflicted upon blacks, seemingly at whim. Two white police officers who forced a black woman into their car and raped and beat her had their charges dismissed. Similarly, a man who raped a fifteen-year-old baby sitter—who later died in shock—was found not guilty.

Montgomery, Alabama, witnessed the spreading climate of repression visible elsewhere. In the wake of the Brown decision, an ex-football star organized a movement to form White Citizens Councils throughout the city. "By the spring and summer of 1955," writes historian Stephen B. Oates, "a flame of discontent was smoldering below the surface of passivity in black Montgomery." Martin Luther King, Jr., recently arrived with his family to step into the pastorate at Dexter Avenue Baptist Church, could sense the growing tension.[43]

Martin Luther King, Jr., had grown up in a professional family in Atlanta, city of the largest and most prosperous black middle class in the South. His father was minister at the prestigious Ebenezer Baptist Church, had long worked for black gains in the city, and believed in standing up to whites, if necessary, to assert his dignity. One day, when Martin was a child, a policeman stopped the car driven by his father, "Daddy" King. "Boy, show me your license," the officer ordered brusquely. "Do you see this child here?" asked King, pointing to Martin Luther. "That's a *boy* there. I'm a *man.* I'm Reverend King." "When I stand up," Daddy King told his son, "I want everybody to know that a *man* is standing up. Nobody can make a slave out of you if you don't think like a slave."[44]

King undoubtedly learned from his father's example. He also rebelled against his father's strict fundamentalism and autocratic ways, planning a career other than the ministry. For a time, King intended a future as a scholar and college professor, and periodically throughout his life imagined that at some point he would return to the world of academia. But at Morehouse College in Atlanta, he also gained another perspective on the ministry from Benjamin Mays, president of the school. Mays believed that too many black preachers created "socially irrelevant patterns of escape." He saw too many black schools, as well, simply accommodating the system of segregation. In his view, the proper function of education was "liberation through knowledge." And the proper mission of the black church was leading the movement for freedom. King saw Mays as what he wanted "a real minister to be"—a preacher who combined spiritual uplift with social involvement and intellectual rigor and rationality. And he chose the ministry for himself, in the tradition of both his father and maternal grandfather. "I came to see that God had placed a responsibility upon my shoulders," he remembered later, "and the more I tried to escape it the more frustrated I would become."[45]

King continued his education at Crozier Seminary in Pennsylvania, and then in graduate school at Boston University, where he earned a doctorate. At both institutions, he schooled himself in writers who spoke from modern theological and philosophical perspectives—Hegel, Walter Rauschenbusch, Reinhold Niebuhr, and others. Indeed, in many ways his theological education was a model of learned, "liberal" scholarship and discourse. But if King could speak the language of "intellectual rigor and rationality" characteristic of the modern academy, his religious concerns were differently focused, grounded directly in the popular religiosity of the black community and the free social spaces of the black church.

Modern theology, as Harvey Cox has recently observed, begins with a premise very different from popular religiosity. Since the late eighteenth century, theologians of virtually every major school have had a distinctive and particular objective: the "fervent desire to appeal to the thoughtful, educated, skeptical 'modern' mind." The objective shaped the nature of the audience: "Theology's conversation partner became the dominant classes, and it lost contact with the lower ones. Theology made the problem of skepticism its main challenge." But for King, simply, religion was not a "phenomenon" to be rationally analyzed or justified to the modern, skeptical interlocutor. Rather it was simultaneously a transcendent source of meaning and the wellspring of struggle against oppression. Even in graduate school, King articulated the beginnings of an alternative theory of social change and social conflict, one which was to have far-reaching impact.[46]

King's view of God and faith focused on problems of action. Social gospel theologians such as Rauschenbusch, who imagined the social engineering of a good society, were far too facile, in his opinion, about human evil. But modern Protestant theologians in the vein of Niebuhr had "become too pessimistic, so that they lapsed into a mood of antirationalism and the utter hopelessness of the world and man's incapacity to change it or himself."

In turn, King's concern with simultaneous social and personal change led him to the philosophy of personalism, a strong strand in much of radical Catholic thought with a communitarian cast. In the personalist view, each is made in the image of God. Sin is a reality, but it can be overcome through "man's willing acceptance of God's mighty gift" and recognition that all were "potential sons of God." Such perspectives informed a different view of both social change agency and ultimate goal. Rather than conventional liberal focus on an abstractly conceived citizen and individual rights and liberties, or the left-wing notions of inevitable clashes between abstract aggregates of people thought to have irreconcilable interests ("classes," "masses"), King's developing philosophy emphasized the redemptive power of love and suffering. He rejected Marxism for its depersonalization of the individual and its doctrine of "class conflict." He dissented from left-wing focus on large-scale government as a metaphor for the future, opposing any systems which reduced the individual "to a depersonalized cog in the ever-turning wheel of the state." Instead, he was attracted to the conception of the "Christian commonwealth," a notion drawing on older, populist and biblical themes and traditions. And his strategy for change emphasized Gandhi's belief in *Satyagraha,* the idea that love and truth could be combined in a vehicle for social change that disciplined and directed anger. The practice of *Satyagraha,* in King's terms, would redeem and transform both oppressed and oppressor. Gandhi was his model of a "self-remade man."[47]

King brought such intellectual perspectives to Dexter, a middle-class congregation in Montgomery which was delighted by the combination of erudition and fiery eloquence in their new minister. But King was interested in more than simple preaching. He developed an ambitious social action program, as well as social service committees to care for the sick, help young people with their education, and so forth. And he became active in the broader community, serving on the NAACP executive committee, making contact with a variety of other churches in Montgomery, decrying the "crippling factionalism" which he feared would prevent effective action.[48]

Then, on Friday morning, December 2, 1955, an event occurred which galvanized the entire community and seemed a ready-made opportunity to test one of the most glaring segregationist statutes. The law required blacks to sit in the back of the bus, even if front seats were empty, and to turn over their seats to whites no matter what the age or condition of the black passenger. Bus drivers had long been notorious for the crudity and vulgarity of their treatment of black passengers, who made up 70 percent of the bus company's clientele. The white drivers —and all were white—regularly called Negro passengers, "niggers," "apes," "black cows," and the like. And they were especially prone to focus their humiliating abuse upon black women.

That morning, Rosa Parks, a tailor's assistant in a downtown store, got on the bus and sat down. She had gone shopping after work and her feet hurt. When the bus driver ordered Mrs. Parks to stand so a white man could sit down, she simply refused. He yelled at her, threatening to call the police. "Mrs. Parks sighed," recounts Oates. "She thought how you spend your whole life making things comfortable for white people. You just live for their well-being, and they don't even treat you like a human being. Well, let the cops come. She wasn't moving." Behind Rosa Parks's apparently spontaneous act, however, was a long history of active involvement—she had attended Highlander Folk School, an old, activist institution in the South, and her parents had both been activists in battling segregation. Moreover, her act of defiance came at the moment when many threads merged: growing black resentment, the emergence of a new and articulate generation of black leaders, increasing national unease about segregation, economic and social changes which had increased the capacities for independent and powerful black organization. Together, all these created a historic stage. "When Momma Parks Sat Down, the Whole World Stood Up," ran the words of the civil rights song that was to commemorate that day.[49]

Police arrested her for violating the segregation statutes—the first arrest under that statute, which many in the black community believed could not stand a court test. E. D. Nixon, a regional official of the Brotherhood of Sleeping Car Porters, was convinced that this was an opportunity long needed. "We can go to the Supreme Court with this," he argued, "and boycott the bus line at the same time." A number of ministers that Friday afternoon urged people to stay off the buses in protest. When the judge made the mistake of finding Mrs. Parks guilty of violating the ordinance, fining her $14 and court costs, she refused to pay. The ministers met to form the Montgomery Improvement Association, named "to stress the positive, uplift approach of their movement." The organization soon became an organization of organizations: E. D. Nixon was the first treasurer; Rufus Lewis, head of the Citizens Committee, chaired the transportation committee; Mrs. Jo Ann Robinson, a leader in the Women's Political Council, served on the executive board. To his surprise, Martin Luther King, Jr., was chosen president, despite his youth. According to some present, his eloquence and ability to talk to people "from any direction" and his freedom from white politicians (according to one, he hadn't been in the city long enough "to be spoiled . . . so many ministers accept a handout, and then they own their soul") were the decisive factors. Others saw King as a compromise candidate between middle-class men and others like Nixon who represented poorer constituents.[50]

All that Monday, the boycott, which had been hurriedly called the Friday before, had proven amazingly successful. Buses along the South Jackson line through the black section of town were empty; bands of youths from Alabama State, the all-black college in the city, hitchhiked to school or stood at the bus stops singing and cheering. That night when the Improvement Association called its first mass meeting, Holt Street

Church filled to overflowing two hours before the meeting was to begin.[51]

King's speech to the gathering, combining, as he put it, "militancy and moderation," reflected the sort of communitarian and democratic themes that had long formed major themes of the black church. He grounded the struggle's aims in patriotism and biblical teachings. "We're here," he declared, "because first and foremost we are American citizens, and we are determined to acquire our citizenship to the fullness of its meaning." Drawing on biblical notions and a sense of their *rights* as citizens, King challenged blacks to discover in themselves a new "sense of somebodyness" that would transform in unalterable ways the relations between whites and blacks. He grounded such a call directly in the power of American traditions and religious faith. "If we are wrong," he declared, "the Supreme Court of this nation is wrong. If we are wrong, God Almighty is wrong. If we are wrong, Jesus of Nazareth was merely a Utopian dreamer who never came down to earth. If we are wrong, justice is a lie." He contrasted the movement's spirit with the violence of the White Citizens Councils and the Ku Klux Klan. "In our protest, there will be no cross burnings. No white person will be taken from his home by a hooded Negro mob and brutally murdered. . . . We will be guided by the highest principles of law and order . . . our actions must be guided by the deepest principles of our Christian faith. Love must be our regulating ideal." Moreover, King summoned up the vision of the historic moment, the challenge which was also a unique opportunity. "If we protest courageously, and yet with dignity and Christian love, when the history books are written in the future, somebody will have to say, 'There lived a race of people, of black people, of people who had the moral courage to stand up for their rights. And thereby they injected a new meaning into the veins of history and civilization.' "[52]

The meeting discussed three demands, so moderate in tone that the NAACP declined to become involved at first: that passengers be served on a first-come, first-served basis, with

Negroes from the back forward, and whites from the front backward; that bus drivers treat Negroes with courtesy; and that Negro drivers be employed at once on the mainly Negro routes. But despite the moderation—there was no proposal at this point, for instance, that segregation itself be banned on the buses—the boycott leaders grasped a deeper significance in the event that transcended particulars. "The real victory was in the mass meeting," King observed, "where thousands of black people stood revealed with a new sense of dignity and destiny."[53]

"Comes the first rainy day," said the mayor, "the Negroes will be back on the buses." It rained the day after. And people walked with umbrellas and papers over their heads. The city's police commissioner ordered black taxi drivers to charge the legal rate, ending any chance of cheap fares and anticipating that many would take buses of necessity. The Improvement Association instituted a car pool to help transport people. Many chose to walk anyway, "demonstrating with their feet." "I'm not walking for myself," explained one elderly woman when she was offered a ride. "I'm walking for my children and my grandchildren." Old Mother Pollard, told to go back to the bus because "you have been with us all along [and] 'cause you are too old to keep walking," responded, "Oh no, I'm gonna walk just as long as everybody else." Asked were not her feet tired, she replied, "My feets is tired, but my soul is rested."

Many whites supported the black movement. "Would you believe," said one black leader, "that many native-born members of prominent southern families with links that dated back to the cavaliers of Virginia helped and encouraged us and made anonymous contributions? They would call and say, 'Don't reveal my name but go to it. We're all for you.'" A young white librarian, Juliette Morgan, wrote in the Montgomery *Adver-tiser:* "One feels that history is being made in Montgomery these days. . . . It is hard to imagine a soul so dead, a heart so hard, a vision so blinded and provincial as not to be moved with admiration at the quiet dignity, discipline and dedication with which the Negroes have conducted their boycott."[54]

But despite such sentiments, the dominant reaction from white Montgomery was adamant opposition. King's house was bombed and there were regular threats on his life. And there were many other acts of violence and threats. Nat King Cole was dragged from the stage in Birmingham. A black pedestrian was mutilated in the genitals. A local judge declared that "in Montgomery, it looks like all the niggers have gone crazy." And the three city commissioners joined the White Citizens Council in a rally at the Montgomery Coliseum, where James Eastland denounced the boycott, and thousands of racist handbills circulated. "When in the course of human events, it becomes necessary to abolish the Negro race, proper methods should be used," it read. "Among these are guns, bow and arrows, sling shots and knives." That spring, King and eighty-eight others were arrested for violating an ancient law against "boycotts."[55]

The leaders of the bus boycott had an adroit strategic sense that did not depend upon moral appeal alone. They were fully aware that Montgomery was not going to change on its own, and appealed to a broader public audience throughout the nation to strengthen their actions on the streets and in the courts. That spring, King toured the country, giving a history lesson which recast the terms of standard textbooks. Whites, according to King, had finally realized the "monstrous moral contradiction of slavery" in a land founded on the principle of equality, and the Emancipation Proclamation had resulted from the long and bloody Civil War. But the promises of Emancipation had also been overturned by the U.S. Supreme Court and the "Pharaohs of the South." It had taken generations—and involvement in another war, fought in part against racism—for blacks to begin to "realize they are somebody." The publicity which his speeches and the unfolding drama in Montgomery generated formed a powerful backdrop for the court deliberations. And the courts themselves formed an invaluable system of alternative justice. When King attended the opening hearings in federal court on May 11, 1956, he observed that with "the tragic sabotage of justice in the city and state courts of the South

. . . in the federal courts the Negro had an honest chance for justice."[56]

When victory finally came on November 13—the Supreme Court ruled to sustain a lower-court decision that the bus laws were unconstitutional—people wept for joy at Holt Street Baptist Church. A sympathetic white minister, Bob Graetz, created a "sensation" when he read from First Corinthians: " 'When I was a child, I spoke as a child; but when I became a man, I put away childish things.' "[57]

Black churches were typically the foundation of the movement in communities across the South. Even where ministers proved hesitant, the churches became drawn into the struggle through the activities of church members, and the language of black religion furnished the central themes of the movement. Moreover, most activists had gained their skills and aspirations in the church. As William Chafe described in Greensboro, North Carolina, for instance, "The churches provided a training ground for political leaders and a meeting place where the aspirations of the black community could find collective expression.* The Southern Christian Leadership Conference formed in early 1957 out of discussions among King, Ella Baker, Ralph Abernathy, Fred Shuttlesworth, Bayard Rustin, and others. In-

*Two of the four students who sat in at the Greensboro Woolworth's in 1960 —the act that sparked the student sit-in movement—went to Shiloh Baptist Church and had been inspired by Martin Luther King when he spoke there in 1958 (William Chafe, *Civilities and Civil Rights* [New York: Oxford University Press, 1980], p. 25).
    Steve Max has pointed out the difference in the social and class character of free spaces used by students on the one hand and black working-class church-goers on the other—and especially the problems ultimately caused by students' relative detachment from deep communal roots. "Just as the black worker was free of many of the restraints which existed in the rural areas, the black student was freer than the worker. Few had full-time jobs, owned homes or had families to support. Black students, like white students, could afford to be both radical and mobile, restrained mainly by the dependence of black colleges on white philanthropy." Subsequent themes of African dress, revolutionary campus politics, and preoccupations with violence were possible, for a constituency detached from such communal responsibilities, in ways that differed markedly from the black clergy (see Steve Max, *Civil Rights* [Chicago: Midwest Academy, 1978], p. 13).

tended to expand "the Montgomery way" across the South, the organization consciously built on "the most stable social institution in Negro culture—the church," as its first working paper put it. Its idea was to coordinate and strengthen local efforts, bringing ministers together to share stories and experiences and focusing attention on particular local campaigns. "You get a sort of camaraderie," as Abernathy put it. "You get strengthened, backed and supported because you see a Kelly Miller Smith from Nashville and C. K. Stelle from Tallahassee and T. J. Jemison."

But early leaders like Ella Baker, a veteran of decades of organizing activities in the North and South who became SCLC's executive director in 1959, countered with a strong stress on development of local leadership among ordinary people. "Instead of 'the leader'—a person who was supposed to be a magic man," she argued, referring to what she saw was an overdependence on King, "you would develop individuals who were bound together by a concept that provided an opportunity for them to grow into being responsible." Baker saw broader possibilities in SCLC's first undertaking—a campaign called the "Crusade for Citizenship" that sought to register tens of thousands of new voters. "The word Crusade connotes for me a vigorous movement," she explained, "with high purpose and involving masses of people. . . . It must provide for a sense of achievement and recognition for many people, particularly local leadership."[58]

Along with other civil rights organizations—NAACP, the Congress of Racial Equality (CORE), and the Student Nonviolent Coordinating Committee (SNCC), formed by students in 1960 as an outgrowth of the sit-ins at segregated lunch counters in Greensboro by a group of black college students—SCLC spearheaded a variety of local protest movements. As the movement spread across the South, it tapped and built upon ancient traditions of resistance and community strength in ways that intimated new, far-ranging experiences of democratic activity.

Women, in particular, had played invisible but crucial roles throughout black history in the South in sustaining family ties at home and much of the religious life in the broader community. Though they rarely achieved the public recognition accorded male black preachers, black community women had long been symbols and models of strength and courage, sometimes attaining the stature of legend within the community itself. In the movement, such women came into their own, gaining new skills, voice, and, frequently, public visibility. As SNCC staff member Charles Sherrod wrote, describing southwest Georgia, "There is always a 'mama.' She is usually a militant woman in the community, outspoken, understanding and willing to catch hell, having already caught her share." He profiled, for instance, "Mama Dolly," an elderly woman, "who can pick more cotton, 'slop more pigs,' plow more ground, chop more wood, and do a hundred things better than the best farmer in the area." Building on such models, women like Septima Clark, Dorothy Cotton, Fannie Lou Hamer, Diane Nash, Ruby Doris Smith Robinson—and later civil rights leaders like Gwen Patton, Cynthia Washington, Annie Pearl Avery, and a host of others—became powerful, inspiring public figures as the movement developed.[59]

The changes that occurred within communities were embodied in a variety of new movement practices and institutions accompanying the democratic cultural sensibility. Songs, often adapted from old Negro spirituals, would echo the point: "Over my head, I see dignity in the air. There must be a God somewhere." "Ain't going to let nobody turn me 'round." "Just one thing that we did wrong. Stayed in the wilderness a little too long. Keep your eyes on the prize, hold on." Role-playing before every demonstration would teach the basics of nonviolence. In Montgomery, before blacks returned to the buses, "sociodramas" presented the potential conflicts. Leaflets counseled blacks to be courteous and dignified, to rely on "moral and spiritual force" instead of violence. At the center of the movement, were "schools" of a different sort, which taught new conceptions of democracy and citizenship, and symbolized them with their names.

In Montgomery, on the anniversary of the bus boycott, movement leaders organized an event they called the Institution on Nonviolence, which brought white and black theologians, political leaders, social scientists, and other professionals from around the country to discuss the relevance of nonviolence to American problems. Such precedent had established the notion of an alternative "educational process" from the beginning of SCLC. But it took on extensive life when SCLC adopted a program that Ella Baker had urged from the beginning, creating an enormous program of "Citizenship Schools" across the South.

The Citizenship School model had originally been developed by Esau Jenkins and Bernice Robinson, leaders in the black community of Johns Island, South Carolina, with help from Miles Horton and Septima Clark of Highlander Folk School, an organizing training center in the Tennessee mountains which had aided grass-roots movements for decades. The citizenship education program taught blacks—largely illiterate on the island—to learn to read and write in order to pass the arduous literacy tests that authorities used to disenfranchise poorer citizens of both races. But from the beginning, the organizers had been convinced that literacy and voting had to be connected to rich, living notions of citizenship. "They believed that blacks on Johns Island would learn to read and write if they came to view voting, writing and reading as an obligation and a political responsibility," as Aldon Morris described. To that end, they junked normal academic approaches to literacy and treated "students" as adults who could come and go as they pleased, chew tobacco, use snuff, and bring their sewing to classes. Classes held in the back of Jenkins's small store used, as their primers, documents like the Declaration of Human Rights of the United Nations and the constitutions of South Carolina and the United States, which then became sources for extraordinary discussions of what "citizenship" was all about.

Demand for such classes spread rapidly across the South, soon swamping the capabilities of Highlander. In 1961, with funding from the Marshall Field Foundation in New York, the Southern Christian Leadership Conference adopted the program as its own. It hired Andrew Young, Dorothy Cotton, Septima Clark, Bernice Robinson, and Wyatt Walker to develop the effort. They traveled all over the South, using spirituals and the basic documents of American democracy as their source material, and bringing in thousands of prospective local "teachers" to the SCLC training program at Dorchester, Georgia. Through such experiences, people learned far more than the mechanics of how to register and vote. Students learned a whole array of other organizing skills—how to conduct voter-registration drives, combat illiteracy, win government benefits for the poor, and talk about the meaning of American citizenship. And they learned new confidence. As Cotton put it, "people were going back saying they're not gonna take segregation and discrimination anymore. . . . It meant just a whole new way of life and functioning."[60]

In small towns across the South, such discussions would become electric. Illiterate sharecroppers, domestic workers, janitors, and others learned to read the American Constitution and talked about the right to vote as an intrinsic part of being a citizen. In projects organized by the Student Nonviolent Coordinating Committee, analogous "Freedom Schools" encouraged people to register, as well, and combined such discussion with courses in black history, poetry, and other cultural and social topics. Through these sorts of experiences, literally and figuratively new education in citizenship, people's sense of themselves was often palpably transformed. "We got our heads up now and we won't ever bow down again," explained one janitor. "No, sir—except before God!" A study by one research team of psychologists discovered a dramatic decline in the levels of crime and social pathology in communities involved in the civil rights revolt.[61]

Such organizing efforts remained largely invisible in the national mass media and in many accounts of the civil rights movement. But they led to enormous, visible public activity as well. By the summer of 1963, in the aftermath of the massive demonstrations and arrests in Birmingham, Alabama, when police dogs and fire hoses had been turned on young children and others, nonviolent direct-action campaigns had occurred in over 900 cities and towns, with an estimated one million participants. Campaigns forced thousands of desegregations in 261 cities, and mounted growing pressure on Congress to pass legislation that would ban segregation in public facilities and guarantee the right of blacks to register and vote. As *Time* magazine put it, "The invisible Man has now become plainly visible."[62]

Important as any changes in public law and formal code were the transformations in the life of communities themselves. Local protests began to generate a democratic movement culture. But the nature of the movement, for all its accomplishments, also imposed severe limitations on how fully it could realize its goals. On the broadest level, the civil rights revolt was intended, as Martin Luther King put it repeatedly, to "make real the promise of democracy." By democracy, those involved in the movement meant not simply formal rights, like the right to vote, but participation and the transformation of power relationships which kept some in a dependent and inferior position. "The more important participation was to be not just at the moment when the ballot was cast but in all the moments that led up to that moment."[63]

The movement was a spontaneous, dramatic, and in many ways transitory phenomenon, dependent upon mass media attention. There were intimations of an approach to social change that differed from normal "voting blocs" or "issue constituencies"—the beginnings of what might be called a democratic populist vision, embodied in the Citizenship Schools which connected diverse communities and taught ordinary people new skills of public life. Leaders like Andrew Young and Ella Baker believed, indeed, that the Citizenship Education program was the foundation on which the entire movement was built. And the Student Nonviolent Coordinating Committee sought to create a stable political organization in Mississippi, the Mississippi Freedom Democratic Party, which mounted a challenge to the regular Democratic Party delegation from the state in the national party's convention in 1964.

In practice, however, the communities moved into action during the civil rights protests had no way to sustain their activity over time, nor to make ongoing connections with other communities similarly mobilized. Scattered attempts to build enduring organizations through which poor and powerless people could take action after the end of mass demonstrations received scant support. In the face of tremendous repression and the overwhelming need for changes in federal law and support from other areas of the country, the strategic focus inexorably came to be placed upon mediagenic events which would garner broad sympathy. Doing something "dramatic enough to command national media attention," Oates pointed out, was the great skill of King and SCLC.

More generally the structure of the movement itself reflected its goals. Despite the broader *vision* of leaders like King and Ella Baker and many of the rank and file, the civil rights movement was designed to address problems of legal segregation. Like the suffrage movement of women a half century earlier, it used language of republicanism that stressed formal participation, not transformation of substantive relations of power. In its own terms, the civil rights movement *succeeded* in abolishing the segregated statutes, in registering hundreds of thousands of new black voters, and in redefining normal "democracy." Broader problems of economic and social power · required new forms of strategy and new sorts of alliances, which King sought to create in the last years of his life.

Meanwhile, with no mechanisms for remaining directly accountable (SCLC itself had debated becoming a membership organization, but decided that jealousy from other civil rights groups like the NAACP would make such a step counterproductive), the SCLC leadership often took on the autocratic character not uncommon among the black clergy. For all of Ella

Baker's arguments and exhortations, leaders often defined themselves as the movement. As the Reverend C. T. Vivian, an SCLC leader, observed retrospectively, "Who could tell us anything? We were the movement." And as expectations often outran capacities to address problems like lower-paying jobs and overcrowded, deteriorating houses, even the most popular leaders were prey to accusations of betrayal. "The white man pays Reverend Martin Luther King, subsidizes Reverend Martin Luther King, so that Reverend Martin Luther King can continue to teach the Negroes to be defenseless," Malcolm X told receptive audiences in northern ghettoes.[64]

On balance, then, the modern civil rights movement proved a dramatic success in raising issues of "democracy" with a moral power that resonated the world over. That it also failed to fashion enduring forms of association that could link particular spaces like the church into organizations for broad, democratic change after the television cameras left had largely to do with the complexities of transition from one form of movement to another. The sort of populist protest that King envisioned, linking blacks and poor whites, remained for the future. On its own terms, the movement made vivid once again the lesson which weaves through the black freedom struggle from its inception: There can be no democracy without dignity and self-respect, and such values are the measure of a people's own determination to resist oppression. For people who have been rendered invisible by the dominant culture, gaining such a transformative sense of themselves requires more than exhortation or experiences of being oppressed. A new sense of self is sustained and augmented in particular sorts of public places where people can discover "who they are" and to what they aspire on their own terms, and where they can begin to think about what democracy means.

CHAPTER 3

BEYOND THE DICTATES OF PRUDENCE

JUST AS BLACK SLAVES created sustaining kinship networks and drew on the liberating themes embedded in Christianity and republican political ideas, women have developed visions of equality out of the changing dynamics of their daily lives. Historians have recently begun to explore the complex intersections between public and private where this takes place. Since women's identities as women have historically tended to draw on familial, daily, traditional identities, emergent group consciousness often occurs in sex-segregated "female spaces" which have a quasi-public character.

Female group consciousness is not necessarily feminist, of course. Indeed, most often it asserts and defends tradition, for example in mothers' clubs or women's auxiliaries. Yet under certain conditions these same environments provide the experiences from which women can imagine and begin to demand equal rights and democratic participation.

The tensions and contradictions within the ideological tradition of feminism are rooted in this struggle to define appropriate public roles for women. One version has sought simple incorporation into the male-defined political arena, emphasizing women's individual rights as citizens. This republican feminism draws upon the heritage of the Revolution. Other strands lead from women's traditional familial roles and responsibilities and the values associated with them as the basis for a critique of the public arena and an alternative vision. Feminism has historically been born in this tension between rejecting and embracing tradition, between assertions of sameness and assertions of difference, between female subculture and individual freedom, between private and public. A democratic, transformative feminism not only must draw on both sides of that tension. It also reworks conventional understandings of "public" and "private" themselves. Yet feminists on all points of the political spectrum frequently find themselves drawn toward one of the poles and insisting that the other represents a mortal danger to female liberation.

Thus, for example, the exchange between Jean Bethke Elstain and Barbara Ehrenreich, in *Dissent* magazine in 1982 and 1983, took on remarkably personalized overtones. Elstain began by "honoring the integrity of my grandmother," whose life in a German-American community in northern Colorado's sugar-beet country was suffused with a "populist pietism" hostile to the logic of capitalist rationality. But by the conclusion of the exchange the focus had turned. "Ehrenreich is blind to the pathos of homelessness, to the alienation of deracination," Elstain charged. "With the liberal technocrat, Ehrenreich can think of no better response to the radicalizing force of capitalism than to redefine the family in line with the market imperatives." In turn, Ehrenreich offered her own "paradigmatic image of a 'strong woman' "—a neighbor, originally rooted in a conservative, blue-collar Catholic community, who had pulled herself together, found a job, and become active in the antiwar movement after being abandoned by her husband. Ehrenreich charged that Elstain had thrown out the window any notion of the "historically responsible individual" of the sort represented by her neighbor. "With all due respect to Elstain's grandmother," she wrote, "this image evokes for me a cult that was vastly more evil and destructive than anything Jim Jones managed to organize."[1]

Each writer eloquently defended a dimension of feminism. Elstain argued that the child-centered family provides a crucial vantage point from which women can critique the modern state and its tendency to destroy richly textured communities for which family life is a bedrock. Ehrenreich, on the other hand, emphasized the assaults on women's individual dignity and self-expression, and the necessity for liberation from repressive tradition. In each case, the claims of the other point of view seemed fraught with intolerable peril. Both ultimately posited a fundamental antagonism between individual and community, freedom and historical identities. Yet in reality, women have historically moved between these poles in their search for the deeper meanings of freedom and sexual equality. When feminism has found its most authentic and democratic voice, it has changed the terms of the discussion entirely.

For nearly two centuries in the United States, women have been creating institutions which simultaneously defined themselves in terms of tradition and stretched the definitions past the breaking point. In the name of their sacred duties to home and family, women built a series of extrafamilial institutions where female solidarity permitted the reinterpretation of personal experience into larger patterns and where women could develop the essential skills for participation in public life. Throughout this process, they moved within the creative tensions and the limitations of their peculiar vantage point at the intersection of public and private life.

Prior to the American Revolution, white women's lives and identities were tightly merged with the realities of rural and artisanal family life. Their days were filled with hard, often repetitive, work and constant childbearing. Not only was it considered inappropriate for women to become involved in the political arena outside the family, but also they had little access to the education and training which prepared men for public roles. Women might be powerful within their families, but rarely outside of them. With other women they shared responsibilities for attending births and deaths, but their collective life had no organizational base.[2]

It was the Revolutionary War which linked politics to domesticity. Inevitably, women were drawn into the political discourse which surrounded them. For example, Sarah Jay, with a deft apology, acknowledged that as a woman in 1783 she was by definition "out of place" in the world of politics. Yet she could hardly suppress the observations prompted by her lively curiosity and intense commitments:

> I've transgress'd the line that I proposed to observe in my correspondence by slipping into politicks, but my country and my friends possess so entirely my thoughts that you must not wonder if my pen runs beyond the dictates of prudence.[3]

Six years earlier, Anne Emlen had written in a similar vein: "How shall I impose a silence upon myself when the subject is so very interesting, so much engrossing Conversation—& what every member of the Community is more or less concerned in?"[4]

Consumer boycotts of British goods, especially the famous tea boycott, required that women exercise political judgment in the purchase of household goods. Spinning, weaving, and sewing became patriotic duties to clothe the ragged rebel army. Women eagerly seized the opportunity to prove their loyalty.

In 1780, Philadelphia women proposed to create a national women's organization to raise money for the troops. In a broadside entitled "Sentiments of an American Woman," they claimed the mantle of patriotism for women "born for liberty, distaining to bear the irons of a tyrannic Government." Women's loyalty and courage would be more visible "if the weakness of our constitutions, if opinions and manners did not forbid us to march to glory by the same paths as the Men." The time had come, they urged, "to display the same sentiments which animated us at the beginning of the Revolution, when we renounced the use of teas . . . ; when our republican and laborious hands spun the flax, prepared the linen intended for the use of our soldiers; when exiles and fugitives, we supported with courage all the evils which are the concomitants of war."

Women in Philadelphia and later in New Jersey, Maryland, and Virginia, raised substantial sums by going door to door. When General Washington refused Philadelphia women's stipulation that the money go directly to the troops, they bought linen and inscribed each shirt with the name of the woman who made it to emphasize their personal gesture of support and solidarity.[5]

At the same time that domestic production and consumption assumed a political cast, the political theories of the Revolution raised new questions about women. Colonial society had been deferential. The "better sort" were expected to rule whether by election or by appointment. Puritans spelled out in numerous sermons the necessity of hierarchy and proper subjection of children to parents, women to men, and people to God: "He to God; she to God in him."[6]

Enlightenment thinkers in Europe, however, offered a powerful critique of definitions of corporate society premised on subordination. Articulating a worldview rooted in the rising commercial middle classes, they emphasized the infinite perfectibility of the individual. Through education, people could abandon the superstition and irrationality of tradition and make a rational social order possible.[7]

Revolutionary political theorists drew on Enlightenment thought to argue about the nature of a legitimate government. Rejecting notions of rights rooted in inherited wealth or position and believing in individual capacities, they turned to ancient theories of the republic, the state whose legitimacy rests on the consent of the governed. That, in turn, led them to elaborate the duties and rights of the citizen. Even in conservative formulations, republican principles referred to popular will. "All power is derived from the people," said one Federalist. "Liberty is everyone's birthright. Since all cannot govern or deliberate individually, it is just that they should elect their representatives. That everyone should possess, indirectly, and through the medium of his representatives, a voice in the public councils; and should yield to no will but that of an actual or virtual majority." The justification for revolution in such theories received one of its most powerful expressions in the Declaration of Independence.[8]

The future of a government established on such principles clearly lay with the "virtue" of its citizens, which could only be expressed and renewed by constant participation in the life of the community. Yet the founding fathers shared a restricted vision of "the citizen." In their view, women, slaves, and propertyless men, along with children and the mentally ill, lacked the capacity for independent and rational judgment for the general good. As generations of feminists noted in subsequent centuries, the ringing declaration that "All men are created equal" used the word "men" quite literally. Indeed, as historian Linda Kerber has pointed out, every statement of republican principles implicitly presumed that women were exceptions. Rousseau presumed that the citizen was necessarily also the head of a household, a husband-father. His definition of the "public" and the ideal polity presumed the existence of a private world which sustained the "softer" values. According to Jean Bethke Elstain, "the flip side of a coin that features the public-spirited visage of the male citizen and dutiful father is the profile of the loving, virtuous, chaste, selfless wife." Female participation in civic life, then, could destroy this essential relationship. "Without someone to tend the hearth, the legislative halls would grow silent and empty, or become noisily corrupt." In turn, the woman who participated in politics violated her nature. "A witty [i.e., articulate] woman is a scourge to her husband, to her children, to her friends, her servants, and to all the world. Elated by the sublimity of her genius, she scorns to stoop to the duties of a woman, and is sure to commence a man."[9]

Only a few educated women at the time noted the logical contradictions. In 1776, Abigail Adams wrote her husband John that the new laws should curb the "unlimited power" of husbands over wives and threatened that "if particular care and attention is not paid to the ladies, we are determined to foment a rebellion and will not hold ourselves bound by any laws in which we have no voice, or Representation." In this famous exchange, John Adams replied with a joking dismissal. Only in a letter to a male acquaintance did he develop the theoretical position that women and children, like men without property, were lacking in independent judgment and "their delicacy renders them unfit for practice and experience in the great businesses of life."[10]

Nevertheless, white women in the propertied classes did present a problem for the new nation. If they were not citizens, what was their relation to the state, particularly in light of their highly visible patriotic activities during the war? The resolution of this dilemma moved well beyond the common-law assumptions which subsumed women's legal identities into those of husband or father. The politicization of domesticity catalyzed a new conception: the republican mother. Her patriotic duty to educate her sons to be moral and virtuous citizens linked her to the state and gave her power over its future.

The image of the republican mother flourished in the early nineteenth century, developing in the midcentury middle class into a full-blown domestic ideology, the "cult of true womanhood." As domestic production gave way to commercial and then industrial capitalism, women's increased segregation from public, social, and economic life diminished the political and increased the moral dimensions of their "mission" as mothers. The emergence of party politics in the early nineteenth century accompanied both a diminution of governmental oversight of moral conduct in favor of the growing market economy and, at the same time, a dramatic expansion of the right to vote. Political activity came to be identified as both partisan and male. Paula Baker has argued that "parties and electoral politics united all white men, regardless of class or other differences and provided entertainment, a definition of manhood, and the basis for a male ritual."[11]

While men bonded together in the electoral rituals of partisan politics, the separateness of women's lives, centered on the vocation of motherhood, provided the basis for the beginnings of a distinctively female culture. Suzanne Lebsock's study of free (white) women in St. Petersburg, Virginia, in the first half of the nineteenth century, shows the operation of a distinctly female value system in such activities as writing wills, acquiring or establishing separate estates, managing real estate, and organizing benevolent associations. That value system is best described as personalism, "a tendency to respond to the particular needs and merits of individuals." Personalism drew its power from the daily realities of female social networks and familial roles. And it bears a striking similarity to Carol Gilligan's descriptions of contemporary women's moral codes based on the primacy of relationships rather than abstract rights and principles.[12]

Shared values did not necessarily imply collective consciousness, however. The latter evolved as women increasingly met one another in specifically female institutions. The special mission of republican mothers justified, for example, the growth of female academies in the late eighteenth and early nineteenth centuries, to which upwardly mobile middle-class families sent their daughters for training in their new domestic responsibilities. Removed from their families to the world of boarding schools, young women developed intense relations with each other and with teachers, who emphasized the special importance of their roles as women. As one young student wrote to her cousin in 1832:

> The school is all I could wish and one in which I feel deeply interested. The teachers I cannot tell you how much we all love. They all love us and are willing to make any sacrifice for our good. There is a great degree of love & friendship manifested for each other. I feel as if I needed to be here a year or more. . . . I find kind friends here, better than I ever expected to find among strangers.[13]

According to Nancy Cott, such schools "fostered women's consciousness of themselves as a group united in purpose, duties and interests. From the sense among women that they shared a collective destiny it was but another step (though a steep one) to sense that they might shape that destiny with their own minds and hands." Within women's schools and academies, young girls also developed literacy, skills in public speaking, and broadened spheres of interest. They had access to powerful female role models in their teachers, and a sense of collective solidarity which influenced them throughout their lives. Emma Willard, founder of Troy Seminary, encouraged graduates to enter teaching and maintained contact with a wide-flung network of former pupils, many of whom went on to found institutions of their own.[14]

Middle-class women's sense of shared mission as republican mothers and their growing access to basic literacy facilitated an unprecedented growth in collective activity in the early nineteenth century. In the face of social dislocations of an intensely competitive, secular, and unpredictable political economy, women moved to assert the values of nurture and cooperation. Personalist values, whether in the form of concern for the salvation of their children or homes for widows and orphans, shaped the explosive growth of prayer groups, missionary societies, benevolent societies, mothers' clubs, Sunday schools, and moral reform associations.

The dynamism of female activism grew in part from its roots in the massive revivals known as the Second Great Awakening which spread throughout the states between 1800 and 1830. The Great Awakening represented a moral, middle-class, and often specifically female revulsion against the consequences of unbridled industrialization and the use of republican rhetoric about individual property rights to justify rapaciousness. A Presbyterian newspaper reported in 1816 in Connecticut: "In many places, 'devout and pious FEMALES' have formed themselves into praying societies and obtained in the discharge of duty— comfort to themselves, and light, and direction to others." When Upper New York State burned with evangelical fervor in the 1820s, preacher Charles Finney permitted and even encouraged women to pray and speak publicly before "mixed" or "promiscuous" congregations of women and men. The intensity of women's participation can be measured both in their willingness to engage in such unprecedented public activity and in the fact that there were twice as many female as male converts.[15]

Encouraged to bear witness to their conversion in good works, women founded missionary societies, benevolent and charitable associations for widows and orphans, moral reform societies to rescue "fallen sisters" (i.e., prostitutes) and to control the sexual behavior of men, and reform societies of all sorts. A writer in a religious publication in the late 1820s imagined a little girl's puzzlement: "Mother, there are so many societies! . . . I longed for you this afternoon when I came home from school, and they told me you were gone to the Maternal Society: you go very often. Mother, what is a Maternal Society?"[16]

Religious reform activities strengthened women's sense of sisterhood and common purpose. Within them they developed many essential political skills: writing constitutions, electing officers, running meetings, raising money, recruiting members, voting, planning and coordinating campaigns. They also began to analyze the sources of moral corruption in the world from the perspective of the female victim. Not surprisingly they frequently found men and male institutions to be at fault. Moral reform societies moved from timidly distributing tracts to drawing up legislative petitions and publicly confronting men who frequented brothels. They justified this moral surveillance of the community by reminding themselves of the ubiquity of their cause:

> Even our small children are infected by it. Who among us have not had our hearts pained by the obscenity of little children; who among us does not tremble lest some who are dear to us should be led away by the thousand snares of the destroyer. Who among us can tell that our sisters and daughters are safe while the seducer is unhesitatingly received into our society and treated with that attention which virtue alone can claim.

By 1839, more than 445 local societies joined together in the American Female Moral Reform Society.[17] Like other reform associations, moral reform societies engendered a sense of sisterhood and collective power, taught women skills, and raised their self-esteem. The proto-feminism of their analysis and activity derived from their clear sense of gender solidarity and their use of middle-class women's traditional roles and values as the basis for their critique. At the same time, their defense of the female victim in many ways "accommodated them to a limited, clerically defined role."[18]

Schools and religious reform associations within the emerging white middle class, thus, were paradoxical institutions. Each was seen as, in itself, an extension of tradition. Yet they also constituted arenas outside the family in which women could develop a collective consciousness, political skills, and a growing sense of their rights. Lydia Maria Child wrote in 1841 about the contradictions of unintended consequences:

> In modern times, the evangelical sects have highly approved of female prayer meetings. In the cause of missions and dissemination of tracts, they have eloquently urged upon women their prodigious influence and consequent responsibility, in the great work of regenerating a world lying in wickedness. Thus it is with those who urged women to become missionaries, and form tract societies. They have changed the household utensil into a living, energetic being; and they have no spell to turn it into a broom again.

Historian Mary Ryan concluded that in Oneida, New York, the charitable institutions women created "allowed them to exercise their abilities outside the home, brought them into contact and sympathy with working women from another class and culture, and led them on to criticize industrial capitalism and the men who managed it. They had, in sum, significantly remodeled the sexual division of social space."[19]

For the most part, women did not interpret their new roles as a political challenge to the restrictions on their citizenship rights. The female political culture which they had created relied on indirect modes of influence and moral sanctions congruent with their sentimental vision of women and the home as guardians of virtue. Nancy Hewitt, in a careful examination

of female activism in Rochester, New York, makes it clear that
the private identities on which women drew were simultaneously embedded in class relations which inhibited their further
politicization. Upper-class settlers in the 1820s, for example,
initiated a Female Charitable Society, evolving a mode of activity that in effect provided careers for several women and represented no threat to the structures of power dominated by their
male relatives. Later in the 1830s, women from the rising entre-
preneurial class became fervent advocates of evangelical reform. They conducted massive petition drives for abolition and
moral reform, applying domestic values to public activity. But
they became less active when discouraged by men of their class
who, in the 1840s, shifted their own reform activities into the
political arena.[20]

Nevertheless, all of this activity provided a necessary background to the initiation in the 1830s and 1840s of a tiny but
vociferous women's rights movement. While relatively large
numbers of women began to define public roles for women as
extensions of domestic values, a few took the additional step of
measuring their new sense of possibility against the political
heritage of the Revolution. The precondition for this was participation in the radical, Garrisonian wing of the abolition movement, whose principal constituency in Rochester lay with the
Hicksite Quaker community. The rural Hicksites were a radical
Quaker group that had split from their more orthodox colleagues in 1828, advocating a boycott of slave-produced goods
and an egalitarian spiritual community. Like all Quakers, they
allowed women to exercise leadership as ministers and to meet
together in a Women's Meeting to oversee the spiritual life of
female members. A split in that community in the 1840s was
sparked from two directions. First, many Quakers found that
their opposition to slavery made it impossible to avoid secular
activity as the Hicksite community required. Secondly, the
Women's Meeting voiced increasing demands for equal participation, asking in 1837 at the Genesee Yearly Meeting that "the
discipline be so alter'd that men & women shall stand on the

same footing in all matters internal in which they are equally interested."[21] This resolution, which was postponed year after year, first appeared as Quaker abolitionists Sarah and Angelina Grimké toured New England speaking publicly both against slavery and for the rights of women.

Unwilling to refrain from worldly activity on the pressing moral issue of slavery, many Quaker women broke with their religious community, bringing with them into the abolitionist movement models of female leadership, a willingness to remain socially marginal, and an egalitarian tradition. It should not be surprising, then, that the key leadership of the women's rights movement was trained in the radical, Garrisonian abolitionist movement. There they developed a broad political framework, a critique of social and political institutions which rendered them immune to clerical criticism, an egalitarian ideology which made the incidentals of race and sex secondary to the principle of human equality, and a method of organizing congruent with women's previous experiences in benevolent missionary and reform associations. There they could also make fullest use of biblical themes to challenge the limitations and contradictions of republicanism. Women like Sarah and Angelina Grimké suddenly found that, in the name of Christian duty to speak against sin and evil, they had transgressed the boundaries of acceptable behavior and were forced to defend the right of women to participate in public discourse.

Sarah and Angelina Grimké were devout Quakers, daughters of a Charleston, South Carolina, slaveowning family. When they toured New England in 1836 and 1837, they expressed their sense of moral obligation to speak from their own personal experience against the horrors of slavery. Their stand, defined entirely in religious and moral terms, accented basic contradictions in the image of the true woman, North or South. How could women discharge their moral duty while remaining silent on the fundamental moral dilemma of their time? It was on this ground that Sarah Grimké urged women to participate in the moral and social reform movements of the day.

As they traveled and spoke in New England churches, however, Congregationalist ministers in Massachusetts sent out a pastoral letter denouncing their activity as a violation of the New Testament. "The power of woman is her dependence, flowing from the consciousness of that weakness which God has given her for her protection. . . . When she assumes the place and tone of man as a public reformer . . . she yields the power which God has given her . . . and her character becomes unnatural."[22]

In defense of their actions, the Grimké sisters asserted their kinship with female slaves, eloquently fusing the issues of race and gender: "They are our countrywomen—they are our sisters, and to us as women, they have a right to look for sympathy with their sorrows, and effort and prayer for their rescue. . . . Women ought to feel a peculiar sympathy in the colored man's wrong, for like him, she has been accused of mental inferiority, and denied the privileges of a liberal education." Schooled in a biblical idiom, accustomed to inspire women to activity by drawing on strong female figures from the scriptures, they refused to cede any religious sanction for male domination. "I rejoice that they have called the attention of my sex to this subject," replied Sarah Grimké to the ministers' letter.

> No one can desire more earnestly than I do, that woman may move exactly in the sphere which her Creator has assigned her; and I believe her having been displaced from that sphere has introduced confusion into the world. . . .
>
> The Lord Jesus defines the duties of his followers, . . . I follow him through all his precepts, and find him giving the same directions to women as to men, never even referring to the distinction now so strenuously insisted upon between masculine and feminine virtues: this is one of the anti-Christian "traditions of men" which are taught instead of the "commandments of God." Men and women were CREATED EQUAL; they are both moral and accountable beings, and whatever is *right* for a man to do, is *right* for a woman to do.[23]

A generation of feminist leadership emerged from such processes. Women like the Grimkés, Lucretia Mott, Elizabeth

Cady Stanton, and Susan B. Anthony used the language and the organizing styles they had learned in evangelical reform movements, particularly abolition. Women organized for abolition as they had for many reforms: creating female abolition societies, distributing tracts, passing petitions. Indeed, abolition sharply heightened women's political sensibilities as they exercised their single political right of petition on an unprecedented scale, collecting tens of thousands of signatures in the face of public ridicule and hostility. Yet that same movement was torn with dissention over women's participation and the external criticism which it prompted. The final catalyst, then, for an articulation of women's rights was the failure of the abolitionist movement to accord women full equality even as it raised their expectations.

In 1840, Elizabeth Cady Stanton and Lucretia Mott sat in a curtained balcony at the World Anti-slavery Convention with the female delegates who had been denied voting status. Radical Garrisonians in the American delegation had supported women's rights, but others voted with the British to make the convention one of "gentlemen only." Stanton's youthful, eager intelligence complemented the gentle courage of the Quaker veteran and together they determined that there must be public discussion of women's rights.

The intensity of the ongoing fight against slavery in the 1840s, the pressures of their daily lives, and the unprecedented nature of what they proposed meant an eight-year delay before those formative conversations led to concrete action. Finally, at a kitchen table meeting in upstate New York in 1848, Stanton, Mott, and other women issued a call for a women's rights convention in Seneca Falls. On short notice, two hundred women from the surrounding towns and countryside came to the meeting in the Wesleyan Chapel. They must have known that such an event was radically new, yet they brought with them seventy years of female activity. Many had traveled the same route over and over to attend revivals, missionary meetings, female gatherings in the name of temperance, moral reform, and abolition.

Their mothers had been the leading force in the Great Awakening which swept the area a quarter century before. Their grandmothers and great-grandmothers boycotted tea, spun and wove for the army, and believed themselves "born for liberty." When the organizers of the convention started to write a statement for the body to debate, they returned to the legacy of their revolutionary foremothers. Their "Declaration of Sentiments" clearly and directly claimed for women the promise of the Revolution: "We hold these truths to be self-evident," they wrote, "that all men and women are created equal."[24]

For the next twelve years, radical abolitionism provided organizing methods, constituency, and language for the recurrent conventions on women's rights. Understanding themselves as a prophetic minority, emerging leaders honed their skills and hammered out an analysis and a program which would guide them for several decades. By the end of the Civil War they had developed a clear ideology focused on the symbolic centrality of the right of suffrage. The demand for the vote captured the essence of republicanism applied to women: the right of citizenship.[25]

While pre–Civil War reform movements and women's rights conventions laid the groundwork for feminism in America, the base did not yet exist for the broad and successful movement in the early twentieth century. Only a small number of women had the requisite skills and experiences to find women's rights a compelling cause. Black, immigrant, and working-class women struggled daily for the elemental survival of themselves and their families. The educated new middle class, a result of the growth of industrial capitalism and modern cities, was still quite small. And most women in that class had developed a group consciousness which was not yet politicized. At midcentury they had turned with new vigor to their responsibilities in the privatized and intense life of the family, looking to other women and to the church for support and guidance.

By the latter part of the nineteenth century, however, the middle class had become a hegemonic force in American cultural life and the numbers of women with some education and some leisure was very large. Their organizational sophistication made a significant leap during the Civil War when they volunteered by the thousands for the Sanitary Commission, raised funds, gathered petitions, and provided food, clothes, and nursing services to armies on both sides. Following the war, while women's rights advocates in two small, competing organizations doggedly kept the issue of suffrage alive, a much broader movement began to prepare the way for a mass movement for women's rights.

It was temperance, the fight against "demon rum," rather than the tiny suffrage movement, which transformed and politicized traditional female spaces, making it possible for women gradually to redefine their mission, their rights, and their capacities. In particular, the Women's Christian Temperance Union presented middle-class women with a symbolic issue which condensed many of the dilemmas and antagonisms built into their lives and provided an opportunity to develop an awareness of their cultural, and ultimately their political, power. By the 1890s, with over 150,000 dues-paying members, the WCTU was the largest organization of women to that point in American history.[26]

Temperance had been a reform issue since well before the Civil War and one which feminists like Susan B. Anthony and Elizabeth Cady Stanton had long espoused. Like moral reform, it was an issue which reflected middle-class aspirations for respectability and social control. Values of efficiency and self-control clashed with the cultural norms of southern and eastern European peasants who emigrated to America by the hundreds of thousands in the last half of the nineteenth century. Forced to live in urban slums, working in sweatshops and industries which experienced periodic, severe depressions, working-class people seemed alarmingly restive and unruly. Thus, temperance can easily be interpreted as an attempt to impose behaviors rooted in the white, Protestant, native-born middle class on lower-class workers, immigrants, Catholics, and racial minorities. At the same time, it catalyzed a protofeminist analysis which blamed social problems on the immoral and irresponsible behavior of men toward vulnerable and dependent women. The gender and class dimensions of the issue remained in tension throughout the nineteenth century, and the free social spaces created by the WCTU were limited by this fact.

In the winter of 1873–74, women in small midwestern towns like Hillsboro, Ohio, and Adrian, Michigan, rose up in such numbers that they sent a shock wave through the nation. A depression had begun that year. Women devoted to temperance knew that the Ohio legislature showed signs of yielding to pressure from saloon interests to loosen liquor laws. Many may well have felt that they had a stake in the outcome of a political process in which they had no say. No one knows the exact reason, but suddenly the pent-up frustrations of decades poured out as more than 60,000 women took to the streets. Their goal was to close down the saloons, and by the following summer they had indeed closed down more than a thousand of them.[27]

In Hillsboro, Ohio, where it all began, eighty women met in church the morning after a temperance lecture, signed pledges, prayed, and proceeded downtown double-file to sing and pray in the saloons until the owners agreed to close them. Morning after morning they pursued their task. One young customer told a visiting reporter from Cincinnati about how he and his friends had recently returned to town unaware of the crusade:

> He and half a dozen others . . . had ranged themselves in the familiar semicircle before the bar and had their drinks ready and cigars prepared for the match, when the rustle of women's wear attracted their attention, and looking up they saw what they thought was a crowd of a thousand ladies entering. One youth saw among them his mother and sister, another had two cousins in the invading host, and a still more unfortunate recognized his intended mother-in-law.

Soon the Hillsboro women were joined by sisters from Washington Court House whose crusade had already succeeded in closing saloons. As the local temperance men prayed in the church and rang the church bell, the women visited saloons with increasingly gratifying results.[28]

Throughout the Midwest that winter, the streets literally ran with rum as saloonkeepers "surrendered" to the women, signed temperance pledges, and rolled the casks of liquor into the street to be split open. The crusade represented more a transformative moment than a lasting movement. It lacked any structure capable of sustaining it and left some women feeling almost as if they had been on a binge. One woman confessed, "The infectious enthusiasm of these meetings, the fervor of the prayers, the frankness of the relations of experience, and the magnetism that pervaded all, wrought me up to such a state of physical and mental exaltation that all other places and things seemed dull and unsatisfactory to me." Her participation grew from twice weekly, to daily, to several times each day. "The Crusade was a daily dissipation from which it seemed impossible to tear myself. At the intervals at home I felt as I fancy the drinker does at the breaking down of a long spree."[29]

While the impact on the liquor industry was temporary at best, the women's crusade created a cohort of women permanently changed by their new experience of power. As Frances Willard wrote:

> Perhaps the most significant outcome of this movement was the knowledge of their own power gained by the conservative women of the Churches. They had never even seen a "woman's rights convention," and had been held aloof from the "suffragists" by fears as to their orthodoxy; but now there were women prominent in all Church cares and duties eager to clasp hands for a more aggressive work than such women had ever before dreamed of undertaking.[30]

Like abolition, temperance was a secular reform with evangelical roots, couched in religious language. In addition, it became for middle-class women a vehicle for their accumulated grievances as women, much as moral reform had been for an earlier generation. Protection of the home and family from the violence, financial irresponsibility, desertion, and immorality associated with drink became the keynote of the feminized temperance movement.

The national Women's Christian Temperance Union was founded in 1874 as an organizational response to the women's crusade. Men were not allowed to join. Within the boundaries of the white middle class, the WCTU created a free social space for women. Under the inspired and charismatic leadership of Frances Willard, president from 1879 to 1899, the WCTU was an open and democratic female environment within which women experimented and pushed their traditional self-definitions past the boundaries of domesticity and into the broadest demand for full political participation.

Willard's election to the presidency of the WCTU signaled the willingness of its membership to expand their concerns and their tactics. She was best known as an advocate of the "Home Protection ballot," a limited suffrage demand which would allow women to vote on local prohibition ordinances. Such a slogan fused public and private, domesticity and politics, the republican mother and the suffragist. Similarly, slogans like "For God, Home, and Native Land" allowed restive, educated, increasingly leisured middle-class women to redefine their boundaries without having to challenge them head on. Willard used women's commitments to clubs and missionary societies and their social definition as moral guardians of the home to bring thousands into public, political activity for the first time.

The breadth of reform activity initiated by the WCTU, with autonomous choices for local chapters, made it possible for large numbers of women to work with the movement on issues of immediate concern. This "Do-Everything" policy, passed at the 1882 WCTU national convention, was a brilliant organizing strategy. According to historian Ruth Bordin, by 1889, Chicago WCTU activities included "two day nurseries, two Sunday schools, an industrial school, a mission that sheltered four thousand homeless or destitute women in a twelve-month period, a free medical dispensary that treated over 1600 patients a year, a lodging house for men that had to date provided temporary housing for over fifty thousand men, and a low-cost restaurant."[31]

The sharply polarized gender roles of the mid-nineteenth-century middle class which the WCTU and other female reform groups drew on for ideals and visions allowed them to posit a universal sisterhood, a sex-class whose "sacred claims," in the words of Julia Ward Howe, bound them to one another. Estelle Freedman, in her study of nineteenth-century women's prison reformers, describes the arrival of "the first inmate of an exclusively female prison in the United States" in October 1873. Mrs. Sallie Hubbard and her husband had murdered a family of seven. When she arrived at the prison bowed down with manacles, superintendent Sarah Smith ordered the men to "Take off her shackles; she is my prisoner; not yours." She then "embraced her fallen sister, prayed for her, and showed her to a room decorated with bedspread, clothed table, curtains, a pot of flowers, a Bible, and a hymn book." In a similar spirit, the WCTU also took up the cause of prison reform, agitating effectively for the presence of police matrons to deal with incoming prisoners of their own sex.[32]

It seems clear that, as Barbara Epstein has argued, the WCTU drew on and politicized cultural antagonisms between women and men in the middle classes. In cities and small towns alike, women's economic and social dependence on their husbands generated an undertow of anxiety. Anger at men who failed to fulfill their familial responsibilities (alcoholics) thus grew into a challenge to the male mismanagement of the entire political/public arena, a criticism easy to sustain in the heyday of city bosses, robber barons, and corrupt legislatures.[33]

Willard consciously used domestic imagery, both verbal and visual, to encourage women's special sense of moral and political mission. She contrasted, for example, a national WCTU meeting with "any held by men": "Its manner is not that of the street, the court, the mart, or office; it is the manner of the home." The first sign of this distinction lay in "the beauty of decoration . . . ; banners of silk, satin and velvet, usually made by the women themselves, adorn the wall; the handsome shields of states; the great vases bearing aloft grains, fruits and flowers; the moss-covered well with its old bucket; or the setting of a platform to present an interior as cozy and delightful as a parlor could afford." In addition, she argued, not only the setting, but the political methods employed in the "Do-Everything" policy were distinctively female: "Men take one line, and travel onward to success; with them discursiveness is at a discount. But women in the home must be mistresses, as well as maids of all work; they have learned well the lesson of unity in diversity; hence by inheritance and by environment, women are varied in their methods; they are born to be 'branchers-out.' "[34]

The WCTU appealed to a broad range of women, small-town and rural as well as urban, western as well as eastern, wives of artisans and laborers as well as wives of businessmen and professionals. Its leadership, however, was predominantly upper-middle-class, educated, native-born white Protestant, a profile which matches that of other female reform leaders. These educated, increasingly leisured women found in the WCTU an arena in which they could experiment with a redefinition of their roles in light of the changed circumstances of their lives. Ultimately, however, the WCTU could not transcend the biases of its base, with its increasing hostility to the lower classes, to immigrants, and to blacks. Willard was never able to bring the WCTU as fully into electoral politics as she wished, nor to win a majority to her increasingly radical, socialist perspective.[35]

Nevertheless, the WCTU's radical legacy lived on in the populist movement of the 1880s. According to Mari Jo Buhle, populist women, whether on farms or in cities, shared "a universal commitment to women's enfranchisement that found its ideological and organizational base for women of varying backgrounds within the WCTU." When the farmers' revolt shifted from cooperatives to partisan politics, however, unenfranchised women had fewer roles. Campaigning for the Populists in 1892,

Mary E. Lease offered the populist version of politicized domesticity: "Thank God we women are blameless for this political muddle you men have dragged us into. . . . Ours is a grand and holy mission . . . ours the mission to drive from our land and forever abolish the triune monopoly of land, monopoly, and transportation. Ours is the mission to place the mothers of this nation on an equality with the fathers."[36]

In the early years of the twentieth century, the same legacy continued in the newly founded Socialist Party, where women looked to Frances Willard's "beautiful life" to confirm their view that socialism was "the grandest expression of woman's instinct for moral perfection." Both Populists and Socialists continued the practice of women's "parlor meetings," where in the safety of a familiar setting and the comfort of sisterhood women could learn and practice the political skills of public life.[37]

The urban women's club movement eventually overtook the WCTU, developing an analysis centered on secular economic forces but nevertheless drawing on the same romanticized conception of womanhood that flourished in American Victorian culture. Women's clubs were started in the 1870s by middle-class, often professional, women who sought mutual support and professional advancement. Through clubs, middle-class women began to discard sentimentality and incorporate the values of scientific efficiency associated with their class. "They stressed how scientific motherhood, if translated into efficient, nonpartisan, and tough-minded public action, could bring social progress."[38]

Growing numbers of college-educated women turned their energies toward building institutions and creating professions—teaching, nursing, social work. In the process they developed new dimensions of the politics of domesticity. The settlement house movement, started in 1889 with the founding of Hull House in Chicago, brought middle-class women to live in the urban slums. Jane Addams and Ellen Starr understood the settlement house as homelike, a natural environment for women and an expression of personalist values. As Ellen Starr explained to her sister: "There is to be no 'organization' & no 'institution' about it."[39]

For several decades, settlement houses were centers of female creativity, public spaces in which women (and some men) could challenge the realities of urban industrialism by measuring them against the values of the middle-class home. Settlement work expressed, according to Addams, "the great mother breast of our common humanity." In the name of mother love, then, the residents at Hull House and other settlements initiated a wide range of civic and social institutions, including juvenile courts, public playgrounds, cooperatives, coffee houses, industrial medicine, the union label, mothers' pensions, and investigations into social issues like housing, sanitation, prostitution, and education. Women created public, political roles defining them as "civic housekeeping."*[40]

The result was a reform agenda known as Progressivism, an assertion of corporate, societal responsibility for children, for public health and safety, for factory working conditions, and for the rights of the poor. That agenda played a major role in transforming the previous, gendered definitions of politics. In the name of the moral values of the home, female political culture had assumed responsibility for the destitute and homeless. Ironically, as women demanded social responsibility in the form of government programs, however, they began to turn over the institutions they had created to the government. Their "faith in the scientific method and in professionalism eventually led to a devaluation of voluntary work and to the relinquishment of social policy to experts in governmental bureaucracies."[41]

Another underlying problem with "domestic politics" was the fact that the ideals of sisterhood based in middle-class cul-

*This is also Elstain's model for contemporary feminism. She calls her perspective "social feminism," as Addams did, and she wants a critique of the state based on the roles and responsibilities of the mother. See Jean Bethke Elstain, *Public Man, Private Woman: Women in Social and Political Thought* (Princeton: Princeton University Press, 1981).

ture frequently shattered in the face of class differences. There were few environments where that vision could take on a more concrete reality. Working-class and immigrant women could not be drawn into settings which failed to recognize their own traditions and which presumed politicized sisterly bonds they had yet to experience. While native-born women trained in the WCTU or club movement developed their own indigenous and fiercely feminist Socialist movement, for example, immigrant women clung to radical traditions from Europe and accepted their men's insistence on female subordination within the proletarian family. German women in the 1870s, excluded from politics, pioneered roles as service auxiliaries to the working-class movement. Mari Jo Buhle offers a sensitive and subtle analysis of women's historic roles in creating the cultural infra-structure which gave vitality to the movement and to immi-grant culture. "The Socialist milieu, ostensibly political, also operated as a spiritual home, a relief corps, a marriage broker-age, a recreational center, and in the last instance as a burial service for the loyal members. . . . Here, in what is usually referred to as the fraternal network, women participated avidly and enjoyed a leverage they never gained in the party proper." Yet in the intensity of that counterculture which defined women's rights as yet another assimilationist threat, women had no autonomous public space in which to define themselves and to gain access to political skills. Nevertheless, their activities were the first steps on which their more assimilated daughters could build.[42]

The National Women's Trade Union League, founded in 1903, represented the most successful alliance between work-ing-class and middle- and upper-class women, many of the lat-ter from the settlement house movement. Though rife with class and ethnic tension, the WTUL developed organizing tech-niques which recognized the unique ways in which working women's lives were embedded in family and community life. Frustrated by the hostility of the labor movement, however, the WTUL ultimately turned to legalistic and social scientific remedies as well in the form of protective legislation.[43]

After 1900, the suffrage movement blossomed into a mass movement capable of winning the fight for civic equality. The base for such a movement had been built by women's experiences in the club movement, in reform activities, and especially in the WCTU. The politicized female subculture on which it built, however, was itself disintegrating in the face of widening class differences and the proliferation of "domesticated" public roles for women outside the environments which had nourished female collectivity. The institutionalization and professionalization of settings like settlement houses, for example, both narrowed their vision and detached their activities from the ongoing dynamic of a social movement. At the same time, the emerging consumer culture and changing sexual norms stressed the pleasures of romantic heterosexual relations and increasingly denigrated bonds between women.

Historians and political activists have long pondered the contradiction of the suffrage movement. Hundreds of thousands of women, mobilized for more than a decade, won an amendment to the United States Constitution and then apparently disappeared from the political scene. But a focus on free spaces at the heart of the movement clarifies this discrepancy.

Voting is an individual act, one which defines a critical relationship between the citizen and the state. Republican feminism, born at the Seneca Falls Convention in 1848, had at its core the radical demand for citizenship and for female participation in public affairs. In the nineteenth century, the act of voting defined "male" politics, leaving to women broader concerns for moral norms and the care of dependents. Though women had used their sense of moral mission to redefine the public arena and the nature of politics, the republican theory which underlay their demand for the vote had always taken community-building activities largely for granted. And with the rise of progressive theories of democracy that shifted the locus of civic life from community to state, voluntary female associations were in effect defined as only instrumental to winning the right to women's participation in the "public life" of the state. With victory, such associations were stripped of function. Thus, as the central goal and symbol of the movement, suffrage had no way to translate a communal vision of sisterhood into politics.

In 1920, suffrage leaders joyfully dismantled their social movement organization, the National American Woman Suffrage Organization, and created in its place a nonpartisan instrument for educating women to exercise their individual rights as citizens, the League of Women Voters. In a recent reinterpretation of nineteenth-century political culture, Paula Baker concluded that "in a sense, the antisuffragists were right. Women left the home in a symbolic sense; they lost their place above politics and their position as the force of moral order. No longer treated as a political class, women ceased to act as one. . . . By the 1920s the home was something of an embarrassment. Many men and women rejected domesticity as an ideal. The 'new woman' of the 1920s discarded nineteenth-century womanhood by adopting formerly male values and behavior."[44]

The male and female political cultures of the nineteenth century disappeared as women began to vote and domesticity ceased to provide a platform for social critique. Yet the power relations between the sexes remained asymmetrical. Political parties did not really include women as equals. Rather, they redefined the sexual division of labor to encourage women to use their organizational skills at the grass-roots level. So women became the precinct workers and poll watchers, party housekeepers, so to speak, while political office remained a male preserve.[45]

At the same time, the institutional expressions of middle-class female culture such as the League of Women Voters, church organizations, the YWCA, the Consumer's League, and the Girl Scouts persisted through the twentieth century in a depoliticized and marginal form. In retrospect, one can document that many leaders of the feminist resurgence in the 1960s learned leadership skills in such organizations, but those organizations were not themselves the base for insurgency.

One partial exception illustrates this depoliticization or re-privatization of female spaces. In the southern states, under the leadership of Jesse Daniel Ames, a powerful leader comparable in some ways to Frances Willard, white women organized a campaign against lynching. Working through the networks of church missionary societies, they reached out to women in small southern towns and galvanized them to use their moral authority in their communities to prevent lynchings. Such women publicly disavowed rhetoric which justified lynching as a defense of "white womanhood," made personal calls on sheriffs and newspaper editors to encourage them to enforce the laws, and placed moral pressure on husbands, fathers, and sons not to participate in lynch mobs. While they thus began a crucial process of redefining themselves in relation to the prescriptions of southern culture, their strategy kept them within cultural boundaries which could only bring women into activity based on personalist values and private action.[46]

This depoliticization persisted for several decades even among women in the radical left. Those who became leaders viewed their roles as individual ones, not appreciably different from those of men. The Marxist left, for example, which debated "the woman question" in explicit recognition of the oppression of women, actively discouraged any consideration of personal life in its political culture.

The testimony of activist women presents the painful consequence. Peggy Dennis and Vera Weisbord were organizers and leaders within the Communist Party in the 1920s and 1930s. Like male leaders, however, they were expected to subordinate their personal lives and family commitments for the "greater good." For Dennis, this included leaving her son in Russia to be raised in an institution. Any serious confrontation with the subjective subtleties of sexism became virtually impossible. Furthermore, opposition to sexism within the left remained muted because women developed little or no sense of community with each other as women. In the lingua franca of politics, there was no place for sharing personal hardship and hurt—to do so would be weak, almost betrayal. Women expected themselves to act "like men." While individual women assumed important roles and were held up as exemplary, they were cut off from the legacy of female subculture. It took the highly personalized, and sexist, counterculture of the 1960s to reclaim that legacy.[47]

Women who were political activists, like female professionals in the interwar years, made their commitments at the price of bifurcation of self. In the meantime, however, women in the old left often presented strong, politically active, if ambiguous, role models to their daughters and thus laid important groundwork for the renewal of feminism in the 1960s and 1970s.[48]

The revival of feminism in the 1960s built in many ways on the substructure of women's organizations in a new context of dramatic change and rising stress for women whose social roles diverged increasingly from their daily realities. The massive entry of women into the paid labor force during and after the Second World War rendered domestic ideology obsolete. Yet as the numbers of working women soared, transforming the average "working girl" into an older married woman, popular culture reasserted with powerful force the notion that married women belonged exclusively in the home. In the 1960s, Betty Friedan would name this idea the "feminine mystique."[49]

The problems women faced in the last half of the twentieth century could no longer be defined simply in terms of their access to public and political rights. Technically, women had such access. In the political culture of the twentieth century, party rituals were no longer reenactments of manhood, and the state had taken over many of the functions which nineteenth-century women pioneered. Most professions were open, in some measure at least, to women. Yet traditional assumptions about female nature and women's roles continued to undermine women both in the public realm and at home.

The "feminine mystique" represented a new version of romanticized private life, echoing the nineteenth-century cult of true womanhood. But the blurring boundaries of public and private meant that it could no longer provide a basis for female self-assertion. As the state assumed roles previously assigned to women, as women joined the public labor force, often in the service sector where their jobs mimicked traditional roles, old boundaries shattered. The "domestic sphere" was no longer a female world where women could mobilize in defense of compassion and communal values. Rather it was an arena of consumption for both women and men. Domesticity, in this context, served as a cushion against the anxiety of change and the blurring of boundaries. It also transferred into the public arena assumptions which undermined women's ability to participate as equals. "Women's jobs" tended to be unskilled, often service oriented, and extremely low paid, while housewives coped with the demanding changes of a suburban, consumption life-style, never sure that what they did was really "work." As a result, traditional women's organizations, long embedded in domestic ideology, could provide training grounds for leadership, but were only indirectly the base for insurgency.

The feminist revolt in the 1960s grew in two environments. The first was a small network of professional women whose political activities involved them increasingly in issues of women's rights. The second was the youthful social movements of the Sixties—civil rights, the student new left, antiwar—which served as catalysts similar to the abolition and other reform movements of the nineteenth century.

Professional women were subject to particular pressures during the postwar years as their numbers grew while their position relative to men declined. For them in particular, domestic ideology presented contradictions which undermined their capacity to pursue their chosen work. Subjected to discrimination, isolation, and subtle harassment at every turn, they experienced most acutely the contradictions of a culture which simultaneously endorsed and denied the basic values of individual opportunity and republicanism.[50]

Politically and professionally active women were prominent voices in the rising expressions of concern in the 1950s about the changing work and family roles. Some networks, such as those surrounding the Women's Bureau in the Department of Labor, were the direct descendants of suffragists, still working for a kind of social feminism. Others were a new breed: lawyers, members of Congressional staffs, Congressional wives with ambitions and political careers of their own, the professional staff of unions in the CIO. In the women's department of the United Auto Workers, in the student YWCA, in sociological research on "women's two roles" or conferences on women and work, the dilemmas began to be explored and new perceptions to find a voice.[51]

The creation of a Presidential commission on the status of women and of dozens of state commissions in the early 1960s finally offered an environment in which professional women could use their expertise to reeducate both themselves and the public. The commissions combed the laws, judicial decisions, statistics on labor force participation, wages, marital status, and fertility to create a devastating portrait of inequity, and an agenda for change.[52]

The activities of the commissions linked, broadened, and politicized networks of women in Washington, D.C., and in several states. Women in these networks served on commissions, on the staffs of commissions or sympathetic members of Congress, in the Women's Bureau of the Department of Labor, and, increasingly, in other agencies as well. They began to perceive the need for a more powerful lobby for women.

The creation of the National Organization for Women in 1966 at a meeting of state Commissions on the Status of Women was the first step in the political self-organization of these networks. The original NOW statement of purpose vowed "to bring women into full participation in the mainstream of American society now, assuming all the privileges and responsibilities thereof in truly equal partnership with men." It represented in some ways a modernized version of the Seneca Falls Declaration by reclaiming for women the republican ideals of equal participation and individual rights. The importance and power of these networks grew with the proliferation of groups such as the Women's Equity Action League (WEAL), the National Women's Political Caucus, and Federally Employed Women, all focused on public equality and individual rights.[53]

Modern republican feminism, however, like its nineteenth-century predecessor, failed to mobilize masses of women in part because of its focus on rights and individuals, abstracted from communal relations. The founders of NOW understood that women were seriously disadvantaged in the American political and legal system, but they presumed a model of political activity which was essentially male. In the beginning, the bonds of sisterhood remained unarticulated and depoliticized. Indeed, NOW was very careful to insist that it was an organization "for" women but not necessarily "of" women. Men have always been welcome to join.

Most women, however, could not identify with the clear-cut dilemmas of the professional woman. Trapped in the mystifying complexities of a popular culture which simultaneously endorsed individual opportunity and the feminine mystique, a gender-segregated economy which drew women into low-paid, low-status jobs, and a child-centered family premised on the full-time services of a wife/mother, they could not abstract issues of rights from the underlying questions of identity. They did respond, however, to the angry critique of a small group of radical young women who challenged the very definitions of public and private, of politics and personal life, and who asserted women's needs for personal support and group solidarity as well as for political action.

The young women who proclaimed, in the late 1960s, that "sisterhood is powerful" were children of the postwar middle class. Their parents had achieved unprecedented material success in a culture characterized increasingly by rootlessness. The flip side of the romanticized domesticity of the feminine mystique or women's magazine slogans like "togetherness" proclaimed in the 1950s was the continued erosion of community and its replacement by consumer culture. Tradition was no longer seen as a source of virtue. Rather the search for pleasure emphasized the "new" and the scientific in the ersatz communities of grassy suburbs. As Richard Fox and Jackson Lears have pointed out,

> Life for most middle-class and many working-class Americans in the twentieth century has been a ceaseless pursuit of the "good life" and a constant reminder of their powerlessness. . . . Although the dominant institutions of our culture have purported to be offering the consumer a fulfilling participation in the life of the community, they have to a large extent presented the empty prospect of taking part in the marketplace of personal exchange.[54]

The student movements of the 1960s represented a backlash on the part of middle-class youth against the materialism of American society, the absence of authentic community, and the failure of America to live up to its moral claims. In the civil rights movement and the new left, they not only organized to demand changes but also to experiment with new and visionary forms of democratic relationships.

These movements provided young women with a social space within which they could challenge received definitions of domesticity and female nature. They also shared their generation's intense search for community and discovered there the power of sisterhood. As a result, they challenged the definitions of politics more fundamentally than women had done since the days of the WCTU. With their declaration that "the personal is political" they repoliticized the bonds among women and rediscovered the ground for collective action.

From the beginning, the student movement expressed intense commitment to the power of democratic community. In the civil rights movement the terms "beloved community" and "redemptive community" captured a vision of racial equality which the movement itself strove to embody. The Student Nonviolent Coordinating Committee, founded by southern blacks who started the sit-in movement, established a pattern of prolonged and personally wrenching meetings which ceased only with consensus. The northern student left developed a similarly personal style in its attempt to live out the ideal of "participatory democracy."

Within the black civil rights movement, middle-class white women experienced a politicizing transformation analogous to that of their abolitionist foremothers. Bolstered by a radical commitment to equal rights, often with religious roots, they broke the mold of passive domesticity, organizing voter registration drives and freedom schools, risking arrest, enduring jail, and witnessing firsthand the dignity and self-respect of impoverished rural black communities. They learned from black women upon whose strength much of the movement rested: women who had endured grinding poverty and the humiliations of segregation with their strength and pride intact; who risked their lives to vote, to house white volunteers, and to sustain the movement. For middle-class white women raised in the era of the feminine mystique, these black community women offered a vision of womanhood which further reinforced an emerging sense of self-assertion. Finally, as the young women activists gained in self-esteem and saw new models of womanhood, the continuing sexual division of labor in the movement put them together frequently by themselves. Within the broader social space of the movement, women found a specifically female social space in which to discuss their experiences, share insights, and find group strength as they worked in the office or met on the margins of big meetings.[55]

The activities of southern students inspired the northern student new left to develop in ways that offered similar free social spaces to young women. The student left in the late Fifties and early Sixties had been heavily intellectual and male dominated. But when Students for a Democratic Society (SDS), in imitation of SNCC, initiated community organizing projects in northern cities, it unwittingly offered women an opportunity which they eagerly seized.[56]

The theory behind SDS's organizing projects was one which predicted massive (male) unemployment, generating a constituency for militant, interracial organizations of the poor. Economic conditions, affected by the buildup for the Vietnam war, however, conspired to lower unemployment rates, and college students who went to live in the ghettos of Chicago, Cleveland, Newark, and Boston found a male constituency consisting primarily of street gangs and winos. While male SDS leaders touted an organizing method based on "hanging out on de corners wid de guys," women in the same projects discovered a large, stable, female constituency which they proceeded to organize with some success. Indeed, the only organized legacy of the SDS projects were several groups which joined the welfare rights movement in the late 1960s.

Women's experiences in SDS were, even more than in the civil rights movement, filled with irony and mystification. Publicly, men were acknowledged as the key leaders of almost every project. In reality, women were the most skillful organizers. The battles over organizing strategy revolved around unemployment (Jobs or Income Now) versus community issues (Garbage Removal or Income Now). The higher prestige of the former centered on its presumed male constituency, and its greater connection with the public world of work. Men and women alike worried about the "problem" of having so many women leaders. The acronyms of the two positions, JOIN v. GROIN, summarized the low esteem in which private, community, and female issues and constituencies were held.

Nevertheless, the projects offered women opportunities to develop leadership skills, political analysis, and role models which they later used to begin a new women's movement. The principal female leadership within SDS after 1964 came from community organizing projects where they had tested their own courage, learned to organize and to run meetings, developed strategies, and, along the way, developed confidence in themselves. Within the SDS projects, women also developed communal bonds among themselves and a deep identification with the female leadership of poor communities both in the North and in the South.

The left as a whole became a less hospitable environment for women after the mid-Sixties. In the South, racial anger and the need of the black community for self-definition made it impossible for whites to participate in an increasingly nationalist black movement. In the North, the anti–Vietnam-war movement eclipsed community organizing and left women with no political task comparable to that of the male draft resister. The youthful counterculture celebrated love and community—feminine values—and yet the sexual freedom it proclaimed often exploited women.[57]

The community organizing focus which had provided women with skills, self-confidence, and a new experience of sisterhood disappeared just at the moment when women had begun to apply the egalitarian ideology of the new left to themselves and their condition in American society. Networks of female friendships were critical links between northern and southern movements. Within these networks, as early as 1964, women explored the possible consequences of applying democratic principles to their relationships with men. They discovered the realities of sexual inequality within the very settings which had taught them the value of egalitarian community.

When women raised the question of their equality within the movement, they met a combination of indifference, ridicule, and anger. Women were hooted at, threatened with rape, accused of divisiveness and betrayal. But they were armed with self-respect, considerable organizing skills learned in the movement, a radical commitment to equality, and an appreciation of the power of group solidarity. They transformed the new-left emphasis on the personal nature of political action into the feminist assertion that "the personal is political," and broke away to create a movement for the liberation of women.

Early meetings were intense and exhilarating. In a style they had learned in the civil rights movement and the new left, women explored the political meaning of their personal experience. Again and again, individuals were shocked to discover that their lives were not unique but part of a larger pattern. The warm support and understanding of other women empowered them as they reclaimed the lost legacy of sisterhood.

The small "consciousness-raising" group was the central organizing tool of the women's liberation movement. Its brilliance lay in the fact that it repoliticized informal female networks—office friendships, neighborhood kaffeeklatsches—creating thousands of free social spaces in which women could explore new modes of understanding their lives and new visions for the future. The intellectual task which radical women set themselves was to measure all received knowledge against their own lived experience and to hold nothing sacred. The result was an outpouring of theory and polemic and, in subsequent decades, of feminist scholarship.[58]

The process begun by young radicals in the 1960s also shaped the awakening lesbian community. In consciousness-raising groups, lesbians became visible to themselves and one another. Freed to challenge social definitions of femininity, of sexuality, and of deviance (even when those attitudes persisted in the women's movement itself), they began to articulate the dimensions of a lesbian feminist perspective. They also discovered a preexisting organization, the Daughters of Bilitis, founded in the 1950s by Del Martin and Phyllis Lyon. Since the Second World War, lesbians in America had become an increasingly self-conscious and self-identified community. But the emotional and intellectual energy of thousands of younger women suddenly transformed the tiny and relatively apolitical organizations. Young radicals brought a keen understanding of the importance of sisterhood and the creation of new social spaces which would nourish communal bonds and make a visible alternative to the marginalized and self-destructive "bar culture." They built coffeehouses, bookstores, counseling centers, theaters, musical productions, and a variety of feminist enterprises. Lesbian feminism soon became a central intellectual thread in the new movement.[59]

The weaknesses of the radical branch of the women's movement were related to its strengths. Angry at the increasingly authoritarian and exploitative male leadership of the student movement, radical women revived the democratic ideals of the early new left. They consciously avoided creating organizations with designated leaders. The search for pure democracy, however, meant that the leadership which inevitably arose remained unacknowledged and unaccountable. Where the old left had denied the importance or relevance of private life, the women's liberation movement's intense analysis of the politics of private relations left no clarity about public roles and structures. Personalist values reigned in such a way that the vitality of the new movement achieved no sustained institutional form but rather resulted in a plethora of small groups, each with its own version of "true" feminism.

An additional factor in the inability of youthful radical feminists to build movement organizations was their belief that the creation of feminist community involved the total rejection of tradition. Cut off from traditional communal structures, radical young women had no tangible sense of historical resources and no base in women's traditional spaces. Many consciousness-raising groups spent their first meeting discussing their reluctance to come because their images of "women's groups" were so negative. These upwardly mobile daughters of an increasingly rootless middle class had internalized the cultural denigration of women as trivial, gossipy, and superficial. As a result, they generated an historical dynamic which they could not comprehend as the politicization of informal structures which existed in more traditional environments. In effect, they activated the latent organizing experiences of millions of American women who spontaneously began to initiate consciousness-raising groups, rape crisis centers, and women's projects of all kinds.

Women whose lives were tightly bound into a web of community, family, and ethnic loyalties found that the initial rhetoric of the movement demanded that they reject those ties. Few working-class women were willing to do so. In time, however, some founded groups like the National Congress of Neighborhood Women, claiming that "they wanted to be part of the women's movement but that the women's movement was leaving out women in working-class neighborhoods—there wasn't space. We also felt that the ethnic and neighborhood movement didn't have space for women." Traditional women's organizations, church groups, the YWCA, the Girl Scouts, Business and Professional Women, even the League of Women Voters, began to take on feminist issues and to provide "consciousness-raising" experiences.[60]

Black women, having fewer specifically female spaces within the black movement, deeply aware of the need for racial solidarity, and sensitive to the racism of white middle-class women, moved through a different dynamic to their own feminist consciousness. At the grass roots, women like Bertha Gilkey in St. Louis struggled to raise their children in the dirty and violent surroundings of public housing projects. As a teen-ager, Gilkey started to organize the residents of Cochran Gardens, a project so crime-ridden that even the police avoided coming there if they could. After more than a decade of work, Cochran Gardens is tenant run and completely rehabilitated. Hallways and lawns are spotless. Tenants provide staff for a day-care center, a senior citizen high-rise, a medical clinic, and a catering service that prepares meals on wheels.

In 1981, Bertha Gilkey became involved with the National Congress of Neighborhood Women and discovered the feminist dimension of her work. Today she would say she has a woman's consciousness, aware that the people who transformed Cochran Gardens and run its many businesses are principally women.[61]

Throughout the 1970s and early 1980s, massive numbers of women resonated with the call to female solidarity and seized the opportunity to explore new ways of understanding and organizing their lives. Many simply shifted their activities in church and voluntary associations toward feminist concerns. Others began to organize specific constituencies of women: clerical workers, sociologists, day-care providers, historians. Those interested in republican feminism turned to NOW. The National Organization for Women and its offshoots were from the beginning more thoroughly grounded in the female voluntary tradition than their younger radical sisters and, as a result, they reaped the benefit of the radical upsurge, growing to a membership of more than 250,000 in the 1980s. The power of sisterhood applied to the liberal political agenda generated a wealth of new legislation in the 1970s, a serious national effort to pass the Equal Rights Amendment, and in 1984 the nomination of Geraldine Ferraro for the Vice-Presidency.[62]

At the same time, the basic tension between the individualizing vision of republican feminism and the communal perspectives rooted in women's familial and biological roles remains unresolved. Much of NOW's massive membership is not active. Critics argue that "NOW is feminism impersonalized, divorced from its grass-roots base; feminism institutionalized, rigidly structured, with an internal agenda of its own; feminism professionalized, dominated by a small group of full-time activists. And it is feminism legitimized, locked within the narrow confines of electoral and legislative politics."[63]

It is not simply that the pragmatism of electoral politics has narrowed the vision and internal life of organizations like NOW. Rather, the limitations are part of a long tradition of republican feminism which defines freedom for women in terms of their rights to public, political power as conventionally understood. Like the suffrage movement, liberal feminism commands powerful symbols, attracting a broad coalition. But it lacks the transforming vision which is possible when women draw on their own, gendered experience to create visions of the future. At the same time, contemporary cultural feminism has often become apolitical, disengaged from the process of social change. The splintering of the women's movement indicates both its strength and its weakness. Today, as ever, women mobilize effectively only at the sparking juncture of public and private. And they express their deepest, most democratic vision when they rework the very terms of discussion, challenging and changing conventional notions of what "public" and "private" are about.

CHAPTER 4

CLASS AND COMMUNITY

> As our fathers resisted unto blood the lordly avarice of the
> British ministry, so we, their daughters, never will wear the
> yoke which has been prepared for us.
>
> —Lowell, Massachusetts, 1836

THUS PROCLAIMED several hundred young women, walking
away from loom and spindle in the Lowell mills of 1836. They
knew of no traditions of "labor militancy"—factories were relatively new, and young women came to them from the rural
countryside, enticed not only by the prospect of wages but also
by the owners' idyllic depictions of Lowell as a "republican
community" worthy of self-respecting and virtuous citizens.

But the promise had soured. And Lowell workers, thinking of
themselves not as an abstract "class" of workers but rather as
descendants and heirs of the American Revolution, had shattered the city's professions of communal harmony. Their protests, moreover, presaged things to come. Throughout the nineteenth century, bitter conflicts over the emerging new
industrial order were fought out in terms of sharply competing
views of the meaning and promise of the American heritage—
one, radically egalitarian; the other, emphasizing property
rights and individual advancement.[1]

The turbulent history of American industrial workers furnishes a fine-grained case study in the centrality and complexity
of free spaces in democratic revolt. Yet it also presents a series
of problems for the contemporary analyst and historian of those

struggles, for the normal ways of speaking and thinking about such things involve a set of assumptions about their "normal" and "progressive" process of development which obscure the role of such social space. To clarify the problem, it is useful to begin with an exploration of the actors themselves—a look at who, and what, we are describing.

E. P. Thompson published his pathbreaking work, *The Making of the English Working Class,* in the early 1960s on the complex of traditions, ideas, cultures, and activities that produced the first wave of trade unions and political activity by English workers in the eighteenth and nineteenth centuries. Since then the study of "working-class protest" has undergone considerable change. It has been difficult to treat such conflicts as the simple, reflexive response to conditions of hardship and victimization, or to treat the institutional history of workers' formal, large organizations, preeminently unions, as if those *institutions* were the whole or even main story. Yet there remains an ongoing problem in defining and using such essential terms as "working class" itself.

The concept of class emerged in its modern sense in the period of 1770 to 1840, when critics began to use it to designate fixed groups—the lower class, the middle class, the upper class, and so forth. In particular, it described economic relationships born of the modern age. One cotton spinner in 1781 referred to employers and workers as "two distinct classes of persons." John Stuart Mill and Karl Marx both used an initial class typology of landlords, capitalists, and laborers. For Marx, this division was increasingly superseded by the simple categories of bourgeoisie (the capitalists) and proletariat (the working class).[2]

Here "class" is used in a double sense, and the dual meanings create the problems. First, class is a descriptive category, a way of analyzing what actually happens to people, their institutions, and their ways of life in modern society. However, class is also used to describe a group as organized, self-consciously in conflict with other classes, and dedicated to a particular political and social agenda. In this double meaning can be found great irony.

As a method of description, notions of class detail and name profound experiences and processes of modern life. In the first instance, it was the project of thinkers like Karl Marx to give historical concreteness to the age-old conflicts between social groups and to illuminate certain circumstances that hinder or facilitate group action. For example, in the *Communist Manifesto,* Marx and Engels described the process of working people's aggregation into factories, the increasing polarization of classes, the routinization of the work process—all factors that worked to increase collective linkages among working people. In a section of the *Eighteenth Brumaire,* by way of contrast, Marx analyzed the circumstances, such as bad communications, that encouraged isolation and prevented the French peasantry from forming common bonds. In their treatment of cities, for example, Marx and Engels often suggested that the workers' new freedom and contacts with a diversity of subcultures would create preconditions for "universal" consciousness.[3]

Though Marx and Engels saw such developments as laying the basis for broader, universalist forms of association and identity, they also described with great feeling the pain and hardship involved in such processes. According to Marx, in the factory "men are effaced by their labor." Labor becomes abstract, valued according to money alone. "The pendulum of the clock has become as accurate a measure of the relative activity of two workers as it is of the speed of two locomotives." Under modern factory conditions, people's particular identities, their histories, are, as Marx said, "obliterated." The machines, the rhythm of work, acquire an eerie reality of their own and "appear as a world for themselves, quite independent of and divorced from the individuals." In contrast, "standing over against these productive forces we have the majority, robbed of all real life-content, abstract individuals."[4]

The insights embedded in phrases like these—"abstract individuals," "robbed of all real life-content"—have been developed into powerful analyses. They name people's experiences, and provide a language for describing the anomie, the homelessness, the felt injustice of the modern world. Out of such understanding comes a great wealth of historical investigation into the forms of association that people create in the effort to cope with their new situation: benevolent associations, trade unions, cooperatives, and finally electoral parties, all built upon people's experiences as "workers."

The problem has not been with the attempt to analyze and understand the processes that dehumanize workers, but with the attempt to develop conceptions of action and theories of social change based upon the capitalist definition of working people. The notion of an abstract, universal cosmopolitanism as the end point of true class consciousness draws its theory of group formation and its language from the vast settings where people are organized by modern life. It assumes that a sundering of people from their historical and organic connections—from their "roots"—is the indispensable preliminary to freedom. It proposes, in place of community weakened or lost, an organization based on abstract solidarity. Moreover, the idea that uprootedness is an indication of progress has maintained a compelling hold over much of modern scholarship—Marxist and non-Marxist alike—which sees traditional relations as reactionary obstacles. From such a stance, in turn, workers *must* abandon memories and ties to their communal past as an essential part of building modern movements like the trade unions. Thus, for instance, for Engels the "driving of workers from hearth and home" that accompanied urbanization and industrialization was "the very first condition of their intellectual emancipation." In his view, "modern large-scale industry . . . has turned the worker, formerly chained to the land, into a completely propertyless proletarian, liberated from all traditional fetters, a free outlaw."*

*Both Marx and Engels frequently described the workers' relation to the past with ferocity. For Marx, there had to be a "radical rupture" with what had gone before. For Engels, "tradition is the great retarding force . . . but being merely passive is sure to be broken down." In the *Eighteenth Brumaire*, Marx argued that a revolution by the working class would necessitate a kind of radical amnesia: "the social revolution cannot draw its poetry from the past, but only from the future."

Marx's indifference to working people's roots did not spring from indifference to working people's sufferings. There is a strong feeling for the concrete in the

Following such[5] a legacy, much recent historical research has begun as the effort to discover how the industrial work force

---

historical writings of Marx and Engels that confounds the abstract universalism of their political theory. Yet the point is that the basic theory that saw revolutionary consciousness as a rootless cosmopolitanism has continued to hold sway over the dominant left approach. It appears in Lenin's theory of revolutionary consciousness as the worldview of middle-class, radicalized intellectuals that must be introjected into the working class, and in Trotsky's contention that the Bolshevik Party must be a "moral medium" of its own, guarding against ideological contamination and, implicitly, forming a socializing agent for its members in order to detach them from all prior loyalties. In our time, the leftist view of liberated consciousness as a process of radical separation lies behind Michael Harrington's vision of a "rational, humanist moral code" to replace traditional moral values. It informs conventional criteria used to distinguish social movements. Thus, E. J. Hobsbawm contrasts "primitive" protests grounded in communal ties and "modern, secular" movements like the trade unions and socialist parties that supposedly have severed such connections. Similarly, the Tillys separate "reactive" communal movements from "proactive," modern movements. Ralph Miliband means much the same thing when he argues that "the Marxist notion of a 'most radical rupture' with traditional ideas signifies a break with all forms of tradition and must expect to encounter the latter not as friend but as foe." And this view of social change and its agents is succinctly summarized by Stanley Aronowitz in his essay entitled, appropriately enough, "The Working Class: A Break with the Past." According to Aronowitz, all particular identities—of "race and nationality and sex and skill and industry"—are obstacles to the development of homogenized class consciousness. As he puts it, "they constitute antagonisms which still act as a brake on the development of revolutionary consciousness."

In many practical instances, radicals have overcome such condescension toward traditional relations—in fact, exactly such practical supercession of the theoretical tradition has proved the key to moments of leftist success, again and again around the world. Yet there is, therefore, enormous tragedy inherent in situations of such success, when orthodox left-wing movements, having identified themselves with popular traditions and then having won power, seek to impose theoretical models of "the new man" and of "modernizing" collectivization which pose as *obstacles* those free spaces that are the source of democracy. Indeed, this can be seen as the terrible contradiction at work in nations stretching from Vietnam to Cuba. See Marx, *The Holy Family* (Moscow: Foreign Language Publishers, 1956), pp. 52–53; Engels, "On Historical Materialism," in Lewis Feuer, ed., *Marx and Engels: Basic Writings on Politics and Philosophy* (Garden City, N.Y.: Doubleday, 1969), p. 66; Marx, *Eighteenth Brumaire of Louis Bonaparte* (New York: International Publishers, 1963), p. 15; Michael Harrington, *The Twilight of Capitalism* (New York: Simon & Schuster, 1976), p. 291; E. J. Hobsbawm, *Primitive Rebels: Studies in Archaic Forms of Social Movement in the 19th and 20th Centuries* (New York: W. W. Norton, 1959), Charles and Louise Tilly, *The Rebellious Century* (Cambridge: Harvard University Press, 1975); Ralph Miliband, *Marxism and Politics* (Oxford: Oxford University Press, 1977), p. 44; Stanley Aronowitz, "The Working Class: A Break with the Past," in Colin Greer, ed., *Divided Society: The Ethnic Experience in America* (New York: Basic Books, 1974), pp. 312–13.

moves from a group brought together by modern industry—
what is sometimes called a "class *in* itself"—to a group that
understands its identity in mainly abstract, universalist terms,
a "class *for* itself." Yet in the process, scholars alert to the living
reality they are studying have discovered something else.
Rooted communities and voluntary associations created by
familial, religious, artisanal, ethnic, geographic, and other daily
ties furnish the vocabulary, terms, and sources of inspiration for
conflicts born out of economic change and capitalist development. To the extent broader consciousness of "class solidarity"
has had a power and relevance in working people's lives, it has
taken on meaning and depended for its sustenance upon the
survival (or renewal) and vitality of communal relations and
voluntary associations bridging divisions between home and
work.*

Thus a new generation of social historians documents the
communal origins of labor protests with a richness of detail that
challenges traditional ideas about political agency. In view of
such evidence that the life of communities and not abstract
notions of class have provided the main resources for oppositional movements among working people, the conventional
terms of thinking about politics are themselves called into
doubt. Thus, for instance, the famous question that has vexed
political historians and theorists for more than half a century—
"Why is there no socialist movement in America?"—itself can
be shown to obscure the very issues it purports to examine. The
more basic and prior question is how community ties and voluntary associations bridging home and work worlds have survived
at all, given the extreme rootlessness of American life. In the
face of rootlessness born of extensive migrations, the pressures

---

*Sociologist Craig Calhoun has contrasted notions of community and class
usefully: "Community is built of direct relations; class, on the contrary, is made
possible as a form of social solidarity only by the development of large-scale
systems of indirect relationships." (Calhoun, "Class, Place and Industrial Revolution," in N. Thrift and P. Williams, eds., *The Making of Urban Society: Historical Essays on Class Formation and Place* (London: Routledge & Kegan Paul,
1985).

to assimilate into a "melting pot," the growing culture of consumerism and the like, radicals are those with roots, something to lose—not those who have lost "all but their chains." And to the extent radical alternatives have gained widespread acceptance among American working people, they have typically been framed not in the traditional left-wing language of socialism and class struggle, but rather in a more communitarian, decentralized, and republican idiom. Terms like "cooperative commonwealth" have moved Americans in ways that visions of a Soviet America or nationalized industry never have.

Thus, a closer look at the shifting patterns of working people's insurgencies which accompanied the emergence of modern capitalism in the United States illustrates the ways in which community life and voluntary association at the nexus between work and the world outside provided the bases for serious and sustained opposition. In such free spaces, working people appropriated and redefined their heritage to construct an oppositional way of seeing things—and came to see that their way might indeed be able to succeed.

In the first instance, the heritage which informed organized resistance to factory work and the intrusion of new market forces into community life came directly from the republicanism of the American Revolution. Americans recalled the battle against the English as a fight against privilege in the name of a virtuous republic. The virtue of the republic, in turn, rested on the reality that citizens were freeholders, small landowners or artisans who "owned" their trade and their tools. In the Jeffersonian tradition, the independence—the "freedom"—generated by small-scale property joined with freedom from despotic and arbitrary authority to produce a "commonwealth." In turn, free and independent citizens, zealous in the preservation of their liberties, were the only body capable of acting in the interest of the community and the society as a whole.[6]

Artisans also drew specifically on ancient traditions of craft solidarity when, soon after the Revolution, they had to defend their independence and dignity against the encroaching factory system. In the eighteenth century and early nineteenth century, artisans provided a focal point for community life. Their elaborate parades, for instance, were exciting, colorful public rituals in which masters and journeymen would march by craft under the symbols of the craft and those of the Republic, alike. Indeed, these artisans saw themselves as the very embodiment of republicanism, workers whose independence ensured their virtue. But in the first decades of the nineteenth century, the craft system began to crumble. National markets offered greater profits for contractors and "sweaters" who parceled out portions of the tasks to less skilled workers. By the 1830s, artisanal republicanism had, under the impact of such developments, begun to divide into two opposing interpretations of the Revolution, each of which claimed primacy. On the one side, entrepreneurs emphasized the individualism of equal opportunity in spirited defense of the emerging order. They placed the blame for success or failure squarely on the individual. On the other side, working-class republicans drew on their artisanal traditions to develop what Sean Wilentz has called "a radical critique of that order, saturated with the spirit of cooperative labor and production for the commonwealth." In these terms, speculative capitalists whose primary motives were greed and self-interest represented a mortal danger to the community.[7]

But such ideas were appropriated and developed only under certain conditions. Much, perhaps most, resistance to the emerging factory system was sporadic, individualized, and defensive. In massive numbers, workers refused to bend to the new disciplines of the industrial setting. They came late or not at all to work. They refused to let the factories control their children. Most of all, they quit and moved elsewhere. Mobility studies indicate that in major cities like Boston, 25 percent of the population at any time had not been there a year before. "It is as if working class communities were no more than a gathering of strangers and working class life an ordeal undergone in isolation."[8]

While mobility may have contributed to the gradual homogenization of specific occupational cultures, its most powerful effect was the disruption of the dense relations of village life. According to Jonathan Prude, migrants in the textile industry created something of a "self-conscious occupational culture," for instance, but in the face of "the divisive pressures of factory life [it] was no more than a limited camaraderie: a fraternalism that . . . failed to encourage a 'habit of solidarity' among nonrelatives."[9]

How did it happen, then, that in the land of the uprooted, some people moved beyond defensiveness and toward a radical critique of the way things were that led to continuing, cooperative action? Protest and group solidarity clearly were possible only where communities existed or could be created—communities with associational life capable of appropriating, enriching, and experimenting with democratic traditions and ideas. In the textile towns described by Prude, such communities were largely absent. In Lowell, however, young female workers, migrants from the rural New England countryside, lived together in boardinghouses and worked in settings which required considerable cooperation. The result was a pioneering drama of industrial conflict.

Strikes in Lowell in the 1830s and the ten-hour movement which gained strong support in the city in the following decade grew directly from the close-knit communities where women depended upon one another for companionship, support, and mutual respect. These young women from the New England countryside, moreover, formed a socially and culturally homogeneous work force. The similarity of their backgrounds and the mutual dependence of their lives both at work and in the boardinghouses permitted the creation of powerful group norms. Thus, one local minister described "the power of opinion" in restraining the behavior of young women concerned to maintain the purity of their character and reputations: "A girl, *suspected* of immoralities, or serious improprieties of conduct, at once loses caste."[10]

When wage cuts threatened the economic independence of Lowell workers, however, that same group solidarity became insurgent. Calling on their "patriotic Ancestors," they determined to retain their freedom. By the 1840s, female textile workers had become a political force in Lowell, and the solidarity built through work, leisure, and struggle shifted their self-perceptions from daughterhood to sisterhood. One worker challenged the paternalism of middle-class legislators by arguing that women "have at last learnt the lesson which a bitter experience teaches, that not to those who style themselves their 'natural protectors' are they to look for the needful help, but to the strong and resolute of their own sex."[11]

The spirit and solidarity of women operatives in Lowell lasted only brief decades, undermined eventually by changing patterns of employment which brought dozens of nationalities to the city, men and women alike. Yet the pattern repeated itself elsewhere again and again: those settings which sustained organized protest against the factory system were communities whose dense relationships meshed work and daily life. The most successful examples, indeed, were communities capable of remembering an artisanal past and blending that memory with republican ideology, using it to judge and criticize the legitimacy of what was emerging.

For example, throughout the nineteenth century, Lynn, Massachusetts, harbored a continuing tradition of labor organization and militancy among shoemakers and workers in related industries. It was also a hotbed of radicalism, utopianism, abolitionism, and finally socialism. The story of the Lynn shoemakers vividly recapitulates the powerful and disordering changes occasioned by the changing economy.

At the beginning of the American Revolution, Lynn was a small, rural community whose households combined agricultural pursuits with the skilled craft of shoemaking. Most of the shoes produced by masters and their apprentices and journeymen were custom orders, made for known individuals and often bartered for other goods. The boycott of British goods and sub-

sequent demands of the Revolutionary army signaled the beginnings of a national market and a sudden growth in production from several thousand pairs annually before 1760 to 400,-
000 pairs by 1796. By the early years of the nineteenth century,
shopkeeper entrepreneurs had discovered new possibilities in
aggressively expanding their markets, using shoes in trade for
other goods.[12]

With their access to credit and need for greater productivity,
they began to centralize control over the industry. By the
1830s, the old system of household production had disappeared.
Some of the work had been moved to central shops, while
piecework continued to be hired out to small shops in Lynn and
other New England towns. The introduction of the sewing machine permitted the final shift to the factory system between
1855 and 1865, bringing together all the processes under one
roof and permitting the hiring of large numbers of unskilled
workers.

Throughout this transition, the shoemakers of Lynn drew on
the heritage of dignity and pride in their craft. They believed
in a republican community of independent households and pro-
ducers bound together in intricate webs of mutual dependence
as shoes were traded for cloth and cloth for food. Alan Dawley
describes how "artisans reached out from their own households
to grasp ties of fraternity and sorority in their neighborhoods,
in the community, and among laboring people as a whole. Even
as manufacturers were taking over the central command of
production, artisans successfully asserted control over vital folkways." The ideas were a mix of the labor theory of value—the
idea that all worth comes directly from work—republicanism,
and Christianity. As a result, their periodic protests were constantly infused with a positive awareness of the worth and dignity of the individual and the importance of community. By the
1830s, they had begun to organize political parties, benefit societies, producer cooperatives, trade associations, and newspapers. In articles and songs, they turned the language of their
trade into political puns:

> Now, EQUAL RIGHTS the motto,
> *Wax* your *threads* as true *souls* ought to;
> Though the run-*round* bosses *bristle,*
> We'll raise a *peg* and let them *whistle.*
> > Stick to the last, brave cordwainers!
> > In the end you'll *awl* be gainers![13]

Their republicanism presumed certain inequalities. Thus, the (male) head of the household served as the political representative of all its subordinate members—women, children, apprentices, and servants. Yet the growing numbers of women in the shoemaking industry never hesitated to claim the tradition for themselves as well.

In the late 1850s, as a depression exaggerated the already severe impact of the transition to factory production, shoemakers in Lynn mobilized the legendary "Great Strike," the largest labor uprising before the Civil War. They called the strike on Washington's Birthday in 1860, and soon more than 20,000 workers throughout upper New England had joined. The strike was marked by the rituals of community and artisanal life—great parades in which thousands marched and hundreds came to cheer as strikers, local militia and fire companies, brass bands, and delegations from surrounding towns marched through the center of Lynn. Women organized their own associations and strike meetings and held a parade in which 800 female strikers marched with a banner reading: AMERICAN LADIES WILL NOT BE SLAVES! GIVE US A FAIR COMPENSATION AND WE LABOUR CHEERFULLY.[14]

Whether male or female, shoemakers contrasted their own independence and freedom with the conditions of slaves and called on their Revolutionary heritage. In the words of a song written during the strike:

> > Resolve by your native soil,
> > > Resolve by your fathers' graves,
> > You will live by your honest toil,
> > > But never consent to be slaves.

> The workman is worthy his hire,
> No tyrant shall hold us in thrall;
> They may order their soldiers to fire,
> But we'll stick to the hammer and awl.[15]

Unfortunately, community solidarity was not sufficient. Manufacturers brought in both strikebreakers and state police from outside. While the employers had centralized their power, workers' organizations remained decentralized, and they had few alternative sources of income. After eight weeks, the Great Strike faded away, but it remained a powerful memory of community mobilization which inspired later and more effective organizations after the Civil War.

By the 1870s, the last shred of artisanal existence disappeared with the demise of the piecework system. Still, shoeworkers recalled a time when they controlled the pace of their work. They remembered a tradition of voluntary organization and corporate acts of resistance culminating in the Great Strike. Their ability to form the first real organizations of factory workers, the Knights of St. Crispin and the Daughters of St. Crispin, rested on this historical experience, a legacy which had created "not only the *experience* of organizing but also the stubborn conviction that a worker had as much *right* to organize as anybody else."[16]

The Knights of St. Crispin achieved its greatest successes in the early 1870s. It left a tradition of organizing experiences, of rituals, and of a vision which transformed the artisanal worldview into a growing and radical critique of the inequities of the emerging industrial order. In the 1870s and 1880s, shoemakers and workers in related industries in Lynn had built dozens of organizations. By the mid-1880s, the Knights of Labor enrolled thirty-four different labor unions and associations, and the labor movement encompassed over two-thirds of the city's workforce of 15,000. In these organizations, workers constructed a new kind of communal environment which could replace the dense relations of an artisanal village while still drawing on its memories.

The "habit of association" flourished in Lynn because it remained possible, in the face even of revolutionary transformations in economic and social life, to sustain communities of working people. Union halls became centers of after-work leisure activities, and the relationships created there also carried over into the bars and cafés which dotted the downtown area near the factories. These were the spaces which workers "owned," where they could tell and retell the stories from their proud past and assert their present rights, where newcomers could be socialized, or ostracized if they ignored or insulted group norms, where local shopkeepers and small businessmen understood their essential interdependence with factory workers and where Yankees and Irish immigrants alike could reaffirm their common interests. Fairs, picnics, festivals—all sustained a rich, spirited cultural life which was matched by impressive political power of workingmen's parties. John Cumbler, writing of the leatherworkers' strike in 1890–91, argued that "Lynn's wage earners viewed their city as a community of workers [and] the community gave the workers strength and support to resist the employers; their friends and relatives were workers and union members, and their unions controlled most of the shops in Lynn."[17]

The Knights of Labor

In the 1880s, the Knights of Labor crystallized the insurgent currents. Almost overnight it grew into a major power in communities across the nation. The genius of the Knights was its ability to organize people not only through their workplace associations but also through family, fraternal and sororal, kinship and religious associations as well. Its meteoric rise and fall left only an attenuated memory in the twentieth-century historical imagination: faint images of "romantic," backward-looking and "quaint" people who lacked a "modern" outlook and "mature class consciousness." The reevaluation of the Knights now under way has become possible precisely because historians have begun to look at the broader dynamics and currents in working-class life, the very complexities which the Knights so dramatically expressed. In addition, more recent disillusion with the "mature labor movement" has meant that historians no longer "confuse survival with success."[18]

One of the most dramatic examples of the transforming democratic experience which the Knights made possible took place in Richmond, Virginia, former capital of the Confederacy. There, for a moment, the Knights built popular movements in both the black and white communities and produced a series of victories in workplaces and in city politics. The story of the Knights' rise and fall in Richmond, chronicled by historian Peter Rachleff, reveals much about the possibilities and the vulnerabilities of democratic communities when the memories they have to draw upon harbor both democratic and authoritarian themes.[19]

Richmond had been an industrial center from well before the Civil War, its labor force divided from the beginning between white and black. As a center for the production of iron, tobacco products, barrels, and other packaging materials, Richmond was inhabited by an industrial labor force that included significant numbers of skilled and unskilled workers alike. Beginning with the Civil War, women also occupied an increasingly significant place in industry.

White men in skilled trades such as printing and iron-molding inherited a prewar legacy of self-organization and artisanal pride, but for the most part the organization of political, social, and religious life in the white community consistently undermined lower-class insurgency and solidarity. Poorer whites attended the same churches as the white elite and their political allegiance was continually sought and manipulated in the interests of racial solidarity and planter domination. There was precious little "space" for white workers to develop their own cultural and political life apart. Latent awareness of their own divergent interests, however, appeared in occasional acts of defiance among skilled workers and, during the war, in the

mobilization of women from poor and working-class neighborhoods in a massive bread riot. The women, angered by widespread speculation and crippling inflation, directed their anger
not only against the city government but also against the leadership of the Confederacy itself.[20]

White workers in Richmond, however, articulated a version
of republicanism which had been recast in racial terms. Their
social institutions, like the churches and fraternal associations,
were organized along racial rather than class lines. Though
there were German and Irish neighborhoods, the definition of
community was clearly most importantly "white." The "free"
and "independent" worker thus understood his freedom less in
contrast to some parasitic leisured class than as the antithesis of
slavery. In the postwar period, such perceptions were heightened by the conscious manipulations of the elite which encouraged racial solidarity and set out to abolish the few arenas for
interracial activity, like brothels, dancing houses, gambling
dens, and prize fights. Political campaign rhetoric fostered a
vision of a (mythical) "monoracial, monocultural community in
Virginia, set upon by outsiders like local blacks and federal
government officials."[21]

When the political and manufacturing elite organized a parade in February 1873 to celebrate the completion of a railroad
line to Richmond, however, some workers suggested that they
march under the banners of their trades and unions. Throughout the 1870s, issues arose which undermined the unity of the
white community: the use of convict (mainly black) labor in
industry, the absence of relief during depressions, and the general failure of the white elite to perceive ongoing problems in
the poorer communities. Nevertheless, in 1873, participants in
the parade marched by shop rather than by trade, a symbol of
the leadership of employers and foremen over their employees.[22]

Subsequent attempts at self-organization during the Green-
back and Readjuster campaigns of the 1870s met similar fates,
though each reform attempt schooled another group of poten-

tial leaders. And whereas employers easily controlled the celebrations in 1873, by the late 1870s, growing numbers of working-class whites no longer perceived their interests as identical with those of the white elite. Their activities provoked an organized counterattack by politicians. The assault on the Readjuster movement through which poor whites and blacks sought to ease the burden of Civil War debt raised the specter of "Negro domination" and "social equality." As a leading Democrat spelled it out graphically: "Social equality would lead to intermarriage, and that would lead to the destruction of the white race."[23]

The fears of the white elite and the vulnerability of white workers to racial manipulation are more comprehensible when one also contrasts the dense, potentially powerful self-organization of the black community. The legacy of the slave community, constructed along kinship lines and institutionalized in black churches, had been politicized after the Civil War and found expression mainly through the Republican Party. More important, however, blacks in Richmond not only incorporated large numbers of ex-slaves who flocked to the city, but also achieved an extraordinary level of community solidarity which remained independent of white control. Secret societies were at the heart of such organization.

Secret societies extended the ties of kinship and religion to embrace the black community as a whole, enhancing racial pride and political awareness. By the 1870s, there existed more than 400 such societies in Richmond, with broadly overlapping membership. Secret societies served as trade associations or unions. They provided insurance benefits for those without extended families to draw upon. They served as benevolent associations which cared for orphans, widows and widowers, and the elderly. They worked for political purposes and unity of the black community. Crisscrossing lines of family, religion, and employment, secret societies became the social spaces in which black people could see themselves as a community, where they could develop a common vision and learn the skills of public leadership. The ritual of one political society demonstrated the condensation of religious, political, and labor symbolism: "The altar is draped with the flag, on which lies an open Bible, the Declaration of Independence, a sword, ballot-box, sickle, and anvil or other . . . emblems of industry."[24]

According to Rachleff, "voluntary secret societies, rooted in the working class, had become the central fabric of the black community by the 1870s." Parades and public rituals in the black community were organized by secret societies of all sorts. On April 20, 1870, the leaders of the Colored National Labor Union sponsored a parade to mark the passage of the Fifteenth Amendment. A procession more than a mile long included fifty secret societies and several bands with colorful banners and uniforms. The panoply of the march expressed virtually every concern and dimension of the black community. More than 6,000 spectators gathered to watch them and to enjoy the concluding rally, which opened with a hymn that declared "the year of Jubilee is come/Return, ye ransomed sinners, home." The biblical year of Jubilee, of course, was supposed to occur every fifty years, when all privately held land would be returned to common ownership and redistributed.[25]

Through the free social spaces of the secret societies, Richmond blacks achieved an intense level of self-organization and racial solidarity, but until the 1880s they were repeatedly blocked from finding a public means of expressing their collective power. The Republican Party was controlled by racist and paternalistic whites, and blacks remained divided among themselves about whether to seek an alternative or to battle for greater control.

The meteoric rise of the Knights of Labor in the mid-1880s in Richmond and throughout the nation represented the most significant alternative to the ongoing ravages of industrial capitalism in the nineteenth century. The Knights offered a social and political vision which reinterpreted both republican and religious traditions to create a powerful alternative vision. Vivid memories of an artisanal past and the self-sufficiency of the small farm became critical tools in describing the flaws in the lives of industrial workers, their loss of control over the processes and products of their work. Old images of the commonwealth fused with newer notions of cooperation required by the larger operations of industry into a vision of a "cooperative commonwealth" that was anticapitalist without being anti-industrial.[26]

The Knights' organic view of social relations challenged the atomization of factory and city life, the physical separation of work and community. It also resulted in an organizing method which built on existing strengths and solidarities in working-class communities. Assemblies of the Knights of Labor were open to anyone—male or female, white or black, skilled or unskilled, factory operatives or small shop owners. Thus, they drew in members through multiple networks—familial, religious, fraternal—rather than relying principally on work relations. Because the Knights did not believe that there was or should be a separation between "work" and "community" or "life," their concerns could flow into any available channel— trade unions, politics, community life. And finally, they appeared at a moment when large numbers of workers—from shoemakers in Lynn to tobacco workers and coopers in Richmond—found that the skills and work cultures which they had developed within the factory were again threatened by new machines which heralded further reorganization and degradation of their work.

In Richmond as in Lynn, almost overnight the Knights of Labor had organized virtually the entire working-class community and had transformed the balance of political power in the city. The looseness and decentralized nature of their organization permitted the emergence of two social movements, one white and one black, whose tenuous alliance represented a potentially earthshaking redefinition of Richmond society. The rituals and rhetoric of the Knights of Labor incorporated common practices in both black and white experience which could easily be interpreted in terms of the specific realities of each community.

Richmond blacks, accustomed to secret-society rituals, found in the Knights a vehicle with which to politicize and imbue with new purpose the dense networks they had already created. Through the Knights, they gave public expression to race pride while at the same time building alliances with white workers.

White workers, on the other hand, whose cultural and social spaces were far weaker, created in the Knights of Labor a movement culture which drew on their religious traditions and the weak legacy of republicanism to forge a new vision. For the first time, it became possible for working-class whites on a large scale to break away from their racial identification with upper-class whites. Within the Knights they developed a complex cultural life reinforced by ritual and symbolism that embraced every aspect of their lives.

Each assembly elected sixteen officers with specific duties such as master workman, worthy foreman, worthy inspector, financial and recording secretaries, worthy treasurer, unknown Knight, and venerable sage. Yet members and officers sat in the assembly room or "sanctuary" on the same level. According to Grand Master Workman Terence Powderly, "This is to indicate that there are no degrees or rank, no upper or lower class—all men are admitted on an equal footing. The laborer, the artisan, the Craftsman, and the professional man each has an equal share in the inheritance left to the Order." Rituals emphasized the nobility and holiness of labor: "To glorify God in its exercise, to defend it from degradation, to divest it of the evils to body, mind, and estate . . . ; to rescue the toiler from the grasp of the selfish is a work worthy of the noblest and best of our race." An initiate, hearing these words, would then be asked if he or she was "willing to accept the responsibility, and, trusting in the support of pledged true Knights, labor, with what ability you possess, for the triumph of these principles among men?"[27]

Meeting in a "sanctuary" before an "altar" surrounded by symbols of unity and collective strength, giving the password, and signing one's name as a sign of the "duty" to acquire "knowledge sufficient to prevent the evil-disposed from imposing on [one]," both individually and collectively, Knights were imbued with a sense of mission and a new vision of what could be. Such perceptions took on a new reality as people learned the concrete tasks of governing their own organizations and implementing projects. The Knights initiated cooperative factories and a building fund to pool resources so that workers with little capital could gradually achieve home ownership; even partial success in such endeavors carried critical lessons. In addition, the Knights put on plays, and organized outings and other cultural events which brought people together, making them visible to one another, creating and sustaining community.[28]

The Richmond Knights' most successful tactic was a boycott which catapulted them to the forefront of public life in both white and black communities and began a process through which black and white workers could redefine their interests as common. Whites had long resented the use of convict laborers, most of whom were black. When a local flour mill contracted to buy prison-made barrels, coopers in the barrel industry, one of the few biracial skilled jobs, recognized the threat to their livelihoods and initiated a boycott. The Knights endorsed the boycott, finding in it an appropriate symbol of the deteriorating position of all workers, "an injustice done honest labor," a practical and effective gesture imbued with moral significance. It was also a means of mobilizing entire communities by politicizing household consumption and it provided a practical link between black and white workers. Justifications of the boycott called together the political and religious imagery which the Knights used so skillfully. William Mullen wrote in the *Labor Herald* about the "divine right to boycott [which was] accorded us by the Holy Bible" and cited the seven plagues visited by God on the Pharaoh as his example: "We believe the same just God that aided Moses in bringing the children of Israel out of the bonds of slavery will aid us in our struggles for justice."

Having established the biblical sanction for the boycott he turned to the patriotism of the Revolutionary generation who not only boycotted tea but threw it into Boston Harbor. "Why, the right to boycott is handed down to us by our forefathers," and those who applaud the Revolutionary boycott while condemning actions of the Knights "are the Tories of the present day." By the end of his article, Mullen had concluded that the boycott was not simply a "right" but a "duty." "It is patriotism in us. . . . We are performing a Christian duty and we have the law of both God and man on our side."[29]

The boycott mobilized Richmond's working people as nothing else ever had, and it gave them a taste of victory. Through their newspaper, the *Labor Herald,* they also learned of similar actions and victories by working people throughout the country. At the same time, the concerted action of black and white Knights did not result in structured channels of communication. When the movement shifted quite naturally into the political arena, they found themselves on a terrain where their weaknesses could most easily be exploited.

A reform ticket backed by the Knights Assemblies swept to victory in the city council elections of May 1886. Within months, it had succumbed to racial polarization as the sophisticated white elite moved to split blacks and whites and to create divisions among working-class whites. The old threats of "Negro domination" and "social equality" were still compelling to whites who had only begun the process of forging an identity that was not racially based. According to Peter Rachleff, "the critical internal problem became the ability of white working-class activists to creatively alter the traditional popular republicanism [which had posited the freedom and independence of white labor as the antithesis of blacks who bore the taint of slavery], so as to admit black workingmen and women as equals." The black movement, riding a crest of racial pride and labor militance, demanded an alliance of mutual respect and made it clear that they would not participate from a position of subordination or deference. But on every front, from labor struggles to political patronage, manufacturers and white politicians pushed for racial polarization. "Dusting off deep seated, traditional beliefs, they compelled workingmen and women to choose between their traditional loyalties and new, unpredictable arrangements, short-circuiting the developing flow from the one to the other within the popular movements. By thus freezing and widening the chasm between the 'old' and the 'new,' they placed the leap beyond the ability of most working people of both races."[30]

The Knights of Labor represented a moment of unrealized possibility in the history of the American people. It wove a democratic vision out of strands from the past in a way that spoke to and mobilized hundreds of thousands of working people. In 1886, the Knights at their peak numbered 700,000 members. Their political force was felt in city after city, and they built natural alliances with a growing Populist insurgency in the countryside as well.

On the strength of its rhetoric, ritual, and symbols, the Knights grew too fast; its leadership lacked organizational sophistication and its base needed time to learn new ways. The traditions that the Knights drew upon were indeed complex, harboring authoritarian, parochial, and nondemocratic elements as well as democratic ones. To transcend these, working people had to build a broader communal context where tradition could take on new meanings and where the anxiety of change could be salved with supportive human bonds. Yet its very size represented a threat to structures of power and authority, and as a result, it provoked a response which short-circuited a process that had only started. Whether in the form of political manipulation, of race-baiting, or of violent use of force, the powers-that-be mobilized every mechanism at their disposal. Nevertheless, every subsequent labor victory has drawn, often unwittingly, on the legacy of the Knights.

The demise of the Knights of Labor came at a time of breathtaking change in America. A massive wave of immigration from southern and eastern Europe fueled the explosive growth of cities and of huge, nationally organized corporations. Cities splintered into ethnic enclaves where working people struggled to sustain body and soul by working together in benevolent societies, churches, and synagogues.

Ira Katznelson argues that the split between work and community had the consequence of narrowing union activity to job issues and associating community with political and ethnic rather than class consciousness. His argument helps explain the broad weakness of the American working class, but it ignores the continuing evidence that labor struggles commonly drew on supportive communal ties and in particular on the broad political vision expressed by the Knights of Labor. His work does explain, however, how ethnicity in the North and race in the South were key obstacles to the Knights' success.[31]

A careful examination of labor militance clarifies the inextricable bonds between communal and class consciousness. Communal relations were the key to most large working-class uprisings; they made survival in an alien world possible—both physically by providing social services and insurance, and emotionally by sustaining a sense of identity and communal pride. Such relations, as we have argued throughout, carry both democratic and authoritarian potentials. They are the root of nativism as well as the source of democratic possibility and vision.

The defeat of the Knights of Labor and then of the Populist movement short-circuited a process of democratic change and weakened the sources of communal memory from which working people could draw strength and inspiration. The artisanal tradition continued, shaping the American Federation of Labor's broad claim for the dignity of work and skilled workers' rights to control the work process. But the AFL also turned to an increasingly narrow, job-focused and craft-conscious unionism severed from the inclusive communal ties which could link them to growing numbers of unskilled, immigrant workers who flooded into the growing mass industries.

Such industries have shaped the labor struggles in the twentieth century. Techniques of scientific management and the assembly line splintered the work process into small components while growing numbers of clerical and service workers maintained complex corporate bureaucracies. The loss of craft and pride in work further exacerbated the separation of work from community life. Work, then, became increasingly instrumental, something one did in order to enjoy a consumption-oriented life-style.[32]

AFL unions survived the 1890s and the early years of the twentieth century only in places like Lynn, Massachusetts, where they had deep roots in the community. Yet even there the ability of companies to mobilize state and federal police forces made it increasingly clear that workers needed resources beyond the local community. Between 1890 and 1897, ninety-two people died in strikes.[33]

Even in industries such as steel, where skilled workers had long controlled the work process—pacing their own work, training newcomers, even hiring—craft unions suffered crippling defeats. Already surrounded by unskilled and semiskilled immigrant workers, skilled ironworkers struck in 1901 to preserve their crafts and wages. National steel companies brought their combined resources to bear not only to defeat the strike but to break the union's authority by reorganizing the work. They replaced skilled workers with machines and less skilled workers, and imposed a strict, almost military hierarchy in the plant. From that time until the 1930s, steelworkers were virtually undefended against the predations of an industry known for extraordinary rates of injury and death. (Investigator Crystal Eastman, in 1910, discovered that nearly a quarter of new workers in steel were killed or injured each year.) Immigrant workers found their only sources of support in ethnic and religious benevolent societies. When they did fight back, it was inevitably on the basis of a mobilized community laced with family networks.[34]

Similarly, union organizers, to be effective, had always to draw on the heritages which shaped workers' identities: class consciousness apart from such roots was unthinkable. In New York City, an early generation of Jewish organizers, committed to a purely secular radicalism, failed to create a significant working-class movement. Only when a new group arrived, able to blend socialism with unionism and Yiddish culture, did Jewish workers become a leading force in the creation of industrial unionism. They led the massive strikes in the garment district of New York: the "uprising of the 20,000" in 1909 and "the uprising of the 50,000" in 1910.[35]

Clara Lemlish was only fifteen years old when her family immigrated from Russia to America in 1903. The daughter of an orthodox Jewish scholar, she had secretly learned to read Russian and yearned for more education. But family circumstances forced her to work in the garment trades, sewing intricate shirtwaist blouses in crowded shops on the Lower East Side of New York. By 1909, she had worked in many shops and helped found Local 25 of the International Ladies' Garment Workers Union. She had also taken classes in Marxist theory at the Socialist Party's school. Local 25, almost exclusively Russian Jewish and dominated by skilled male workers, nevertheless began with the leadership of young women like Lemlish to build a constituency among the young women who constituted the vast majority of garment workers.

By the fall of 1909, Lemlish was an experienced organizer. Her shop, Leiserson's, had been the third in a wave of small strikes that fall which met with violent responses. The owner hired prostitutes and pimps to beat up pickets who were then arrested and fined for assault. Clara Lemlish had already experienced seventeen arrests when Local 25 called a mass meeting on November 22. Thousands of teen-age girls filled the hall, spilling out the doors, listening patiently to two hours of speeches. Finally, Clara Lemlish stood up and asked for the privilege of speaking. Officials on the platform were uncomfortable, but the chair granted her request. In eloquent Yiddish she argued for common action and moved for a general strike. The crowd responded unanimously. "The chairman then cried, 'Do you mean faith? Will you take the old Jewish oath?' and up came two thousand right hands, with the prayer, 'If I turn traitor to the cause I now pledge, may this hand wither from the arm I now raise.' "[36]

The unions which grew from these uprisings—the International Ladies' Garment Workers Union and the Amalgamated Clothing Workers (ILGWU and ACW)—laid groundwork for a new sort of industrial unionism. These unions grew out of the self-organization of women workers, but older craft traditions and status hierarchies influenced the emergence of an almost exclusively male leadership. Sidney Hillman, president of the Amalgamated Clothing Workers, for example, was formerly a cutter, a skilled and male-dominated craft in the clothing industry. The emergence of the Congress of Industrial Organizations in the 1930s marked the maturation of this new form and the organization of basic industries. The story of the CIO, however, has traditionally been told in terms of specific leaders like Sidney Hillman, David Dubinsky of the International Ladies' Garment Workers Union, and, of course, John L. Lewis, legendary leader of the mineworkers. Indeed, there are few studies available which explore the grass-roots activity undergirding labor militance of the Depression years with any richness of detail. Histories tend to be institutional—and take for granted the split between home and work. Yet a few recent efforts have begun to examine working people's organizing through these years and have, in the process, indicated the continuing importance of communal spaces and identities.

The wave of industrial militancy which led to the formation of the CIO in the mid-1930s represented an outburst of protest against conditions which had become intolerable. Yet though protest often *began* as defensive resistance, again and again thousands of workers developed definitions of their goals and a vision which transcended the immediate struggle to maintain an eroding standard of living. They pioneered innovative tactics, such as the sit-down, an action which effectively prevented companies from drawing on the large pool of unemployed people to destroy strikes. And, in ways that have yet to be explored fully, they were able to utilize new technologies of communication and elements of the mass culture—movies, radio, and the like—that had also weakened communal identities.*

Indeed, the ferment which spread like a wildfire through industrial communities of the Depression years reconnected with and reinvigorated much older traditions which had virtually disappeared from view. Thus, the demand for civil rights at the workplace drew on the language of the American Revolution and branded its opponents "Tories." Mary Heaton Vorse wrote that "There has been a social awakening throughout the country, the coming of democracy in towns and industrial valleys where the Bill of Rights, such things as free speech, free assembly and even the right to vote as one pleased, had been unknown."[37]

How did such communities develop the capacity to act collec-

---

*In a fascinating, important essay on recent labor history, Leon Fink has pointed out how much more we know about the wellsprings of the labor protests of the nineteenth century, growing out of autonomous workers' communities and drawing upon still-vibrant republican traditions, than we know about twentieth-century movements like the formation of the CIO. "Why, in principle," he asks, "is it easier for us to assess the world of the New York journeyman mechanic in 1830 than that of the Schenectady electrical worker or the Detroit wild-cat striker of the 1940s? Can it be in part that the cultural apparatus at our disposal—with its tight-knit communities, ethnic neighborhoods, moral codes and skilled-worker republicanism—no longer fits but, except for notions of mass embourgeoisement and depoliticization, we have little to put in their place?" (p. 18). Fink's criticisms lead him to useful speculation about subversive messages in the mass culture, the democratizing effects of the erosion of patriarchal community, and the contagion effects of new media like the radio, spreading what Berndt Ostendorf calls "an interethnic consensus" that helps overcome older lines of division. He points out, insightfully, moreover, that too much recent social history has seen workers' cultural traditions in a defensive and static fashion: "By focusing on workers' culture almost exclusively through traditions, origins and inheritances," he observes, "workers themselves have become 'traditionalists,' threatened by what is new and changing around them" (p. 16). Such a static view slights the dynamic ways workers have adapted older traditions. Yet Fink's comments also neglect the evidence that twentieth-century workers' protests also reclaim and revitalize—as well as rework—traditions and create new communal ties. Free spaces are central to such cultural change and connections. "Looking Backward: Reflections on Workers' Culture and the Conceptual Dilemmas of the New Labor History," Future of American Labor History Conference, Dekalb, Illinois, October 10–12, 1984.

tively? Where did their leaders come from? What nurtured the
wildly democratic élan of a union like the United Auto Workers
in its early years? And finally, how was this broad process of
self-organization finally narrowed and institutionalized into the
legalistic, circumscribed relationships which characterize union–management collective bargaining after the Second World
War?

The evidence suggests that the new labor movement of the
1930s drew much of its power from a substructure of ideas and
social relationships embedded in ethnic communities and in
specific kinds of work environments. It depended for its shape,
strategy, and tactics upon groups of left-wing organizers committed to broad conceptions of class action. And it found a
broader responsiveness because radical organizers revived,
adapted, and redefined an older republican idiom.

At both national and local levels, key organizers of the Congress of Industrial Organizations had been schooled in radical
cultural traditions widespread among immigrants from Russia
and Eastern Europe. Most prominent among these immigrants
were Jews. A related and often overlapping group of leaders
consisted of skilled workers like those who led the formation of
the United Electrical Workers, "loosely supervised workers
who possessed considerable freedom to move about and determine the means by which they would execute their tasks."
Especially in the aftermath of the Communist Party's "Popular
Front" strategy after 1935, these groups of radical organizers
wedded their skills and notions of concerted mass action to a
vocabulary that stressed core American themes and concepts.
Progressive political action clubs with names like Thomas Paine
and Abraham Lincoln sprouted across the country; Thomas
Jefferson was described as the ancestor of those "Americans
who are fighting against the tyranny of Big Business with the
revolutionary spirit and boldness with which he fought the Tories of that day"; songs like Paul Robeson's "Ballad for Americans," and "This Land Is Your Land," praising the American
democratic tradition—and broadening it to include all immi-

grants to the land—became part and parcel of the union movement culture. "We used to celebrate every holiday, and use all
our events as ways of educating people about their heritage as
Americans," recalled Terry Pettus, a leader in a successful la-
bor-based political movement called the Washington Commonwealth Federation of the 1930s and '40s. "Later, I used to argue
with the activists of the Sixties. Why give away symbols like the
flag? The Fourth of July was originally the holiday of working
people, celebrating the Revolution!"[38]

Rank-and-file members were mobilized through two sorts of
communal channels: informal work groups and the ethnic community. Informal work groups had been products of the process
of industrial mechanization itself, which had generated settings
on shop floors where the organization of work created space for
considerable socializing. Though the assembly line in the Ford
plants, for instance, fragmented work tasks in a regimented and
extreme fashion and provided scant opportunity for human
contact, most workers in the plants were actually occupied in
small groups which prepared component parts to feed the gi-
gantic line. In such groups they came to know one another, to
develop group norms about the appropriate pace of work, and
to impose a notable measure of collective control over the process in ways which were invisible to management. Group consciousness drew further reinforcement from the bonds of ethnicity and gender that often characterized work environments.

Stella Nowicki got a job at Swift and Company, where she
worked with other women, most of them Polish like herself, in
the sliced bacon department. She was an organizer for both the
CIO and the Communist Party. But she soon learned that the
women in her department had organized themselves already to
exercise control over major features of the work. Thus, the
women maximized their pay by turning out exactly 144 packages of bacon each hour. Experienced women trained the newcomers: "they would help her out so that gradually . . . she was
doing the 144. But they would never let anyone go beyond that
144 packages." When a "smart-aleck girl" tried to exceed the

limit, others on the line ensured that the bacon she received would be "messed up and scrappy," so that she failed even to reach the basic quota. In fact, the whole group "took a loss just to show her."

Nowicki learned from her co-workers the simplest and easiest way to wrap bacon, as well as techniques to introduce "a lot of extra motions" when the time-study checker arrived with a stopwatch. As the older women brought her into the group process, they also taught her powerful lessons about group solidarity—even though they were fearful of unions. Her role as an organizer consisted principally of offering an alternative channel for group activity when the death of a co-worker finally convinced them that they needed the strength of a broader and more formalized group.[39]

Saul Alinsky learned the basic skills of community organizing from the radical CIO organizers in the Chicago packinghouses. While working on a local program to fight juvenile delinquency in Chicago's "Back of the Yards" neighborhood, Alinksy began to attend CIO mass meetings, intrigued by the intensity and skill of the professional organizers there. He admired the breadth of their concerns, which linked specific workplace grievances with social issues that ranged from the problems of southern tenant farmers to the Spanish Civil War—and showed the connections, as well, to local rent strikes and problems in the community. And he learned a language of change, illustrated vividly in later works, like *Reveille for Radicals*, that drew directly upon Popular Front themes of the rights of American citizenship and democracy.[40]

The organizers' efforts to unionize the packinghouses were foundering, however, because of strong opposition from the Catholic Church. Polish and other eastern European immigrants in the Back of the Yards were reluctant to commit themselves to any group which priests regularly denounced from the pulpit as a "communist plot." Alinsky proceeded to form a neighborhood council, winning the support of every local group he could find, "church societies, union locals, ethnic clubs, bowling leagues, a businessmen's association, card clubs, even the American Legion." Accompanied by Bishop Bernard J. Sheil, Alinsky then visited and won support from the local priests for the group, which was intended to address a range of community problems.[41]

At the founding meeting in July 1939, a convention of 350 delegates voted resounding support for the Packinghouse Workers Union. "Two nights later, the Back of the Yards Neighborhood Council marched with a large delegation of Back of the Yards residents to the CIO rally at the Chicago Coliseum. On the stage, Bishop Sheil sat next to CIO president John L. Lewis." The companies vigorously sought to prevent the rally. Key leaders were threatened or shot at. Afterwards, however, as the strike was about to begin, the packinghouse industry in Chicago capitulated. A coalition of neighborhood organizations, churches, and workers had suggested the likelihood of a strike with such power and tenacity that it did not seem worth the battle.[42]

Similarly, organizers in the steel industry discovered considerable self-organization within the "company unions" where authority resided less with the company than with informal work groups. Union activists found that rather than oppose such structures, it was necessary to work within them. In addition, the CIO soon realized the necessity of building broad community support in company towns by working through ethnic associations, churches, and black organizations. John Bodnar's study of Steelton, Pennsylvania, spells out some of the complexities. Prior to 1930 in this company-dominated town, ethnic communities had developed in part as a defensive response to occupational immobility and exclusion from community power. Divisions among ethnic and racial groups, whose mutual suspicions were reinforced by occupational and residential segregation, undermined labor solidarity. At the same time, groups of Slavs, Germans, Irish, Italians, and blacks built on their inherited ties of kinship, religion, and ethnicity that were substantially different from those of the old countries. Broad ethnic identities replaced village identification, for example, while the ethnic group itself became increasingly institutionalized to meet the needs of the strange and unpredictable environment of urban America. One member of the Croatian St. Lawrence Society described the lodge as "a place to express themselves where they 'felt safe from the American class of people.' "[43]

With the second generation came a change in consciousness. Where parents had been transient, children expected to stay in Steelton, and their experiences within the ethnic communities paid off in new ways. "Ironically," Bodnar concludes, "while ethnicity was somewhat of a divisive force before 1930, it was actually laying the basis for the type of cooperation that would be necessary for the eventual triumph of the CIO. The reliance on the ethnic community taught newcomers the value of confronting social problems and economic difficulties with large, formalized institutions and organizations rather than with isolated kin groups."[44]

Thus, while the radical leaders of the Steel Workers Organizing Committee (SWOC) clearly played crucial roles in the formation of the Steel Workers of America, they succeeded mainly by giving new vision and purpose to the organizations and networks workers had already created themselves.

Transit workers in New York City joined the Transport Workers Union of America between 1933 and 1937 also through the dual channels of informal work group and community mobilization. Communist organizers had discovered responsiveness among the repair shops and other workplaces where, despite social diversity, workers exercised considerable autonomy while working in close proximity to one another. Moreover, both organizers and workers commonly drew on similar radical, eastern European immigrant traditions. But the key to the success of the union turned out to lie with the Irish, who dominated the more public and isolated jobs in the transit industry, like ticket-taking. Spatially segmented, ethnically different from other transit workers, recent immigrants from a deferential peasant society, the Irish became mobilized by a process which drew on the networks and loyalties of Irish republicanism and nationalism.

The Irish community in New York, laced together through institutions of church, Democratic Party, fraternal organization, and an Irish-American press, sustained powerful bonds among transit workers. According to Joshua Freeman, however, "the main pillars of the community . . . displayed little immediate interest in the plight of the transit workers as workers." A small cadre of young men initiated on their own the move toward unionization by drawing on their own experience in the fights for national independence of Ireland. Through their activities in the IRA, they had broken ancient patterns of deference and developed a vision of freedom as well as an ingrained hostility to privilege.[45]

By reinterpreting their work experience in republican terms, this young group reached Irish transit workers as no one else had been able to. Workers felt comfortable and familiar with the semiconspiratorial methods of organizing necessary in the early stages when such methods were compared to experiences in the old country. On the other hand, such methods—building on paramilitary organizations of the IRA and the male networks of pub and bar in the Irish community—may well explain why the only unit which voted *against* the Transit Workers was a section of female ticket agents. Had the organizers been able to work also through the churches and other social networks where women predominated and where military metaphors could be replaced with language based on family ties, those young women could well have been more involved.

In the case of both the shops and the ticket booths, thus, TWU organizers located and built upon autonomous spaces at work and in the community where people could draw upon communal memories in reinterpreting their situation and moving to collective action. Yet the fact that no broader "movement culture" emerged also limited their victory. Freeman argues that "though the TWU had enlisted Irish workers in part by mobilizing ties created in a shared national experience, the whole thrust of the union's development was away from the very parochialism that had been one source of its initial strength." What Freeman labels "parochialism," however, contained within it the seeds of a broader democratic possibility.[46]

The potential power of movement culture, the new values and sense of possibility which emerge in the process of movement-building itself, is more visible in the early days of the United Auto Workers. Entire communities mobilized to support sit-down strikes against the industry giants. Through these experiences, we can see that strikes, while usually rooted in communal social spaces, are also themselves contexts which create new forms of democratic sociability.

Strike activity takes on a life of its own. Workers first move into action, often, because they are able to draw upon previously established relationships and communal memories. Once the strike begins, other sorts of educational experiences occur. Daily rounds of picketing, maintaining soup kitchens, raising money, holding meetings, and the like organize every feature of life. Latent communities take on a new vitality and power.

Yet the stories of the greatest sit-down strikes at General Motors in 1937 have usually been rendered in terms that omit the essential nature of the community's involvement. The men who sat down for forty-four days in Flint, Michigan, emerged from that experience with deeply emotional bonds. They were following a practice which had developed spontaneously in the rubber industry and in sporadic work stoppages in auto as well. They maintained a tight discipline throughout: "If anybody got careless with company property—such as sitting on an automobile cushion without putting burlap over it—he was talked to." As the realization grew that their action might succeed, they sang, exercised, and called boisterously out the windows to passers-by. Louis Adamic described the sit-down as "a social affair." Thousands, suddenly idle in the stilled factory, turned to one another in a new way. " 'Why, my God, man,' one Goodyear gum-miner told me in November, 1936, 'during the sitdowns last spring I found out that the guy who works next to me is the same as I am, even if I was born in West Virginia and he is from Poland. His grievances are the same. Why shouldn't we stick?' " Victory in Flint was met with delirious joy. One participant, decades later, told Studs Terkel what it meant: "When Mr. Knudsen put his name to a piece of paper and says that General Motors recognizes the UAW-CIO—until that moment, we were nonpeople, we didn't even exist (laughs). That was the big one. (His eyes are moist.)"[47]

On the fortieth anniversary of the strike, the veterans of the Flint sit-down gathered to commemorate the event. Thousands of strike veterans were startled when a woman wearing a red beret stood up from the audience and demanded to speak. She pointed out that the program had no women on it and as she spoke women all over the room joined in a chorus of insistence that the chair yield the podium. Then she walked to the front to remind her union brothers that they could never have won without the active participation of women in the community. While only male workers remained inside the plant, women organized on the outside to supply them with food and to confront the police. The red berets of the Women's Emergency Brigade appeared wherever violence threatened, and without their alertness this founding event of the United Auto Workers would probably have ended in defeat. A camera crew only the day before had interviewed women in the Emergency Brigade for a film, *With Babies and Banners.* There in the union hall, they also restored communal memory.[48]

By the mid-1950s, what had been a vibrant, grass-roots union movement two decades before had become largely acquiescent. In the interests of stability and particularly under the pressure of wartime production, major unions shifted to a more businesslike operation. In part such quiescence can be traced to the institutionalization of unionism under the legal protection and regulation of the state. The very legislation which promoted unionism in the 1930s, the Wagner Act and the National Labor Relations Board which it created, also conceded elements of control over the bargaining process to the state. Labor legislation essentially defines the parameters for the operation of unions, from the definitions of bargaining units and negotiable issues to the legality of strikes and other militant activities. One consequence is that the process of bargaining has become routinized and the focus of bargaining narrowed while the broader considerations of the organization of work and control over the work process remain management prerogatives. Strikes became essentially a negotiating tool to be used shrewdly by union leaders rather than a spontaneous and powerful expression of collective grievances. With the NLRB, one of the great legal achievements of the American labor movement, one also sees the end of much of the artisanal tradition, with its proud defense of workers' prerogatives, their right to define and control their work. The trade-off was for higher wages, increased job security, and a more predictable labor system for both workers and employers.[49]

Such procedures also represented critical legal lines of defense against a corporate system that previously had often ruthlessly sought to suppress any worker self-organization. And the labor movement's quiescence had at least as much to do with the broader political situation. The McCarthyism of the late 1940s and '50s had as special priority the purge of all radicals and militants from the labor unions, and created an environment in which dissenting ideas of any sort were extraordinarily difficult to express.

In such a setting, organizers like the ones Alinsky admired became technicians. "Their experience was tied to a pattern of fixed points, whether it was definite demands on wages, pensions, vacation periods, or other working conditions, and all this was anchored into particular contract dates." They were no longer good at what Alinsky called "mass organizing" because "Mass organization is a different animal, it is not housebroken." In recent years, however, numerous alternatives to this sort of pattern have begun to emerge.[50]

Farmworkers, for example, despite efforts in the 1930s, had never successfully organized until well after the Second World

War. Excluded from the protections (as well as the restrictions) of the National Labor Relations Board and comprising extremely poor Mexican-Americans throughout the southwestern states, farmworkers were clearly at the bottom of the American labor force. Beginning in the 1960s, however, under the leadership of Cesar Chávez, farmworkers created a union and a social movement which sparked a nationwide boycott of grapes and lettuce. Chávez had been trained by an Alinsky associate, Fred Ross, working first as an organizer and later as director of the Community Service Organization in California's Spanish-speaking community. When he began to build the National Farm Workers Association, he drew on this community-organizing experience. The NFWA rooted itself in the cultural and religious life of Mexican-Americans and used the CSO's well-developed house meeting approach. It also offered services badly needed by the community. Chávez argued, "The union must hold out concrete programs which guarantee a new life. Cooperatives, credit unions, educational programs of a practical nature, money saving devices . . . these are necessary elements of any union planning on capturing the imagination of the farm worker. It must be grass roots with a vengeance." Strongly allied with churches, civil rights organizations, and finally with the AFL-CIO, the United Farm Workers Union waged a highly visible and ultimately successful struggle for union recognition for more than a decade.[51]

In part, the decline in organized labor reflects fundamental shifts in the economic structure as services and information systems overtake heavy industry both as engines of change and as employers of the majority of the labor force. A concomitant of these economic shifts, however, has been the massive entry of women into the labor force. And the mobilization of these women, whose familial and communal identities remain powerful forces, has generated some of the most creative organizing since the Second World War.

The farmworkers provided a model to Day Piercy in 1972 when she set out to build an organization of clerical workers in downtown Chicago. Working closely with the emerging women's movement groups, with the newly founded Midwest Academy training center for community organizers, and with the Chicago YWCA, Piercy led in the creation of a new kind of working women's organization. From their first organizing meetings, the women recognized that clerical workers had historically been unreceptive to traditional union approaches. Consciously, they experimented with a combination of community organizing methods and feminist sensitivity to the gender-specific modes of subordination female office workers commonly experience.[52]

One of the first training sessions at the Midwest Academy was devoted to building the new organization, Women Employed. Ellen Cassidy came from Boston, where she, Karen Nussbaum, and a small core of clerical workers at Harvard had initiated a newsletter (and, they hoped, an organization) called 9-to-5. They, too, wanted to extend the women's movement into the feminized clerical labor force, and in Chicago, Cassidy found a method to move toward that goal.[53]

Women Employed pioneered in public celebrations of Secretary's Day under the slogan "raises not roses." In 1976, they achieved national prominence when they occupied a prominent law firm to protest the firing of a legal secretary who refused to make coffee. They also conducted corporate investigations, beginning with Kraft Corporation, to publicize women's low wages and the failure of companies to comply with affirmative action requirements of law, and to demand compliance.[54]

Nine-to-Five also grew, using many of the same techniques, into a national organization with chapters in most major cities. More recently, through an agreement with the Service Employees International Union, they have begun to transfer their techniques into the more traditional arena of union organizing. Yet even there, a sensitivity to the nature of female networks and office subculture shapes their approach. At a major insurance company in upstate New York, for example, secret organizing was conducted through the medium of Tupperware parties. Management remained unaware of the organizing drive until SEIU, District 925, filed for an election by submitting cards signed by 90 percent of their employees.[55]

While feminists sought new ways of organizing, women in the labor movement also broke through their traditional isolation in the 1970s to form the Coalition of Labor Union Women (CLUW). Its roots lay principally in the United Auto Workers women's department, the only such department in any major union. Through the 1950s and '60s, the UAW women's department had served as a tiny enclave where it was possible for working women to articulate their concerns. They found natural allies in commissions on the status of women and participated in the founding of the National Organization for Women (NOW) in 1966. The shock wave of the new feminism was felt not only in the UAW, but also in unions such as the United Electrical Workers (which had maintained a more radical tradition through the 1950s) and the American Federation of Teachers or the American Federation of State, County, and Municipal Employees, whose constituencies embraced the growing female sectors of the labor force. But traditional union divisions not only prevented concerted action, for the most part they kept female activists in different unions from knowing each other, even when they worked in the same city. The networks which led to the initiation of CLUW were forged as union women like Olga Madar of the UAW and Addie Wyatt of the Amalgamated Meatcutters Union met in activities to end the Vietnam war and to support the farmworkers' organizing efforts. Networks were also enhanced by roundtable discussions of women union leaders hosted by Elizabeth Koonz at the U.S. Women's Bureau in the early 1970s.[56]

When a founding meeting for CLUW was called in 1974, more than 3,000 women showed up—twice the expected attendance. Joan Goodin described the excitement as "electric." "I remember being hugged in a jammed elevator by a stranger who proclaimed: 'Sister, we're about to put trade union women on the map.' "[57]

The subsequent history of CLUW has not fully borne out the hopes of that first meeting. Membership grew slowly in the early years amid a prolonged battle over structure. The decision to work within the labor movement meant that CLUW could not on its own engage in organizing women workers, since to do so would encroach on the prerogatives of established unions. CLUW can and does encourage such organizing, and when invited to, participates actively. But as a result, and for consciously strategic reasons, CLUW is only partially a free social space as we have_defined it. Yet even on its own terms, the consequences can be powerful. Founders of CLUW were surprised at how exciting it was simply to establish a network among union women. Current president Joyce Miller argues that women gain several important things from participation in CLUW: They find there a training ground in leadership skills as well as a support group of women. For many, leadership in CLUW has translated into further leadership roles in local unions.[58]

Certainly the most innovative and successful examples of contemporary organizing show the same characteristics as their predecessors. None are marked by an abstracted "class consciousness," but all manage to merge into the activity of the union the communal traditions central to people's identities. This occurs in particular sorts of voluntary associations, free spaces that link communal life and workplace activity, where people can learn essential public skills and a powerful sense of their own rights and capacities. In the process of organizing, traditional identities and institutions furnish ideological resources even while themselves undergoing democratic transformation. Class as a lived and powerful reality, then, always has a populist cast. It is about peoplehood, multiple identities, and the places in the community that nurture democratic aspiration and capacity, as well as about relations to the means of production.

CHAPTER 5

THE PEOPLE ARE TOGETHER

> The jaws of sheep have made the land rich,
> but we were told by the prophecy
> that sheep would scatter the warriors
> and turn their homes into a wilderness.
> The land of our love lies under bracken and heather,
> every plain and every field is untilled,
> and soon there will be none in Mull of the Trees
> but Lowlanders and their white sheep.
>
> —Angus MacMhuirich, "The Jaws of Sheep,"
> quoted in John Prebble,
> *The Highland Clearances*

W HEN Angus MacMhuirich, bard on the Isle of Mull, composed his lament in the late 1840s, large-scale evictions had become commonplace on the islands off the Scottish coast, spreading from the Scottish Highlands where they had begun. Harriet Beecher Stowe, author of *Uncle Tom's Cabin,* the impassioned, if superficial, novel which had become a world-famous indictment of American slavery, traveled to the Highlands—reportedly planning to investigate.

The evictions were not new. More than one hundred years had passed since the Scottish nobility of the Highlands, defeated at the battle of Culloden in 1745, began to turn villagers and peasants out of their homes to make way for enterprises more profitable. Whatever the force of tradition, the nobles had legal sanction for their undertakings. By the eighteenth century, the land—once held by all the tribe in common throughout the

Scottish Highlands—had become the property of the clan chieftains. Legally, they could do with it as they wished.

After Culloden, the lords had quickly severed the complex, intricate networks of custom, tradition, and family relationship that had bound their class to "the commons," the ordinary families of the clans, for eons. Rather, they looked south—to their counterparts among the nobility of the Lowlands and England, for approval and recognition. There they sent their children for education. And from the southern upper classes, they learned a new acquisitiveness and cosmopolitanism. When, in the vocabulary of the new age which they embraced, they pondered new "productive uses" for the lands, they discovered a number of possibilities.

They tried new arrangements which raised rents sharply— and refused to grant written leases to the middlemen, the tacksmen of the clans, those traditionally responsible for parceling out the land to commoners and raising warriors for battle. Finally, around the turn of the century, the chieftains became especially enamored with the Cheviot, a breed of sheep that turned out to thrive in the glens and among the heather. Villages were razed wholesale throughout the mountainous regions, and tens of thousands of families had to flee the ancient lands, peopled in imagination with characters and legends— "with talking stones, snow giants, and mythical warriors of mountain granite." Crowding the boats that departed continuously from the port cities—"like bales of merchandise . . . four hundred and fifty passengers . . . crammed into a hold measuring sixty feet by eighteen," as one observer described—they set off on the eleven-week journey to the New World. "The scene was truly heartrending," wrote Donald Ross, a populist-style lawyer, who championed the Highland lower classes against the chieftains. Ross crusaded to stir up public opinion about the plight of the Highlanders. "The women and the children went about tearing their hair, and rending the heaven with their cries. Mothers with tender infants at the breast looked helplessly on, while their effects and their aged and infirm relatives were cast out, and the doors of their houses locked in their faces. No mercy was shown to age or sex, all were indiscriminately thrust out and left to perish." Hearing of Harriet Beecher Stowe's visit, Ross sent her pamphlets, explaining that he understood she planned "to make notes on the clearances and to report the result in your future 'Memoirs of a Sojourn to the Highlands of Scotland.' "[1]

Mrs. Stowe's guide through the districts of Sutherland was Harriet Elizabeth Georgina, Duchess of Sutherland, an amateur architect and landscape gardener and a favorite at Queen Victoria's palace. The duchess had organized a mammoth petition campaign, entitled *An Affectionate and Christian Address of Many Thousands of Women in Great Britain and Ireland to Their Sisters, the Women of the United States.* The address, signed by more than half a million women, appealed to Americans "for the removal of this affliction and disgrace from the Christian world," the system of slavery in the American South.[2]

Closer to home, however, the Duchess of Sutherland was more concerned with practical matters. She gave her guest the book by James Loch, general agent of the Sutherland Estates, which explained that "to emancipate the lower orders from slavery has been the unceasing object of the Highland Proprietors for the last twenty years." Replying to critics who had charged that 15,000 people had been forcibly removed from their traditional homelands on the Sutherland Estates in a ten-year period, Loch said the figures were exaggerated. Only 600 writs of eviction had been issued—perhaps 3,000 people—plus 400 or so families who, in his view, had had no right to be on the property in the first place. Most to the point, whatever the complaints, the removals would have the effect of "convert[ing] the former population of these districts to industrious and regular habits," and, moreover, had been "well calculated to increase the happiness of the individuals who were the object of this change." Incidentally, he mentioned, it would "benefit those to whom these extensive domains belonged."[3]

But Harriet Stowe and Lady Harriet did not linger on such

unpleasant subjects. Lady Harriet introduced her guest to other well-born and cultured men and women like the Palmerstons, Russells, and Gladstones. Ross, hearing of her activities, wrote again. "You are brought to see extensive gardens, aviaries, pleasure groves, waterfalls and all that is beautiful and attractive," he warned. "But you have not visited Strathnaver, you have not penetrated into Kildonan, you have not been up Strathbrora, you have not seen the ruins of hundreds and hundreds of houses of the burnt-out tenants." However, Stowe had seen quite enough to get what she considered a comprehensive view. In her book, entitled *Sunny Memories,* she explained that she had heard in America "dreadful accounts of cruelties practised in the process of inducing the tenants to change their places of residence," but could happily report that such stories were slanders. "In all the circles" in which she traveled, Stowe described, "I have heard the great and noble of the land freely spoken of and canvassed, and if there had been the least shadow of a foundation of any such accusations, I certainly should have heard of it."[4]

Beginning with the tacksmen and their families—the middle class of the Highlands—successive waves of Scottish immigrants populated the upper reaches of rivers like Pee Wee, Cape Fear, and Cross Creek in the Americas. West of Pee Wee in North Carolina was known as "Scottish Mesopotamia." In the backcountry areas, the Highlanders practiced simple agriculture— growing crops they had not known in Scotland, like corn and sweet potatoes. Early settlements continued to speak Gaelic well into the nineteenth century—indeed, the last sermon was spoken in Gaelic in North Carolina in 1860, on the eve of the Civil War itself. Along with other peasants from Germany, Ireland, England, Wales, and other countries, moreover, they merged into a southern yeomanry which retained often bitter memories of experiences which had torn them from their homelands—and saw disturbing parallels in the new lands they had chosen. "The autocrat of Russia does not more deserve the name tyrant . . . than does the petty tyrant who is equally regardless of the acknowledged rights of man," said Samuel McDowell Moore, a delegate from the western districts of North Carolina to a state constitutional convention in 1831, denouncing the planters of the east. His sentiments were magnified in the fiery outcry against the slaveowning elite penned by Hinton Helper on the eve of the Civil War: "Too long have we yielded a submissive obedience to the tyrannical domination of an inflated oligarchy. . . . The lords of the lash are not only absolute masters of the blacks, who are bought and sold, and driven about like so many cattle, but they are also the oracles and arbiters of all nonslaveowning whites, whose freedom is merely nominal."[5]

The story recurs. Both the populist conviction among ordinary people that a tyrannical elite has illegitimately usurped power and used it for ends that destroy the ways of custom and community, and the cultured condescension which renders the strivings of ordinary citizens as invisible as were the "commons" of Scotland to Harriet Beecher Stowe, form a continual theme through American history.

In particular, the strident denunciations of populism by those who pose as sophisticated and cosmopolitan interpreters of American ideas and letters is an illustration of such prejudices, across a wide range of political viewpoints. "Populism" is conventionally associated with a cluster of ideas connoting backwardness, prejudice, parochialism, nostalgia, and other negative attributes supposedly characteristic of ordinary Americans.

Indeed, like Stowe—deaf to the partisans of the Scottish lower classes—American intellectuals of widely varying political persuasions have dismissed the language of populist protest with little attempt at discrimination or subtlety. Conservative historian Peter Viereck characterized the first movement using the term "populist"—the farmers' revolt that emerged in the American South and Midwest during the 1880s and 1890s—as motivated by "a mania of xenophobic, Jew-baiting, intellectual-baiting, and thought-controlling lynch-spirit." And his depiction bore obvious resemblance to that of Richard Hofstadter, dean of liberal historiography in the 1950s, who portrayed the Populists as conspiracy-minded, nativist, chauvinist, jingoes, and anti-Semites—"a particularly virulent form" of that "larger complex of fear and suspicion of the stranger that haunted, and still tragically haunts, the nativist American mind." This sort of view remains dominant in much of supposedly sophisticated thinking today. Thus, Richard Reeves described the emergence of neopopulist themes in the 1984 elections in the *New York Times Magazine*. "PreRoosevelt populism seemed variously anti-everything," he noted in comparison. "Antielite, anti-intellectual, antiurban, antiforeigner, antiblack, antiCatholic and antiJewish. Populism was always nationalistic, often to the point of xenophobia. It was closely tied to religious fundamentalism and public apprehension over cultural differences and any cultural change."[6]

To dismiss populism in this way reflects prejudice born of differences of class, education, and social status. But commentators on populist movements have often also failed to grasp the positive currents within them because they have neglected the study of the sources of democratic vision and value—the free spaces within which democratic, oppositional culture becomes possible. Yet only by a focus on the existence and nature of voluntary "schoolrooms for citizenship"—or their absence—can the outcome of populism be understood.

Populism—the call for a return of power to "the people"—by definition contains the ambiguities and complexities associated with the varied meanings of "the people." "Do I contradict myself?" asked Walt Whitman, expressing his self-understanding as the bard of the common people. "Very well then I contradict myself/ (I am large, I contain multitudes)." In America, for instance, populism has always been prone to that myth of lost innocence, the sense that once there was a golden age of democracy, before modern civilization corrupted us, that Thomas Paine was wont to describe. "Government, like dress," said Paine, "is the badge of lost innocence; the palaces of kings are built on the ruins of the bowers of paradise." Unless populism

generates far-reaching redefinitions of whom "the people" includes, the populist impulse tends to reflect the prejudices and
biases of native-born whites against "outsiders" and minority
peoples.[7]

Yet for all of that, the original movement that created both
the term and the legacy had a remarkable democratic spirit. Its
animus, the demand that power should indeed be returned to
ordinary people, was informed by a broader vision of the common good, or commonwealth. And in turn, the notion of the
common good symbolized not only intention but actual experiences that had taught new lessons in citizenship and a sense of
interconnection with other communities. The story of those
free spaces where such schooling occurred, the farmers' cooperatives, or Alliances, that emerged by the tens of thousands in
the 1880s across the South and Midwest, furnishes a striking
example of the importance of new forms of public life through
which people can begin to rework inherited understandings of
the concept of a people, or *peoplehood* as distinct from person-
hood, and citizenship. It also demonstrates the great difficulties
of sustaining such a public life in a world that is organized
around different and antagonistic principles.

Populist anger grows from a sense of aggrieved peoplehood,
the conviction that an elite has dishonored and abused a historically and geographically constituted people, its historical
memories, its origins, its common territory, its ways of life.
Thus, there is a kind of class intuition in the populist sensibility
—a belief that common people are mistreated by the powerful.
But the very vagueness of these notions leads to political ambiguity as well.

"Peoplehood" is radically different from the idea of class.
While class is historically specific, the product of modern industrialization, the notion of "the people" dates back to antiquity.
It has been used by movements and groups with widely varying
aims and compositions. Class is a category subject to statistical
analysis. It can be depicted with charts and graphs and studied
with research questionnaires and computers. But the idea of a

people is associated with a specific place. It is to be understood symbolically rather than abstractly or quantitatively, through stories and legends, oral traditions, folk wisdom, foods, rituals, ways of speaking and remembering. A people has a point of origin and a moment of birth. This is the case with the Hebrew exodus and covenant stories, with the mythic origin of Athens or Rome, and with our own Declaration of Independence. Such a founding moment allows for celebration and for ritual commemoration sustaining memory, connecting the present to the past. A people is also defined by common space, settled by ancestors, claimed, defended, and filled in by subsequent generations and by certain shared ideals and aspirations. This sense of peoplehood is the essence of what Simone Weil meant when she defined roots by saying "a human being has roots by virtue of his real, active, and natural participation in the life of a community which preserves in living shape certain particular treasures of the past and certain particular expectations for the future."*[8]

Consciousness of being part of a national people coexists with and is nourished by the discrete peoples that make up the whole—a tension especially striking in the case of black Americans, for instance. But the tension between a self-consciousness of separate peoplehood and an awareness of common ties with other Americans has always existed within each subgroup. In

*In his recent work, *Populism: Its Past, Present and Future* (Moscow: Progress Publishers, 1984), Vladimir G. Khoros extensively discusses different contemporary meanings of populism. His book also contains a useful treatment of preindustrial themes that are precursors of populism, and a helpful exploration of the reasons that populism has emerged as a distinctive political movement in both Third World and modern industrial settings, in the late nineteenth and twentieth centuries. Khoros's book is a fascinating, positive evaluation of populism, coming, as it does, from a Soviet scholar. Despite its perhaps obligatory and strained efforts to show that Marx and Lenin anticipated the movement, the book clearly demonstrates the difference between populist and Marxist approaches. Moreover, Khoros's argument that populism may gain a new relevancy in the future as the answer to modern industrial societies' discontents has a vivid relevance to the Soviet Union itself. See especially his conclusion, "Populism: A Farewell to the Past or an Invitation to the Future? Prospects for Further Evolution of Populist Trends."

Martin Luther King's terms, the civil rights movement represented "the best in the American dream and the most sacred
values in our Judeo-Christian heritage." Segregation was an evil
"betrayal of the southern heritage" itself.[9]

Appeals to the American or to the southern heritage can have
very different meanings, depending on the social position and
nature of the group making the appeal. In stark contrast, both
Martin Luther King's Crusade for Citizenship and the appeal
that George Wallace made to southern identity could be considered "populist," but in profoundly different ways.

In democratic populist movements, as people are moved to
activism first in defense of their rights, traditions, and institutions, they change. They discover in themselves and their traditions new resources and potentials. They repair their capacity
to work together for collective problem-solving. They find out
new political facts about the world, build networks, and seek
contacts with other groups of the powerless to forge a broader
definition of the people. These processes, in turn, help clarify
basic power relations in the society as a whole. In sum, communities deepen the meaning of what they are doing, from
understanding it merely as a protest against threats, to coming
to see the need for a struggle for a new vision of the common
good, or common wealth. This kind of change is the identifying
mark of democratic movements broadly, those endeavors
which seek a transformation in power relations, not simply a
return to past conditions or the replacement of one elite with
another. In turn, such changes are not abstractly conceived or
taught: they are not "book knowledge." Rather, they become
part of lived experience and belief, emerging out of the sorts of
voluntary associations we have termed free social space.

The story of the movement first to call itself Populist begins
in the 1880s and 1890s among small farmers in the South and
Midwest, uniting descendants of those Scottish immigrants
from the Highlands with counterparts from other immigrant
groups. The Populist movement was precipitated by a series of
economic changes that threatened the loss of family-owned

farms. But the movement gained power, passion, vocabulary, and vision because of a specific understanding of American peoplehood, drawing from imagery and symbols about the land that had been long at the heart of the American tradition. Such imagery, moreover, had taken specific form in the American South.

The republican vision in America had always placed central emphasis on the land. In the view of Thomas Jefferson and others, a certain amount of business enterprise was probably inevitable. But the commonwealth could only survive if the great bulk of the population remained rural, a self-governing network of communities composed of freeholders. "Those who labour in the earth are the chosen people of God," wrote Jefferson, "whose breasts he has made his peculiar deposit for substantial and genuine virtue. It is the focus in which He keeps alive that sacred fire which otherwise might escape from the face of the earth." Cities, for Jefferson, were the home of "the mobs [which] add just so much to the support of pure government as sores do to the strength of the human body." Capitalists, if anything, were even more dangerous. "Corruption is the mark set on those who, not looking up to heaven or to their own toil and industry for their subsistence, depend for it on the casualties and caprice of customers." Elsewhere, Jefferson issued strong warnings against the "aristocracy of the new monied corporations" which he feared would crush democracy in its birth.[10]

Agrarian republicanism took a specific form, however, among the southern yeomanry, those middle classes who populated the southern Piedmont region which stretches from the coastal plains to the foothills of the Blue Ridge mountains. The yeoman farmers composed the considerable bulk of the white population in most southern states, even on the eve of the Civil War. In North Carolina, only 2 percent of agricultural families owned 500 acres of land, more than two-thirds owned less than 100, and over 72 percent of the white farmers held no slaves. In Kentucky in 1860, 72 percent of the farmers cultivated less than 100 acres and 65 percent were nonslave owners; in Virginia, 59 percent belonged to the nonslaveowning class.[11]

Anger at the pretensions and power of the larger slaveowners formed a continuing thread through the rural backcountry of states like North Carolina, Tennessee, Georgia, Virginia, and South Carolina, erupting periodically in political conflict. Unease with a society increasingly defined by planters combined with soil exhaustion in much of the Piedmont to send tens of thousands of small farmers from the Deep South to points further west during the decades before the war. Between 1820 and 1860, nearly one half of those whites born after the turn of the century—some 200,000 people—emigrated from the state of South Carolina.[12]

For those who stayed, however, the dynamics of race dominated other social questions. The specter of black competition for jobs, land—and white women—proved a potent glue, as spokesmen for the powerful were apt to note in more candid moments. "It is African slavery that makes every white man in some sense a lord," wrote the *Columbus Times* in 1850. "It draws a broad line of distinction between the two races . . . every white is, and feels that he is a man." And the alternative was commonly invoked to bring in line the white population. "Do you desire the millions of negro [sic] population in the South to be set free among us?" asked the *Wilmington Journal* of any who harbored doubts about slavery or secession in 1861. Abolition would mean "lowering white men's level to that of the Negro." And the consequences would be stark indeed, allowing blacks "to stalk abroad in the land, following the dictates of their own natural instincts, committing depredations, rapine and murder upon the whites."[13]

Thus, for southern yeoman whites, the republican tradition had a specific twist that emphasized with precision who was part of the "commonwealth" and who was its antithesis. Joel Chandler Harris described one Georgia farming community as a "Greek democracy" populated by "the most democratic people the world had ever seen." Tom Watson, whose career as a

rural advocate and populist leader followed closely the vicissi-
tudes of the movement, remembered his family homestead in
Georgia as "just a plain house," where the rhythms of the land
formed a stark contrast with the pace and commerce of the city.
"It seems to me that there was neither feverish haste upon it
nor vagrant leisure, exactitude nor slipshod looseness, miserly
gripping nor spendthrift waste." But the Watson family's original opposition to slavery in the pre-Revolutionary period, nourished by their Quaker religion, had long since given way to
participation in the slave system. By the third generation of
Watsons on the land, the family owned a number of slaves
directly, and Tom Watson's own formative memories of politics
during Reconstruction revolved around images of the northern
troops as an occupying force, opposed by all "good citizens."[14]

Thus, the legacy of the Old South was fraught with ambiguity
for the southern white yeomanry. On the one hand, there were
themes of dissent and rebellion under the surface. "The war
was a rich man's war and a poor man's fight," reminisced one
man of Scottish ancestry who had been born and raised in
Charlotte, North Carolina, just after the Civil War, describing
his relatives who had fought. His perspective was a common
one, combining retrospective regrets about slavery with apolo-
getics for the South. "This war proved something: that slavery
is intolerable. It ruled out secession forever. It was the greatest
test our country ever had—the preservation of freedom for the
American people." He viewed "the fashionable part of town"
along North Tryon Street, where his father worked for a time
as a laborer after the war, as peopled with those who "considered themselves the aristocrats, the elite." But themes in his
reminiscence obscured populist conflict and struck regional
chords, binding all whites together. "The South had nothing to
be ashamed of," he wrote many years later, at the age of ninety.
"The North had the money and the soldiers, but the South had
the best generals and the 'guts.'" During Reconstruction, he
remembered, "federal soldiers were in control. Negroes
roamed the streets in small towns, causing trouble. . . . Carpet-

baggers were doing all they could to take everything the South had." And the anger he felt toward the rich and well-born was qualified. "The people of the South were the Negroes' best friends," he averred. Moreover, though the people of North Tryon were "envied by the people on the other side of the track," he insisted the reader "not get me wrong. There were really lots of fine people there—'worthwhile people'" who "helped build the town and supported the churches."[15]

The conflicting elements in such views, threading through the white southern middle and lower classes throughout the years after the Civil War, had one moment when they became dramatically separated out. In the late 1880s, enormous networks of farmers' cooperatives developed across the region, as farmers struggled to maintain family farms in the face of worsening economic hardship and indebtedness. At the same time, moreover, a distinctive new version of the South as a white community took shape in multiplying numbers of mill villages. The different settings embodied and symbolized radically different cultural and social alternatives for the South's future. Each rested, in turn, directly upon the nature of communal institutions—in particular, the existence or nonexistence of free social space in which the southern yeomanry might discover an identity that was distinguishable from that of the white elite.

Like the clan chieftains of Scotland, the leading figures of the South reacted to wartime defeat by adopting the ways and outlook of their conquerors after the period of Reconstruction. "The future of the South is commercial and manufactural," proclaimed Patrick Calhoun, grandson of that fierce defender of "Southern civilization." Quickly forgotten were the diatribes against northern capitalism and acquisitiveness. The South, according to Calhoun, "will exchange the modest civilization of the country gentleman for the bustling civilization of the towns." Others waxed ever more enthusiastic. Henry Grady, who used the Atlanta *Constitution* as a central organ for the articulation of a vision of a "New South," foresaw "a South the home of fifty millions of people; her cities vast hives of industry;

her country-sides the treasures from which their resources are drawn; her streams vocal with whirring spindles." Partisans of the "Old Lost Cause" like Charles Colcock Jones, former Confederate colonel, might complain that "behind this fanfare of trumpets proclaiming the attractions and growth of the New South may too often be detected the deglutition of the harpy and the chuckle of the hireling." But they were seen as quaint anachronisms in the bustling centers of commerce like Atlanta and Charlotte.[16]

New South strategists, however, could not simply discard wholesale the republican values of independence, thrift, communal relations, and the notions of rough equality between whites. The mythology of industrialization had somehow to honor the agrarian republican legacy, even as the factory system undermined its living substance. The solution was a crusade proclaimed to "rescue the region" through textile mill villages, which would preserve the best of the old world in new embodiments.

In four southern states especially—North Carolina, Georgia, South Carolina, and Alabama—industrialization built around textiles after the war. There had long been a modest textile industry in the South, organized in the distinctive mill-village form pioneered by men like William Gregg of South Carolina, who saw such "republican communities" as the South's alternative to "class warfare" in large northern cities. After the war, the combination of technical experience, capital—often of northern origins—proximity to raw materials, water resources, and technological changes like the ring spindle and the automatic loom enabled a rapid expansion in the southern industry.[17]

But as important as the technological and economic factors of the industry were its ideological accompaniments. Like the Old South, the mill village was built on a rigid and unyielding racial caste system which kept symbols of the white yeomanry in a new context. In fact, the mill crusade was intended to strengthen this symbolism. As one Alabama advocate of textile industrialization put it,

It was considered a fact of tremendous significance in the history of
Alabama that the agricultural and industrial forces conspired to
transfer economic supremacy from the black belt to the white
northern counties . . . [the symbolic area of the yeoman]. The political slogan of the white counties "This is a white man's county" was
in a large sense as true of the economic life of the state as it was of
the political.

The mill village was portrayed as a kind of commonwealth,
where the whole white community became involved in salvation of the region—not for profit or individual aggrandizement
but for the common good. The reality was harsh indeed. In
1885, adult male spinners in North Carolina made $2.53 a week.
Women made $2.38 in Alabama. The profits from the mills built
in the 1880s were often phenomenal—the historian Broadus
Mitchell estimated that they commonly ran from 18 to 25 percent a year. But the myths of textile industrialization emphasized a grand crusade for independence of the region. In 1880,
Braxton Craven, president of Trinity College in North Carolina,
the Methodist institution in the state, dedicated a mill to "Almighty God." The Raleigh *Christian Advocate* editorialized
that capital in mills "should have divine blessing." Another
enthusiast described "Southern industry as a moral venture. It
is an adventure in the realm of human possibility. The pioneers
of the Southern industry were the prophets of God doing what
God wanted done." In reality, northern capital and the wealth
of former slaveowners played the central role in creating new
mills—a pattern widely documented by the 1920s. But the notion that capital came from the entire white community remained at the heart of the New South imagery. "They were
built from the combined capital of many of little means for the
social and economic betterment of the region rather than primarily for private profit," repeated one prominent southern
historian as late as the 1950s.[18]

The mills became closed, white-only worlds where blacks
were not welcome. Mill owners sought to control every form of
social space in a clear mimicry of the totalitarianism of the Old

South. Indeed, in the first decades of textile industrialization, they commonly owned and rented out stores, houses, churches, and schools, and frequently paid a portion of the minister's salary. The Cannon family of Kannapolis, prominent members of the textile mill-owning community in North Carolina, received daily reports on school attendance. The paternalism of the Old South was redefined in such contexts in ways which simultaneously emphasized the notion of a "white kinship" and the bonds between owners and supervisors and workers. Recent research suggests that workers constantly created their own mechanisms of communal identity and solidarity, distinguishable from management, and often declined to use company facilities. But the structure of the villages dampened social protest, nonetheless, leading to escape through high rates of mobility, or simply "keeping to themselves."* Later industrial strife most commonly occurred when older norms were violated by new industrial policies and scientific management. "To be deprived of one's dignity as an individual and made into a sort of automaton," was the worst possible fate, according to W. J. Cash, the brilliant interpreter of the white southern sensibility.[19]

The imagery of the mill village as a white commonwealth was one pole of the South emerging from war and Reconstruction. The other, however, was the development of an agrarian radicalism which gave the textile crusade some urgency. The white elite in the 1880s and 1890s faced the specter of a growing revolt among farmers, and the first signs of an alliance between whites and blacks—developments that revived the most troubling dimensions of the republican heritage.

*Even when workforces were integrated, the racial dividing line fragmented working people's common identity. As Dolores Janiewski put it in her study of Durham, N.C., tobacco workers: "Denied a common meeting place, in both a spatial and a cultural sense . . . [black and white] workers never evolved a sense of their collective identity as members of the same community. . . ." From "Flawed Victories: The Experiences of Black and White Women Workers in Durham During the 1930s," in Lois Scharf and Joan Jensen, eds., *Decades of Discontent: The Women's Movement, 1920–1940* (Westport, Conn.: Greenwood Press, 1983), pp. 98–99.

Despite the statistics that southern apologists of the New South used to chart the growth of southern manufacturing, the reality facing most southerners was a rapidly worsening economy. The number of farms had increased, and along with the increase the portion of the agricultural population involved in sharecropping had grown dramatically. By 1880, sharecroppers worked about one-third of southern farms. In the Black Belt, that stretch of counties where slavery had been most entrenched and where blacks often formed the majority of the population, conditions had returned to a state which resembled the old plantation days. One study of manuscript tax assessment roles in Louisiana found that between 1860 and 1880, the number of plantations had increased three times. Henry Grady remarked in 1881 that the large planters were "still lords of acres, though not of slaves."[20]

In both Black Belt counties and the upland areas, "the financial question" was at the heart of the crisis facing farmers. Issues having to do with how money was created and circulated reflected both the particular economic history of the South and, more broadly, the emerging patterns of an industrializing society. In the Piedmont region, extending between the mountains and the Black Belt, small family farmers found themselves under siege from a crop-lien system which threatened to turn the southern economy into a "vast pawn shop," as one observer put it. After the war, the South found itself with only twenty-six banks in the states of the Carolinas, Georgia, Alabama, Louisiana, Texas, Arkansas, and Mississippi—compared to 829 in New York, Massachusetts, Pennsylvania, and Ohio. Massachusetts alone had five times the bank circulation of the entire South; Bridgeport, Connecticut, had more than the states of Texas, Alabama, and North and South Carolina combined.[21]

As a result of tight credit, the figure of the town merchant, or furnishing merchant, became a nemesis for tens of thousands of small and moderate-sized farms. Everything—clothes, food, implements, fertilizers, seeds—had to be bought through the merchant, who put a lien on the farmer's future crop. The merchant, with claim to the crop, then sold the crop himself. Price inflation on the goods sold was often astronomical—up to 100 or even 200 percent of the value of the merchandise. Credit given for the crops ran typically far below the market price. In ways people outside the South had difficulty understanding, the crop-lien system became for millions of southerners something akin to slavery. One contemporary wrote: "When one of these mortgages has been recorded against the Southern farmer, he has usually passed into a state of helpless peonage. With the surrender of this evidence of indebtedness he has also surrendered his freedom of action. . . . From this time until he has paid the last dollar of his indebtedness, he is subject to the constant oversight and direction of the merchant." "Never mortgage," families of farmers were told. "Whatever happens, don't mortgage." But the advice was easier to give than to follow. In Mississippi, Alabama, and Georgia, studies found that up to 90 percent of the farm population had gone into debt.[22]

Such a state of affairs hit at the very foundations of the farmer's identity. Virtue, fairness, rough equity, respect—all rested upon independence, the possibility of being "one's own man," not bossed, not looked down upon. The economic changes occurring in the South undermined precisely that independence. Farmers were desperate to retain their land and escape peonage. And as the solution, they devised a new method, called the Farmers' Alliances, of cooperatively marketing their crops and purchasing their supplies. Through such Alliances, farmers hoped to escape the lien system.

The "gospel of cooperation" swept the South and spread through much of the Midwest as well in the late 1880s, taken by men like William Lamb and S. O. Daws from Texas. By 1885, Lamb had organized 100 suballiances in Montague County, Texas, alone. In the state meeting of the Alliances that year, the largest gathering of farmers in the history of Texas came together. Five hundred and fifty-five suballiances were represented. Alliancemen adopted a resolution calling on all members to act as a unit in the sale of their produce. Moreover, it

developed an innovation which distinguished the new cooperatives from older farm organizations like the Patrons of Hus-
bandry, or Grange. The Alliances themselves extended credit
to farmers, allowing a margin of freedom from the lien system.[23]

By 1887, the Alliances had organized 200,000 farmers in
Texas. Organizers, with a series of successes which reached
from the county storehouse to the giant cooperative for the
whole state, the Exchange, determined to spread "the gospel of
cooperation" across the South. "I hold that cooperation, properly understood and properly applied, will place a limit to the
encroachments of organized monopoly," explained Charles
Macune, president of the newly formed National Farmers Alliance and Cooperative Union. "[It] will be the means by which
the mortgage-burdened farmers can assert their freedom from
the tyranny of organized capital, and obtain the reward for
honesty, industry, and frugality, which they so richly deserve."
The National Alliance sent six lecturers to Mississippi, six to
Alabama, seven to Tennessee, and more to Missouri, Arkansas,
the Carolinas, Georgia, Florida, Kentucky, and Kansas. Lecturers like Cyclone Davis, Mary Blease, S. O. Daws, and Kate
O'Hare became known across whole regions.[24]

Results proved spectacular. Within three years after the first
lecturer arrived from Texas, Georgia Alliances had signed up
more than 100,000 members and had spread to 134 of the
state's 137 counties. In Tennessee, 125,000 members had joined
3,600 suballiances. By the end of the fifth year, lecturers had
campaigned in forty-three states and territories and involved
some two million farm families in what historian Lawrence
Goodwyn aptly described as "the most massive organizing
drive by any citizen institution of nineteenth century America."[25]

The Alliances were concerned with the most practical and
immediate of issues. But from their inception, they taught new
skills of public life, economic planning, agriculture, and a series

of broader lessons about the emerging shape of economic power and financial institutions in America. Put simply, the Alliances created a new form of free social space that the farmers owned themselves. The cooperatives simultaneously were outgrowths and carriers of the movement. Moreover, they were bound together by an interconnecting set of other movement institutions.

Social events had long been central to the life of farming areas. "Court week was a great time," read one reminiscence of Charlotte, North Carolina, in the 1870s, when the city was still a small town and county seat. "The farmers would come in covered wagons, sometimes bringing their families. They would camp in vacant lots (there were plenty of them). They built fires, did their own cooking, slept in the wagons, and stayed for several days." Building on such traditions and similar ones, like southern parades and revival meetings, a rich cultural life accompanied the growth of the new cooperatives. At the largest, thousands of families would gather to hear about "the financial question," new cooperative experiments, marketing ideas, crop rotation, and American history. Such lessons were reinforced continually, moreover, by the flowering "Alliance Press" which sprang up—numbering something like 1,000 newspapers—in farming regions throughout the South and Midwest, with names like the *Advocate,* the *American Nonconformist,* the *Progressive Farmer,* and the *Appeal to Reason.* [26]

The discussions which took place within the farmers' institutions were suffused with animated and impassioned reflections on American history, talk of the country's basic values, and poignant personal testimonies that, in sum, gave the organizing process the character of a self-conscious educational crusade. As one lecturer put it, "The suballiance is a schoolroom." When lecturers arrived in a small town or rural church, they would tell what they had heard in the community before. "Did you know about Joe's new lien?" "They repossessed the old McPherson place." And the assembled farmers would recount their own tales of personal hardship and misfortune. With the combining of such stories, biblical themes, quotes from Jefferson, and the like, an entire view of the world took shape. Farmers reworked the closed and static vision of the South as a "brotherhood" where the things which bound white men together far surpassed any differences of value or interest. They came to believe that America faced a threat to its fundamental values of self-government and participation by free and independent citizens. Such a sense of crisis was vividly expressed in the preamble to the Populist Party platform, written at the founding of the party in 1892. "We meet in the midst of a nation brought to the verge of moral, political and material ruin," read the document.

> Corruption dominates the ballot box, the legislatures, the Congress and touches even the ermine of the bench. Assembled on the anniversary of the birth of the illustrious general who led the first great revolution on this continent against oppression, filled with the sentiments which actuated that grand generation, we seek to restore government of the republic to the hands of the "plain people" with whom it originated.[27]

The sort of educational process generated through the Alliances and related institutions took on life and power because of the heightened sense of possibility among farmers who had once despaired of the future. Out of the concrete experiences of the organizing process—the creation of cooperatives in county after county, the new cooperation with communities and regions one had never seen before, the courses that taught men and women to make sense of and master economic forces that had seemed mysterious and arcane—the conviction grew that ordinary people could, indeed, control their future. "The old order of things is passing away," said Tom Watson, leader of the Georgia Populists. "The masses are beginning to arouse themselves, reading for themselves, thinking for themselves." Goodwyn analyzed the transformative sense which generated what he called the "movement culture" of populism:

When a farm family's wagon crested a hill en route to a Fourth of July Alliance Day encampment and the occupants looked back to see thousands of other families trained out behind them in wagon trains, the thought that "the Alliance is the people and the people are together" took on transforming possibilities. Such a moment— and the Alliance experience created hundreds of them—instilled hope in hundreds of thousands of people who had been without it. It was hope itself, the sense of autonomy it encouraged and the sense of possibility it stimulated, that lay at the heart of populism.[28]

Just as the activists of the Knights of Labor had broken open the political and cultural life of communities across the country, in the apt phrasing of historian Leon Fink, separating out the sharply contrasting meanings of republicanism in the process, so too farmers in the free spaces of the Alliances broke open the culture of the white commonwealth. Both elements of continuity and the distinctive and novel features of the Alliances, alike, were key to such a process.

The free spaces of the Alliances drew directly and deeply on the traditions and institutions of rural areas. Alliance meetings were commonly held in the schoolhouse, corner store, or local church. Biblical themes and imagery were central to the movement. "When He multiplied the loaves and the fishes" said one North Carolina Allianceman, "None went away hungry. God does not create disparities." The rich were often compared to Pharaoh or Cyrus and the Persians who "will listen to no warning until Daniel strides into the Hall." Even the southern heritage furnished material for the movement. Thus, Watson sought to draw upon the "fighting spirit" of the Old South in new ways. "To you who grounded your muskets twenty-five years ago I make my appeal," he told a group of farmers. "The fight is upon you—not bloody as then, but as bitter; not with men who come to free your slaves, but who come to make slaves of you."[29]

But despite the continuities in heritage and setting, the ways in which the Alliances were separate and distinct from traditional community institutions were equally crucial. In most rural areas, social environments were not as rigidly controlled as within the mill village—an environment whose absence of free social space was, in many respects, its most striking feature. But patterns of political and social acquiescence had shaped institutions of political life, farm organization, and church for generations, cementing all whites together in self-conscious opposition to blacks. Thus, for example, though the farmers claimed Christianity as their wellspring—indeed, the movement was often described as "Christianity in action," or possessed of the "politics of Jefferson" and the "morals of the Bible"—the Populists found it necessary to challenge organized religion again and again, despite its cultural roots in the South. The church, said Cyrus Thompson of North Carolina, had become "the ready handmaiden of monarchy, aristocracy and tyranny; of gorgeous greed and human oppression." Thompson appealed "to the historic Christ, Christ the Reformer" and said the church must learn to redeem the world, as well as save souls. "Plutocracy has bribed the church with fine buildings and big salaries and many churches and ministers are now working for the devil," said one Alliance editor in Alabama, advocating a Christianity that took up "root causes" of sin and oppression in the world.[30]

The relative freedom from traditional institutions of the free social spaces at the heart of Populism generated wide-ranging democratic experiments. It meant that the movement, for its time and context, was able to explore a remarkable set of questions and themes within the movement culture, making unprecedented ties with workers, encouraging a measure of women's participation in public roles, even raising tentative questions about the bedrock cultural premise of the white South, racial superiority. When the Knights of Labor struck against Jay Gould's Missouri Pacific rail lines in 1886 after Gould had fired a union spokesman, the railroads mobilized thousands of militia. Newspapers denounced the strikers across the country. But the Farmers' Alliances moved to support. "Knowing that the day is not far distant when the Farmers Alliance will have to use the Boycott in order to get goods direct," wrote William Lamb, "we think it is a good time to help the Knights of Labor in order to secure their help in the near future. We know of a certainty that manufacturers have organized against us, and that is to say if we don't do as they say, we can't get their goods."[31]

From the beginning, women were not only involved in the traditional roles of community-building and sustenance in the Alliances—organizing the socials, working behind the scenes in rallies, helping with the encampments. The Alliances had grown from decades of rural farm organization, especially the Grange, organized in the 1860s, which had seen women "with a mystical significance rooted in ancient lore" and taught Eleusianian mysteries, including the divinity of Ceres, goddess of agriculture. Moreover, for the Grange, women's value was not only inspirational. "Because the Grange emphasized the unity of the family," observed historian Mari Jo Buhle, "women served jointly with their husbands. A local assembly . . . could acquire a charter only by demonstrating that at least four women as well as nine men were ready to enroll." Though apparently women's participation in the Grange was more widespread in the Midwest than in the South, everywhere it created precedents for the Alliances to draw upon.[32]

Following such precedents, the National Alliance defined its goals explicitly in gender-inclusive terms—"to elevate to higher manhood and womanhood those who bear the burdens of productive industry." The organization adopted a virtually unprecedented structure which granted women full rights of membership and participation in the cooperatives. When Texas organizers arrived in North Carolina in May 1887, Harry Tracy, a national lecturer, told the farmers that "The ladies . . . must join the order before we can succeed." A steady stream of letters to *The Progressive Farmer,* the Alliance newspaper edited by L. L. Polk, North Carolina leader, questioned whether such language was indeed meant literally. Polk again and again affirmed that women had full rights—including the right to vote on new members, participate in Alliance business, run for Alliance office and be initiated into "all the secret words and signs."[33]

The detailed story of women's participation in the populist movement has yet to be told, but there is suggestive evidence that women moved rapidly and vigorously to take advantage of the new possibilities. "'Tis not enough that we should be what our mothers were," said Katie Moore to the Failing Creek Alliance in North Carolina in 1891. "We should be more." "Words would fail me to express to you, my Alliance sisters, my appreciation of women's opportunity of being co-workers with the brethren in the movement which is stirring this great nation," Mrs. Brown, secretary of the Menola Suballiance, explained to women at a Hertford County Alliance meeting. "We find at every hand fields of usefulness opening for us . . . as Frances Willard says, 'drudgery, fashion and gossip are no longer the bounds of women's Sphere.' " Women wrote regularly in populist newspapers, often held office in Alliances and suballiances (though rarely positions of president), and were employed as Alliance lecturers. Figures such as Mary Lease, Fanny Randolph Vickery, Marion Todd, and Sarah Emergy became well known and widely respected leaders.[34]

The democratic sensibility incubating within the movement culture of Populism crossed other boundaries as well. At their most expansive, Populist spokesmen could challenge fundamental notions of "manifest destiny" and American foreign policy. Thus, for instance, Tom Watson opposed a threatened war with Chile on the grounds that "it would arouse the military spirit everywhere" and argued on the floor of the House of Representatives that "the time is approaching . . . when wars —those barbarous settlements of disputes by appeal to arms— . . . will be just as much a relic of the past . . . as are now the old, rude ways of trial by combat and dueling." One study of Kansas Populism found that the party, though lukewarmly supportive of America's intervention in Cuba, was "strongly opposed [to] the imperialism that the war engendered." The

Populists at their convention in 1894 took strong stands against the main nativist organization, the American Protective Association, and had among their leadership "large numbers of every politically consequential foreign-born group then in Kansas, with the exception of the Mennonites."[35]

Finally, when the hardpressed southern white farmers sought to make common cause with poor blacks, they evidenced some insight into southern racism. As Tom Watson put it in calling for an alliance between the Negro and the white:

> Now the People's party says to these two men, you are kept apart that you may be separately fleeced of your earnings. You are made to hate each other because upon that hatred is rested the keystone of the arch of financial despotism which enslaves you both. You are deceived and blinded that you may not see how this race antagonism perpetuates a monetary system which beggars both.[36]

Like the story of women's participation, the nature and details of black farmers' participation in the movement have yet to be told. Indeed, the narrative is further complicated by the secret activities of the Colored Farmers' Alliance, the main organizational expression of a parallel movement which spread among the rural black population.

The Populists were far from racial egalitarians—or free of other sorts of prejudice. Indeed, at times, People's Party spokesmen sought to counter the charge that they advocated "social equality" through race baiting themselves. In Watson's campaign for Congress, he attacked immigrants of all sorts. "The scum of creation has been dumped on us," he thundered. "The most dangerous and corrupting hordes of an Old World have invaded us." Even at best, the white farmers viewed their potential black allies with no small paternalism. "The Bourbon Democracy have used the Negro very successfully in keeping their supremacy over us," said the Alabama *Sentiment.* "We propose to use him in turn to down them for the good of whites and blacks alike." "What we desire," explained Andrew Corothers, "is that the Farmers Alliance men everywhere will take hold and organize or aid in organizing the colored farmer, and placing in him an attitude to cooperate intelligently and systematically."[37]

But in the Deep South of the 1880s and 1890s, even the *act* of participating in the Farmers' Alliance or the People's Party was seen as subversive to the racial order. And at points, Populists raised specific issues and implemented practices which went far beyond narrow economic concerns. In Mississippi in 1895, the Populist gubernatorial nominee, Frank Burkitt, crusading against the "putrid, putrescent, putrifying political moribund carcass of bourbon democracy," proposed not only measures challenging economic privilege but also free public education for both black and white children and an end to the restrictions on black voting rights embodied in the 1890 state constitution. In Arkansas, the People's Party took an official position "for the downtrodden, regardless of race." The Texas state party platform of 1894 included measures such as the end of white control over black school districts and a demand for "public free schools for six months in the year for all children between the ages of six and eighteen years."[38]

for all the remarkable innovations which the Alliance networks incubated in thought and activity, their very novelty and distinctness from traditional institutions also meant a precarious existence. In the first instance, the cooperatives came under steady and sustained siege from financial interests who refused to extend credit. Even as the Texas Alliance sent lecturers across the South, leaders discovered that while local organization could make some marginal difference, concerted statewide action was essential to overturn the entrenched lien system itself. Thus, they mobilized an effort to form a statewide exchange through the vast lecture circuit which had developed over several years. Each business agent from every county was to acquire from each suballiance member who wanted to purchase supplies on credit a statement of his needs and a pledge of cotton worth "at least 3 times as much" as the amount; the notes were to be paid in the fall after the crops were harvested and sold, in entirety, through the state institution.

It was an enormous undertaking—and a doomed one without enough credit to purchase supplies. Banks throughout the state adamantly refused to extend loans, and the state exchange proved unable to meet its obligations to the suballiances. On June 9, in desperation, farmers held a "day to save the exchange," with rallies in every corner of the state. More than $70,000 was raised, and more than $200,000 pledged, by the combined efforts of tens of thousands of impoverished farmers. But the exchange remained in trouble. In August, it drew back from its plan, declaring that "all purchases from branch exchanges must be for cash. Notice is hereby given that the books of the exchange are closed against any further debit."[39]

Such failures of strictly economic action led inexorably into politics. And the sense of dignity and possibility that had grown within the movement bred the spirit necessary for independent action, despite the intensely emotional bonds which the Democrats, the "Party of our Fathers" held for southern whites. In December 1889, in St. Louis, the Alliance met with labor groups to call for a "great confederation of labor organizations" and to declare that "cooperation has aroused the hostility of the greedy and avaricious trust, rings and monopolistic combinations to such an extent that great and persistent efforts are put forth by them to thwart us in every attempt at reform." Wide-ranging proposals for government action to control monopolies over land, currency, rails by financial and corporate giants became the basis for holding politicians accountable; when Democrats and Republicans alike betrayed their early promises of support, the logic of the movement resulted in a third party.[40]

But the movement into third-party politics entailed major risks. For example, as the focus narrowed, women were excluded. The terrain shifted to "male activity" and the range of community-building activities which the cooperatives had engendered subsided. Leon Fink has observed, indeed, that the People's Party was the first of the nineteenth-century democratic movements to begin to define "the movement as politics," to identify the aims of the movement with the conquest of elections rather than the self-organization of the community.

Such definition brought with it a series of other problems. To organize a successful third party required ways to reach immigrant and working-class groups in eastern cities, in a time when the Knights of Labor were in dramatic decline.[41]

The fragility of the cooperative base of the movement coupled with the vagaries of electoral politics meant the movement was prey to the machinations of politicians within its own ranks. Even at best, the movement ideology was a pastiche of notions, some grounded in sophisticated economic analyses of finance capitalism, others accepting without deeper examination ideas like "technological progress," middle-class respectability and economic self-interest as the motive force of human behavior. The language of Populism—the vision of a "cooperative commonwealth" of small-scale production and simple market exchange between neighbors and friends—held few resources for dealing with the growth of massive corporations and the new professionals who were reshaping the culture and outlook of towns and cities. Indeed, the new middle class of the cities, made up of white-collar, professional, clerical, and management employees, articulated an individualist ethos of success and advancement that Populists, even at their most radical, often echoed.[42]

Where cooperatives had not organized widely, the movement became what Goodwyn calls a "shadow movement," largely the captive of superficial proposals like the demand for coinage of silver. Even in states where Populism had developed deeper roots, demagogues, appeals to southern racism and regionalism, and other tactics took a severe toll. The rhetoric of the yeomanry had always tended to conceal divisions within communities along class lines, divisions which were acutely aggravated by racial caste. Blacks were most often sharecroppers and tenants; white Populists mainly struggled to own their own land. With such a diverse class base, it is not surprising that the Farmers' Alliance opposed a strike by farm laborers for higher wages in 1891.[43]

Thus, beset by problems within and without, the Populists

were vulnerable to rapid decline. After the fusion with the Democrats in 1896 around the candidacy of William Jennings Bryan, the Populists lost their power and momentum. Again and again, the ideology of the New South asserted itself with vigor and racist crudity and hastened the end.

In Mississippi, Burkitt's gubernatorial campaign of 1895 began hopefully. Populists had proven their strength in much of the eastern hill country and had gathered more than one-third of the votes in the previous year's Congressional elections. Yet conservative Democrats, desperate to stop Populist advances, renewed rhetoric of white supremacy with a vengeance —and succeeded in splitting the movement. By the turn of the century, the state's *Official and Statistical Register* could boast (in revealingly direct acknowledgment of the class dimension of disenfranchisement):

> Mississippi was the first state in the Union to solve the problem of white supremacy in the South by lawful means. The Constitution of 1890 disfranchises the ignorant and vicious of both races, and places control of the State in the hands of the virtuous, intelligent citizens.

For four subsequent generations, Mississippi politics was the preserve of white and affluent men. For seventy years after 1890, its governors were elected with votes from an average of 12 percent of the adult population.[44]

In North Carolina in 1898, the state's leading citizens proclaimed the "vital interest" of everyone in uniting behind white supremacy, after several years of electoral success by a Populist–Republican fusion ticket. "The redemption of North Carolina," argued the *Wilmington Messenger,* "is the imperative demand of civilization and honor and liberty itself." In Raleigh, before the election, preachers and other citizens of "high standing" patrolled black communities. The Rev. C. W. Blanchard of Kingston thundered that it was "doubtless best for a minister of the Gospel to be as nonpartisan in his politics as possible" but when "our white daughters can't walk the streets, free from the insults that a stripling negro girl, as black as the ace of spades,

much younger than themselves, is to heap upon them" something simply had to be done. At one rally in Goldsboro, a Methodist trustee of Trinity College gloried in "the vibrations of our
coming redemption from all wicked rule, and the supremacy of
that race destined not only to rule this country but to carry the
Gospel to all nations and maintain Civil and Religious Liberty
throughout the world." Tensions flared across the state. In Wilmington, all Republican city officials resigned; the new Democratic mayor, Alfred Waddell, bragged about "choking" the
Cape Fear River with black corpses, and a white-instigated race
riot killed between eleven and thirty blacks. The election itself
resulted in overwhelming victory for the forces of the New
South. "Businessmen of the state are largely responsible for the
victory," the *Charlotte Observer* proudly proclaimed. "Not before in years have the bank men, the mill men and the businessmen in general—the backbone of the property interests of the
State—taken such sincere interest in affairs." In the aftermath
of the triumph, business interests held unchallenged power
over dissident elements in the Democratic Party itself. The mill
village—not the farmers' cooperative—became the preemi-
nent symbol of the twentieth-century development.[45]

With the demise of the farmers' cooperatives in the 1890s,
Populism did not entirely disappear from the South. In the early
years of the twentieth century, areas of previous Populist
strength proved, at times, foundations for Socialist Party politics. In the 1930s and 1940s, an interracial movement emerged
among poor whites and black tenant farmers, who unionized in
a number of states in the Southern Tenant Farmers Union.
Southern mill towns remained divided along lines of power and
class in ways that led to periodic protest and even large-scale
mobilization, as in the wave of strikes through the Piedmont in
the early years of the Great Depression. The mood of Populist
anger was even more widespread. Indeed, it animated large-
scale protests like Huey Long's Share the Wealth organization,
as historian Alan Brinkley has described.[46]

Yet the differences in the populists of the 1880s and 1930s

were more important than the similarities. Brinkley contrasted the two. The Farmers' Alliances of the 1880s and '90s "encouraged an active process of community-institution-building. From them emerged marketing cooperatives, community cotton gins and flour mills, cooperative stores and credit unions" and together they constituted "an alternative to the emerging centralized corporate economy." In the 1930s, however, little actual effort at community building took place. "What was most conspicuously absent was a genuine belief in possibilities." Brinkley attributes such lack of hope to the great concentrations of power, bureaucracy, and mass communications that had reshaped American society as a whole in the intervening forty or fifty years.[47]

Such an analysis may have some insight, but it fails to explain why large-scale democratic populist movements did emerge elsewhere in the nation—movements like the midwestern farmer labor parties and the Washington Commonwealth Federation. More important, perhaps, than generalized public hopelessness was the fact that protests of the Thirties in the South had no large networks of free spaces that could generate a sense of hope and build connections among diverse communities of black and white. "Racial segregation . . . made virtually impossible a bi-racial working-class mobilization of the type attempted by the Knights of Labor and the Farmers Alliance," observes a new, richly detailed study of southern mill workers by Jacquelyn Hall, Robert Korstad, and Jim Leloudis. From the late nineteenth century through the 1960s, opposition to the "Solid South" of white supremacy and elite domination was confined to the margins and the underside of society.[48]

Though Huey Long and other self-professed populists who emerged from time to time in southern history did not always descend to the bitter racial demagoguery which resulted from the immediate aftermath of the Populist defeat, their protests remained parochial and narrow. It was a long way from the "gospel of cooperation" and the vision of a people in control of their destiny.

CHAPTER 6

FREE SPACES

IN 1849, one of Herman Melville's characters in his novel *Mardi* presented to the people of Vivenza—the United States —a document that reminded them "freedom is more social than political," meant to suggest that democracy depended upon the virtue and intelligence of the citizens themselves. In outrage, the Vivenzans shredded the document. The book's dismal sales in the mid-nineteenth century seemed to Melville a disgusting confirmation of his warning. Today, the same idea sounds to some a distant echo from the past.[1]

"Democracy" is a term used frequently and with little content. American Presidents like Ronald Reagan, who, shortly after his election, declared to the British Parliament his intention to launch a program to spread "democracy throughout the world," invoke it to separate the "free world" from "communist totalitarianism." The idea of citizenship, however, was entirely missing from the President's discussion of democracy. Yet, as Sheldon Wolin has observed, "the silence on the subject is not peculiar to conservatives or reactionaries. . . . Most Marxists are interested in the 'masses' or the workers, but they dismiss citizenship as a bourgeois conceit, formal and empty." The problem has a simple source. Notions of active citizenship and the common good have all but disappeared from our modern vocabulary because we have come to define the arenas in which active citizenship is nourished and given meaning as entirely outside of "politics" and "public life."[2]

More than thirty years ago, Baker Brownell, a philosophy professor at Northwestern University who had been involved in a number of community development projects, wrote a book entitled *The Human Community*. It polemicized angrily against the academic world from which he came. "Truth is more than a report," said Brownell. "It is an organization of values. Efficiency is more than a machine; it is a human consequence." Captivated by technique, procedure, method, and specialization, Brownell argued, the educated middle class had lost sight of actual face-to-face relations—the actual life of communities themselves—which create the most important criteria for judging any innovation or change. "It is the persistent assumption of those who are influential . . . that large-scale organization and contemporary urban culture can somehow provide suitable substitutes for the values of the human communities that they destroy," he declared. "For want of a better word I call these persons 'the educated' professionals, professors, businessmen, generals, scientists, bureaucrats, publicists, politicians, etc. They may be capitalist or they may be Communist in their affiliations, Christian or Jew, American, English, German, Russian or French. But below these relatively superficial variations among the 'educated' there is a deeper affiliation. They are affiliated in the abstract, anonymous, vastly expensive culture of the modern city."[3]

Brownell stated the case starkly. He largely neglected motivations other than a narrowly individualist search for power and achievement that leads people away from settled communities.* And he paid little attention to the enormous com-

---

*In particular, Brownell neglected what Robert Bellah and others have termed the "expressive individualist" strain in American culture that is embodied in much therapeutic language—notions that the basic commitments and purposes of one's life come through the search for *self-realization* and self-expression. The focus on expressive individualism in American culture, especially as it has melded with consumerism and high rates of mobility and the like, may have contributed to the weakening of what Bellah and his associates call "communities of memory and hope," more stable, continuous sets of relationships characteristic of working-class (and, interestingly in different terms, upper-class) life. But at times it is also the source of creative intellectual and artistic energy—much of the protean American spirit that is so attractive to other

plexity of community life. Ties of place, gender, memory, kinship, work, ethnicity, value and religious belief, and many other bonds may in different contexts be sources of communal solidarity or of fragmentation. Communities can be open, evolving, and changing—or static, parochial, defensive, and rigid. They can encourage new roles for those traditionally marginalized or powerless within their midst, or they can reinforce patterns of exclusivity and parochialism. Without attention to the specific features and processes that democratize community life, any invocation of communal values is prey to telling criticisms of sentimentality and naïveté.

Despite the complexity of communities, however, Brownell accurately identified an intellectual stance that has characterized thought across the political and social spectrum. Close-knit communities where people live in multidimensional relations with one another—what is called *Gemeinschaft* in social theory —are thought to give way with "progress" to relations based on reason, functional identities like work and profession, and voluntarily conceived association. As a result, conventional approaches marginalize or ignore particular identities of all sorts. As Arthur Schlesinger put it in 1949, "Modern technology created free society, but created it at the expense of the protective tissues which had bound together feudal society. . . . New social structures must succeed where the ancient jurisdictions

peoples in the world. And the fusion of expressive individualist and communal themes in free spaces gives public life a remarkable dynamism and vitality. The effort to balance communal commitments and individual expression has informed some of the richest explorations of the meaning of democracy. Thus, for instance, for D. H. Lawrence, "the first great purpose of Democracy" was for each to be "spontaneously" themselves: "each man himself, each women herself. . . . None shall try to determine the being of any other." But Lawrence defined "freedom" in terms sharply different from contemporary cultural radicals who marginalize communal ties. Humans are free, he argued, "only when they belong to a living, organic, believing community." Simple individualism for Lawrence led to commercialism, sex without relationship, and death of the spirit. Lawrence quoted in Raymond Williams, *Culture and Society* (New York: Harper Torchbooks, 1972), pp. 208–10, 212.

Robert Bellah et al., *Habits of the Heart: Individualism and Commitment in American Life* (Berkeley: University of California Press, 1985), especially chap. 11.

of the family, the clan and the guild and nation-state have failed." Marshall Berman's celebration of the modernist sensibility in 1982, *All That Is Solid Melts into Air,* conveys the same message. "He [modern man, personified in figures like Goethe's *Faust*] won't be able to create anything unless he's prepared to let everything go, to accept the fact that all that has been created up to now—and, indeed, all that he may create in the future—must be destroyed to pave the way for more creation. This is the dialectic that modern man must embrace in order to move and live."[4]

From a democratic perspective, more is lost through the eclipse of community than a sense of belonging and secure identity. Citizenship itself disappears from view. And the very arenas where it is nourished and given meaning—communally grounded voluntary associations of the sort we have called, throughout this work, free spaces—are defined simply as bulwarks of order and the status quo. Such a perspective, for instance, characterizes much of contemporary conservatism.

Neoconservative thought has as its central theme a reassertion of the importance of voluntary associations and communally based groupings like family, religious congregations, and neighborhoods. These are said to stand between, or "mediate," the private world of the individual and the "public" world of large institutions like bureaucracy, profession, trade union, and corporation.

The intellectual roots of neoconservatism lie in the 1950s, when social critics like Robert Nisbet argued that totalitarianism depends upon the elimination of voluntary and autonomous communal ties of all sorts. Even the most innocuous, like musical clubs, were outlawed by the Nazi government, for example, because they were organized "for purposes, however innocent, that did not reflect those of the central government." Current theorists like Peter Berger, drawing on such work, have maintained that communal groups create a bulwark against the discontents and dangers of modern life. "The best defenses against the threat are those institutions, however weakened, which still give a measure of stability to private life. These are, precisely, the mediating institutions, notably those of family, church, voluntary association, neighborhood and subculture."[5]

But in Berger's perspective, like that of other neoconservatives, such smaller-scale settings are seen entirely in static, narrow, and defensive ways. For order and stability, one must have a generally accepted pattern of "morality," and such morality can only be taught effectively through experiences close to home. "Without mediating structures, the political order is [unsettled] by being deprived of the moral foundation upon which it rests." Thus, Berger sees change and social upheaval as a function of the weakness or disappearance of community institutions. Such a solely defensive perspective, ironically, produces a political and social vision which contributes to the erosion of the very community institutions neoconservatives purport to support. In a view like Berger's, every community is ultimately left on its own. Government becomes simply "the problem." And the marketplace and acquisitive individualism become the measure of "public" life. Such a perspective offers no model of collective action to regain control over massive economic dislocations, from plant closings to toxic waste dumps, nor any notion of how different communities might join together to pursue a common good.[6]

In mainstream liberal and left-wing thought, as well as neoconservative approaches, the emphasis has been on the ways voluntary associations and communal ties undergird and stabilize the status quo. Douglas Kellner summarized the usual argument: "[Dominant] ideology is transmitted through an ideological apparatus consisting of the family, school, church, media, workplace and social group." Thus, the left tends to see the delegitimization of such associations as the necessary prerequisite for progressive action. The notion of the collectivity is a solidarity based upon rational association by "masses": individuals whose ties to their communal roots of place, religion, ethnicity, and so forth have become sundered. The good social order is imagined, as John Rawls recently put it, as "a voluntary scheme [whose] members are autonomous and the obligations they recognize self-imposed." Such a vision of abstractly conceived individuals, in turn, is easily absorbed into an abstract "public" realm, defined as the state.[7]

Thus, a fascinating convergence of views, left and right, about such voluntary groups exists. Conservatives believed in defending voluntary, autonomous groups against the force of the modern state (though they slighted capitalism's impact on such structures). Radicals have tended to see their disruption as necessary for the creation of cosmopolitan consciousness. But both traditions have defined such institutions as bulwarks of the existing order.

Thinkers on both sides overlook the dynamic character of communal spaces. Under certain conditions, communal associations become free spaces, breeding grounds for democratic change. Indeed, the historical evidence now suggests that popular movements with enduring power and depth always find their strength in community-based associations. As sociologist Craig Calhoun has put it, "communities give people the 'interests' for which they will risk their lives—family, friends, customary crafts, and ways of life."[8]*

Thus, for instance, the new labor history demonstrates clearly that people draw upon a range of ethnic, kinship, religious, and other traditional relations in fighting back and in developing a collective consciousness: even within the factory, people are never merely "workers," and other aspects of their identities

*Throughout *Free Spaces* "community" is intended as a concept suggesting density and texture of a relationship. Thus, though community in this sense most often has a spatial dimension—a "neighborhood" implication—such a dimension is not part of the definition; rather, communal ties depend on a complex set of social relationships that overlap and reinforce each other. Craig Calhoun has characterized community in these terms as meaning a "greater 'closeness' of relations" than is true for society as a whole. "This closeness seems to imply, though not rigidly, face-to-face contact, commonality of purpose, familiarity and dependability." Craig Calhoun, "Community: Toward a Variable Conceptualization for Comparative Research," *Social History* 5 (January 1980): 111.

prove centrally important. In turn, capitalist development has, indeed, fragmented such identities, distancing workplace from community life. Such fragmentation has reinforced and facilitated the growth of large-scale, bureaucratized unions and political parties, which normally work carefully within the framework of the system and see their members largely as clients, not active participants. One strong theme in democratic movements, as we approach the present day, in fact, has thus been the repair and revitalization of memories, communal ties, and voluntary associations weakened by modern corporate and bureaucratic institutions. The labor protests of the 1930s, the civil rights movement of the 1960s, and the farm workers' movements of recent years all have had, as an essential component, "bringing our country back to the wells of democracy," as Martin Luther King described the purpose of the sit-in demonstrators.

Our concern in *Free Spaces* has been to understand the ways in which the defensive and limited impulses which spark most social protests, especially in their early stages, can be transformed into democratic initiatives. What are the features of the environments in which people discover their capacities to overcome deferential patterns of behavior, outgrow parochialisms of class, race, or sex, and form a broader conception of the common good? How do people develop new visions in which elements of tradition become resources for democratic activity?

In the course of *democratic* movements, as a people move into action, they change. They discover in themselves and in their ways of life new democratic potentials. They find out new political facts about the world. They build networks and seek contacts with other groups of the powerless to forge a broader group identity. In turn, for such processes to occur requires more than local, communal roots. Such spaces must also be relatively autonomous, free from elite control.

Thus, the *voluntary* aspect of such community environments is an important element. Unstructured by the imperatives of large and bureaucratic organizations, communal groups that people own themselves allow them to rework ideas and themes from the dominant culture in ways which bring forth hidden and potentially subversive dimensions. Thus, black churches have served as the organizational and visionary heart of the movement from slavery to civil rights. There, black ministers were able to draw on insurgent, populist themes within the very Christian tradition that had been taught to slaves as a method of pacification.

, Some social spaces have a long history of autonomy. Within them, collective action seems almost as natural as breathing. Groups which have had little experience of collective strength and self-confidence, however, remain vulnerable to manipulation by demagogic appeals. Their democratic self-consciousness —not only of themselves but of themselves in egalitarian relation to other powerless groups—is weak. Among lower-class southern whites, for example, where voluntary associations and communal life remained largely under elite control, movement culture in the Knights of Labor or the populist cooperatives depended upon newly created free spaces. The defeat of these movements, in large part because of successful elite manipulation of racist traditions in the South, cut off a historical process of self-discovery that had only begun. By contrast, where free social spaces were deeply embedded in community life—as in the Richmond black community—the Knights of Labor served as a catalyst to bring the mobilized power of the community onto a stage of broader action.

With the emergence of enormous institutions of government and economic life in the twentieth century, the difficulties in maintaining autonomy have taken new form. Government programs, the lure of subsidies, commercialized packaging of candidates, corporate grants, the mass media—all such pressures can severely erode the freedom of action and initiative possessed by voluntary associations, and can obscure the broader civic and democratic implications of civic involvement. Yet in the very different environment of 1960s activism, young organizers at times also gained an understanding of the need for free space that recalled the insights of activists a century or more earlier. Casey Hayden, a young white southerner who spent years working in the civil rights movement, argued in 1965:

> I think we've learned a few things about building and sustaining a radical movement: People need institutions that belong to them, that they can experiment with and shape. In that process it's possible to develop new forms for activity which can provide new models for how people can work together so participants can think radically about how society could operate. People stay involved and working when they can see the actual results of their thought and work in the organization. . . .[9]

Finally, movements also require means for developing a broader public vision and sense of the common good. While certain forms of older divisions, like ethnic cleavages, may no longer be as sharply etched, new problems stand in the way of any broader sense of community. Many traditional public meeting places, from village town square to neighborhood grocer, have largely disappeared. Citizens have few ways to talk about public values and purposes across their immediate lines of friendship and private life. On the one hand, in "normal" times mass culture imposes a chilling silence on public discussion. Politics resembles a "marketplace" where citizens become consumers and are encouraged to think of themselves in the most narrowly self-interested of terms. On the other hand, in times of widespread social unrest like the 1960s, the weakening of deep communities and communal discourse can lead to a rapid commercialization and trivialization of protest, where "media stars" and rapidly shifting political fashion replace deliberation and responsible democratic politics.*

*Todd Gitlin examines this phenomenon in detail in his work on the student movement, *The Whole World Is Watching: Mass Media in the Making and Unmaking of the New Left* (Berkeley: University of California Press, 1980). "The media brings a manufactured public world into private space," Gitlin argues. "From within their private crevices, people find themselves relying on the media for concepts, for images . . . for guiding information, for emotional charges, for a recognition of public values, for symbols in general, even for language" (pp. 1–2). Gitlin, however, neglects the role of free spaces as an

Communal roots and independence are insufficient to generate Walt Whitman's large-spirited and generous citizenry. Indeed, authoritarian and parochial protests—the Ku Klux Klan,
book burnings, religiously bigoted movements and the like—
also emerge from communal settings where people have capacity for independent action. Thus, democratic action today, as in
the past, also depends upon an open and participatory public
life that can bring together diverse communities and nourish
the values of citizenship. The richness and vitality of public life
in free spaces stands in marked contrast to the static and thin
quality of "public" in reactionary protests.

"The reabsorption of government by the citizens of a democratic community," Lewis Mumford once wrote, "is the only
safeguard against those bureaucratic interventions that tend to
arise in every state." Democratic movements have always expressed this sensibility—in contrast to the conventional assumptions that "public" and "government" are virtually identical.
They have seen government as properly the agency and instrument of the self-organized community, neither itself the problem (as conservative ideology tends to view it) nor the solution
(the typical perspective of modern liberalism). Thus, for instance, as the nineteenth-century Knights of Labor engaged in
electoral activity, they understood such involvement to be an
expression of values and community life, not as an end in itself.[10]

For a well-developed consciousness of broader community
and generalized, active citizenship to emerge requires ways for
people to build direct, face-to-face and egalitarian relationships,
beyond their immediate circles of friends and smaller communities. Thus, a prelude to democratic movement, visible in
different times and settings, has been the emergence of ave-

intermediate place between private identities and large-scale institutions.
When free space has deep roots in ongoing "communities of memory and hope"
—as in the black church base of the civil rights movement, for example—
movements are much more resistant to media fads and rapidly changing fash-
ions, and the possibilities for serious alternative media are far greater.

nues for wider sociability. From the Hicksite Quakers and female abolition networks to benevolent societies in Richmond's
black community or the large-scale ethnic associations in Steelton which laid the groundwork for the steelworkers' unionization, such associations create a consciousness that many people
can act together. Moreover, when public arenas that allow active participation become politicized in the context of changing
conditions, they offer broad opportunities for the acquisition
and development of basic skills of public life. People learn to
speak in public, run meetings, analyze problems and their
sources, write leaflets, and so forth—the sorts of skills that are
essential to sustaining democracy.

As democratic movements develop, they create movement
institutions and networks that generate still more inclusive understandings of "the people." The Women's Christian Temperance Union, the Knights of Labor, and the Farmers' Alliances
in the nineteenth century found counterparts in twentieth-
century movement institutions such as the CIO in the 1930s,
the Southern Christian Leadership Conference, and the Students for a Democratic Society in the 1960s. The public life that
emerges out of such networks constitutes an alternative movement culture, an identifying feature of democratic movements.
Movement cultures have been visible in the lecture circuits,
newspapers, and mass encampments of the 1890s Populists, the
celebrations, labor press, and labor education schools of the
1930s, the Freedom Schools of civil rights, and the alternative
institutions of the women's movement, alike. In movement cultures, a newly open and vital intellectual life takes hold. Alternative media, like newspapers, magazines, and movement
schools, offer forums for new ideas and an ongoing process of
movement education. Diversity and difference may help people simultaneously to experiment with novel and unorthodox
ideas and to think differently about their histories and traditions. They unearth buried insurgent elements in their own
traditions, find out new facts about the world, debate alternatives, develop a vision of the common good that transcends
limited and particular interests.

The nature of free social space also shapes specific leadership styles, with powerful consequences for social movements. From the time of slavery, the black church served as the training ground for black leaders, creating a unique, powerful, and largely male rhetorical style. The charismatic tones of the preacher, from Andrew Bryan to Jesse Jackson, have led hundreds of diverse struggles. Yet the dispersed nature of black churches and religious associations also guaranteed the constant production of new leaders, curbing in some ways the antidemocratic dimensions of charisma. By way of contrast, populist movements, whose underlying culture had little opportunity to develop such strengths, proved vulnerable to the manipulation of a long line of southern demagogues, from Ben Tillman to George Wallace.

Leaders have played crucial roles in articulating the democratic and empowering threads within the American ideological heritage. Republicanism and the biblical themes of justice, community, and equality have provided democratic resources for an extraordinary range of movements. At the same time, such traditions also provide the ideological underpinning of antidemocratic impulses. For example, the right-wing version of republicanism justifies unbridled economic individualism and greed, just as biblical themes can be used by those who advocate racial and sexual subordination. The appropriation of democratic possibility depends on the collective experience we have identified with free social spaces. Simply, democratic ideas only make sense in the context of democratic experience. When people begin to see in themselves the capacity to end their own hurts, to take control of their lives, they gain the capacity to tap the democratic resources in their heritage. Thus, workers drew on biblical, artisanal, and republican traditions throughout the nineteenth century and on ethnic cultures shaped to the new environments of urban, industrial America. The separation of home and work spaces made the existence of community institutions such as taverns, churches, reading rooms, clubs, and other groups all the more essential in order to create a vocabulary in opposition to the emerging industrial order, with its focus on individual achievement and consumption. That women were excluded from most of these spaces, that few environments permitted much cross-cultural sharing, that republican traditions themselves were filled with contradictions —all represented limitations on democracy.

The richness and complexity of these processes has become apparent to a new generation of social historians, exploring the lives and experiences of those whom traditional historical approaches largely overlooked. As Gerda Lerner noted some time ago, "The very term 'Women's History' calls attention to the fact that something is missing from historical scholarship, and it aims to document and reinterpret that which is missing."[11]

But the broader implications have yet to be explored in detail. Conventional social-science approaches to the study of social movements normally assume that there is no analytical difference between democratic and nondemocratic movements, and thus manage to obliterate the issue. Even when the question of democratic participation is posed, themes of citizenship, "citizenship education," and the common good are rarely explored. Conservatives and leftists, convinced that the communal associations of daily life represent bulwarks of the status quo, fail to see the sources of democratic change. None of these perspectives can comprehend the tragedy built into the logic of many social movements throughout modern history. As social movement leaders over time became distanced from the communal foundations of democratic revolt, and adopted dominant categories and vocabularies of change that rendered the experiences in such foundations largely invisible, they often forgot or dismissed the very histories that had shaped them, thus hastening the process of bureaucratization and incorporation of protest into the language and terms of modern, centralized authority.

Yet the processes of communal transformation that generate democratic change continue to grow in modern America, sometimes despite great difficulties. These "experiments in democracy" regenerate community and create a space linking public activity and private identities that also has an integrity and specific existence of its own. They maintain some measure of autonomy, and revive notions of citizenship and civic virtue. Most free spaces remain embedded in the institutions of daily life: voluntary groups, religious congregations, union locals, schools, neighborhoods. Others represent new experiments, redefining communities and asking new questions about the past. Whether their insurgent and visionary possibilities will be realized remains impossible to predict, but it is important to recognize the existence of these free spaces, and to develop an understanding of democracy that appreciates their crucial role in reviving active citizenship and conceptions of the common good.

A public housing project in St. Louis provides one dramatic example of community renewal leading to broadened forms of civic involvement. This area in St. Louis is perhaps most famous for Pruitt Iago, a housing project so violent, filthy, and damaged that the city decided to blow up the buildings, erasing its existence. Cochran Gardens was an older project in the same area of the city, also a high-rise, with many of the same problems. By the 1960s, its tenants were all black and the city housing authority had virtually abandoned its maintenance responsibilities. Terrorism by youthful gangs, alcoholics, and drug addicts shaped tenants' lives. Killings were common. Graffiti covered the walls, and elevators reeked of urine. Social workers, service companies, even the police feared to go there. Cochran Gardens was a prime candidate for demolition.

Yet today Cochran Gardens is meticulously clean. Its twelve-story high-rise buildings have been renovated according to plans developed by committees of residents working with architects and planners. Playgrounds were moved, for example, to locations that could be observed from within the apartments. A senior-citizens' building has its own small enclosed play area for visiting grandchildren. Green grass and flowerbeds have replaced dirt, mud, and broken glass. Hallways are always freshly swept, each family taking their allotted turn.

Behind these surface evidences of order and mutual respect lies the story of a community that reclaimed itself. Today Cochran Gardens is tenant run. A tenant manager lives in each building. Tenant councils decide and enforce policies for admission, standards of behavior, and plans for the future. Tenants run several day-care centers, programs to bring together the elderly and the young, food service companies to provide meals for seniors and day-care, a security service, and a new community center. It all started when Bertha Gilkey, herself a young mother on welfare who had grown up in Cochran Gardens, began to organize in a single building. Their first victory was the installation of a laundry washer in an abandoned first-floor apartment. They celebrated with a ribbon cutting and party. Then she organized tenants, floor by floor, to paint their hallways. Gilkey remembered the days when Cochran was a safe and clean and friendly place to live. She was determined to convey that memory, and to see tenants gain control over those forces which had rendered them helpless and dependent. As people began to win specific victories, looking to each other for strength and support, they came to share the vision. And their participation led to active involvement with other poor communities around the country.

Bertha Gilkey now serves as national co-chair of the National Congress of Neighborhood Women, a different kind of experiment. An organization of women in an ethnic, blue-collar area of Brooklyn with affiliates in several cities, the National Congress has consistently avoided taking stands on issues which many see as basic to feminism as conventionally conceived, such as the Equal Rights Amendment and abortion. It began in 1974 when Jan Peterson and other feminists sought to extend the women's movement to working-class and poor women in a manner that would respect their high commitment to neighborhood and family.[12]

As the organization became ethnically more diverse and began to place a positive value on that diversity, organizers developed a sharing process which extends in new directions the notion that "the personal is political." At NCNW meetings and conferences, "identity groups"—defined as participants choose to do so—meet to discuss the meaning of their shared heritage, both the hard parts and the positive dimensions. Each group then presents to the whole what they would like others to know about themselves and their culture. The result is a series of histories: the spiritual values of traditional Lakota culture and their long history of resistance against the loss of their land, their hunting economy, and their sacred places; the racial diversity of Puerto Rico and the importance of Spanish as a mother tongue; the experiences of Italian immigrants on Ellis Island; the historic strength of black women in their communities. And in each case there is also an explanation of the pain caused by stereotyping: the Mafia jokes, the blame heaped on "black matriarchs," the combination of romanticism and disrespect for Native Americans in our popular culture. The impact for many participants is a rediscovery of the bonds among women in a context which does not require the shedding of other identities. For Bertha Gilkey, involvement in the National Congress revealed the feminist dimension of her work. Most of the residents in Cochran Gardens are women. The movement they organized was led by women, and today women occupy most positions of leadership. This recognition also broadened their sense of who could be their allies.[13]

The growth of numerous neighborhood and citizen efforts in recent years that transcend barriers of parochialism, defensiveness, and powerlessness are other instances of free space. The reclaiming and redefinition of citizen participation in public life is evident, for instance, in what has come to be called "value-based community organizing." This method adapts participatory understandings of democracy to the dilemmas of modern culture and the era of large-scale institutions like government and corporations, recognizing as problematic such terms as "community," "tradition," and "public life." In recent years, such groups as the Communities Organized for Public Service in San Antonio, East Brooklyn Churches, the San Francisco

Organizing Project, and others have linked particular issues of concern to their members with extensive processes of community renewal, value discussion, and "citizenship education."

Ernesto Cortes, the first organizer of Communities Organized for Public Service (COPS), distinguished between "self-interest" and "narrow self-interest," or selfishness." He argued that people's basic concerns are not only financial or narrowly for themselves but also include communal ties such as the happiness of their families, the well-being of their neighbors and friends, the vitality of their faith and their traditions, and their own feelings of dignity and worth. Workshops that Cortes and others in COPS have conducted reflect on the communal and civic values people learn from American democratic traditions, their churches and neighborhoods—participation, pluralism, civic involvement, the dignity of the individual, equality, community, love of neighbor, concern for poor. People talk about the ways in which such values are constantly undermined by the dominant principles of corporations, large bureaucracies, and the mass culture. And COPS combines such value and ideological discussion with a tremendously detailed process of what they call "citizenship education," teaching tens of thousands of people the basics of running meetings, analyzing problems, dealing with the press, conducting research, and planning campaigns around issues.

COPS defines itself as a new sort of "public arena" that in many ways is self-conscious of the dimensions of "free space." COPS sees itself reflecting the values of the democratic tradition and the Judeo-Christian heritage, and it advances the concrete needs of families, neighborhoods, congregations, and individuals. But is also takes on an independent life of its own, different from private life, on the one hand, or large "public" institutions, on the other hand. Though it intervenes with remarkable effectiveness in the political process—COPS has won more than $400 million in community development projects in the Mexican communities, mounting an extraordinary challenge to traditional political and economic elites in the process

—it makes a clear distinction between its notion of political involvement and "politics as usual." COPS, according to Cortes, "is like a university where people come to learn about public policy, public discourse, and public life."[14]

The result has been not only material changes in the barrios but also changes in mood and spirit. Leaders speak about the "cultural changes" they have seen, as people have come to value the broader community good and ask what areas of town are most in need of aid. Young people increasingly remain, rather than fleeing for the northern areas of town. Women have taken on unprecedented leadership roles, including the last several presidencies of the organization. Individual congregations have seen a democratization of their internal life, with lay leaders emerging in every aspect. This sort of activity, making affirmation of democratic values integral to its definition, begins to repair bonds that have been gravely weakened by mass culture and economic pressure.[15]

The COPS model of community renewal, citizenship, and cultural revitalization has begun to have significant impact elsewhere in the organizing world. For example, the San Francisco Organizing Project (SFOP) has applied such techniques to the heterogeneous communities of the Bay Area. The organizing effort began with in-depth community renewal and work on issues in specific congregations, community groups, and labor union locals. In parishes like St. Elizabeth's, for example, a largely white ethnic area in the southeast section of the city, congregation members were trained to interview residents in the neighborhood about their concerns and problems, whether or not they were Catholic. Through such interviews they developed a detailed sense of community issues and created ties to people who were all but invisible. Workshops on values gave people a unique chance to talk to others, often for the first time in any public setting, about what had been troubling them. "One day, we had fifty people show up for a brainstorming session that lasted five hours," related one woman. "We talked about what we believe in—our families, neighborhoods, love, respect for each other, being tolerant. And we talked about what threatened those values. Large corporations. How much of society today is being run by media hype. How can you bombard children with all of this and not have them buy into it?" For some months people held such discussions and others on concrete organizational skills, and combined them with work on particular issues like the uses of an abandoned school building. Then the parish held a large convention. It recognized and celebrated different groups in the community, and made decisions about priority areas for action.[16]

This kind of organizing process not only involved traditional community "activists," but as in the case of COPS and similar groups, it built directly upon the core leaders involved in sustaining and renewing community life. These are the people—often women—who work, frequently behind the scenes, to keep the PTAs going, to organize block parties, to run children's sports activities, and so forth. Value-based organizing gives such community leaders new skills, support, and public recognition, changing the very definitions of "leadership" and "public" in the process. Moreover, in the context of a pluralist and diversified organizing effort like SFOP's, such organizing introduces people to other communities in ways that allow serious dialogue.

Nationally, citizen initiatives have now resulted in efforts like Citizen Action, a diverse coalition of community, labor union, senior citizen, rural, environmental, and other groups which defines itself as a "new democratic populism." Since its formation in late 1979, Citizen Action has developed a presence in twenty-five states, and has played a key organizing role in campaigns from toxic waste and farm foreclosure to energy prices and plant shutdowns. Indeed, the changing economic and political environment of the 1980s has tended to generate this sort of larger-scale coalition, in ways that may presage the formation of new citizen movements. "It's a very different time than when I started out organizing ten years ago," recounted Robert Hudak, Citizen Action's field director, in 1985. "In the 1970s, if your community group had a problem you'd go to the county board. They made a decision and it made a difference in people's lives." But Hudak had seen a rapidly growing recognition that coalitions are the only possible way to win against intransigent opposition. "You take a local dump site activist who's been concerned about kids being poisoned by toxic waste. They go to the bureaucracy and get a runaround. It's very easy for them to understand that the only way this sort of problem is really going to be solved is if the government clamps down on corporations and establishes a cleanup fund."[17]

In sum, the historical and contemporary record calls for a new attentiveness to the life of rooted communities themselves, whose institutions are the foundation and wellspring for any sustained challenge to autocratic power. It is through the structures of community life, which sustain and reproduce a group's shared bonds of historical memory and culture, that an oppressed people begin to come to self-consciousness. Through their activity in new contexts, groups may acquire public skills, reinforce democratic values, and form new links between subcommunities into larger networks and organizations. And it is through such processes that a powerless people constitutes itself as a force for democratic transformation of the broader social structure and as a school for its own education in a democratic sensibility. Loss of organic connection to the communal sources of social movement can lead to the amorphous and rootless stridency of the late new left on the one hand, or to the bureaucratic stagnation apparent in many contemporary trade unions on the other.

Yet the evidence also draws attention to the *complexity* of community life, and the relative powerlessness of communities by themselves, from a democratic perspective. If democratic movements necessarily draw their strength, vision, and power from communitarian settings, these also limit the nature of such movements. Leaders, organizational forms, and broader strategies may help movements overcome parochialism and ethnocentrism, may expand the democratic processes within the group life, may make the decisive difference in how effectively the movement influences the broader society. But the requirement for such developments is a willingness to admit and address communities' limitations, as well as a respect for communities' importance.

In present-day America, recognition of both the centrality and the limitations of communities assumes no small urgency. Where are the places in our culture through which people sustain bonds and history? What are the processes through which they may broaden their sense of the possible, make alliances with others, develop the practical skills and knowledge to maintain democratic organization? What are the languages of protest, dissent, and change that express moral and communal themes in inclusive ways that reach beyond particular boundaries of race, ethnicity, gender, and class? Such questions confer the dignity of historical authorship upon ordinary people.

Finally, democratic movements, drawing their spirit from voluntary associations of all sorts, have not only sought structural changes to realize a wider, more inclusive and participatory "democracy." From the commonwealth vision of the WCTU, the Knights of Labor, and the nineteenth-century Populists, to the Citizenship Schools of the Southern Christian Leadership Conference in the 1960s and the citizenship education programs in community groups today, such movements have also illustrated the inextricable links between participation and citizenship. Thus, such movements, and the free spaces at their heart, suggest the need for a basic reworking of conventional ideas about "public life" and "democracy." They call attention to that vast middle ground of communal activity, between private life and large-scale institutions, as the arenas in which notions of civic virtue and a sense of responsibility for the common good are nourished, and democracy is given living meaning. And they remind us, repeatedly, how ordinary people can discover who they are and take democratic initiatives, on their own terms.

SOURCE NOTES

1: "The People Shall Rule"

1. Judge quoted from Vincent Harding, *There Is a River: The Black Freedom Struggle in America* (New York: Harcourt, 1981), p. 71.

2. Royas quoted from ibid., p. 72.

3. Ibid., pp. 43, 60–61.

4. John Cobbs, "Egalitarianism: The Corporation as Villain," *Business Week,* Dec. 15, 1975.

5. Aristotle and Plato quoted in Raymond Williams, *Keywords: A Vocabulary of Culture and Society* (New York: Oxford, 1976), p. 83.

6. Ball and Winstanley quoted in George Woodcock, "Democracy, Heretical and Radical," in C. George Benello and Dimitrios Roussopoulos, eds., *The Case for Participatory Democracy: Some Prospects for a Radical Society* (New York: Viking, 1971), pp. 16, 18.

7. Dickinson quoted in Herbert McClosky and Alida Brill, "Citizenship," in *Russell Sage Foundation Report Program Areas* (New York: Russell Sage Foundation, 1977), p. 87; Marsiglio of Padua quoted in ibid., p. 91.

8. Williams, *Keywords,* p. 84.

9. For useful recent discussions of the concept of citizenship, see for instance Robert N. Bellah, Richard Madsen, William M. Sullivan, Ann Swidler, and Steven M. Tipton, *Habits of the Heart: Individualism and Commitment in American Life* (Berkeley: University of California Press, 1985), chaps. 7–10; "The Democratic Citizen," *democracy* 2 (Fall 1982); Ralph Dahrendorf, "Citizenship and Beyond: The Social Dynamics of an Idea," *Social Research* 41 (Winter 1974): 673–701; Robert Nisbet, "Citizenship: Two Traditions," *Social Research* 41 (Winter 1974): 612–37; Carole Pateman, *Participation and Democratic Theory* (Cambridge: Cambridge University Press, 1970); J. G. A. Pocock, *The Machiavellian Moment: Florentine Political Thought and the Atlantic Republican Tradition* (Princeton: Princeton University Press, 1975), and "The Machiavellian Moment Revisited: A Study in History and Ideology," *Journal*

of Modern History 50 (March 1981): 49–72; "Citizenship and Public Administration," *Public Administration Review* 44 (March 1984); Robert Pranger, *The Eclipse of Citizenship: Power and Participation in Contemporary Politics* (New York: Holt, 1968); Michael Walzer, "Civility and Civic Virtue in Contemporary America," *Social Research* 41 (Winter 1974): 593–611.

10. Franklin quoted in Bruce Johansen, *Forgotten Founders: Benjamin Franklin, the Iroquois and the Rationale for the American Revolution* (Ipswich, Mass.: Gambit, 1982). An extensive historiographic discussion and debate has developed in recent years over the influence of republican themes on the American Revolutionary generation. Pocock's work, *The Machiavellian Moment*, remains the classic argument for the centrality of such themes, while Rowland Berthoff, "Peasants and Artisans, Puritans and Republicans," *Journal of American History* 69 (Winter 1982): 579–98, is a splendid summary and an argument about the continuing "subterranean" power of more radical republican themes into the twentieth century. For critical perspectives, see for example Joyce Appleby, "Ideology and Theory: The Tension Between Political and Economic Liberalism in Seventeenth-Century England," *American Historical Review* 81 (June 1976), and "Jefferson: A Political Reappraisal," *democracy* 3 (Fall 1983); and, most recently, John P. Diggins, *The Lost Soul of American Politics: Virtue, Self Interest and the Foundations of Liberalism* (New York: Basic, 1985).

11. Jefferson quoted in Johansen, *Founders,* pp. 102, 112.

12. On religious themes of the colonial era and the American Revolution, see for instance Robert N. Bellah, *The Broken Covenant: American Civil Religion in Time of Trial* (New York: Seabury, 1975); chap. 1, Bellah, et al., *Habits,* chap. 9. Winthrop quoted in *Newsweek,* special issue on "The Bible in America," Dec. 27, 1982.

13. For a discussion of this aspect of Puritanism, see, e.g., Sheldon Wolin, "America's Civil Religion," *democracy* 2 (April 1982): 7–18.

14. Emerson quoted in Larzer Ziff, "Sloven Continent: Emerson and an American Idea," *democracy* 1 (April 1981): 128, 136. Robert Bellah discusses Emerson's views on individualism at length in "The Quest for the Self: Individualism, Morality, Politics," a paper delivered at the Claremont Institute Conference "Democracy in America: Alexis de Tocqueville Observes the New Order," Claremont, California, Jan. 23–26, 1985.

15. Hamilton quoted in Vernon Louis Parrington, *Main Currents in American Thought: An Interpretation of American Literature from the Beginnings to 1920* (New York: Harcourt, 1927), vol. 1, pp. 298, 302.

16. Ibid., vol. 2, p. 79. Gilder quoted from *Democratic Visions: Progressives and the American Heritage* (Minneapolis: Citizen Heritage Center report #1, 1981), p. 14.

17. Lippmann quoted in William A. Schambra, *The Quest for Community and the Quest for a New Public Philosophy* (Washington, D.C.: American Enterprise Institute, 1983), p. 5; Leon Fink, *Workingmen's Democ-*

racy: The Knights of Labor and American Politics (Urbana: University of Illinois Press, 1983), p. 34.

18. Lippmann in Schambra, *Quest,* p. 5.

19. Herbert Croly, *The Promise of American Life* (New York: Macmillan, 1909), p. 139; Taylor in Schambra, *Quest,* p. 8.

20. Croly, *Promise,* p. 453.

21. C. B. Macpherson, *The Political Theory of Possessive Individualism* (New York: Oxford, 1964), and *The Life and Times of Liberal Democracy* (Oxford: Oxford University Press, 1977); and, in a similar vein, Carole Pateman, *Participation and Democratic Theory* (London: Cambridge University Press, 1970).

22. See, e.g., Peter L. Berger, *Facing Up to Modernity: Excursions in Society, Politics and Religion* (New York: Basic, 1977), and Frances Fox Piven and Richard A. Cloward, *Poor People's Movements: Why They Succeed, How They Fail* (New York: Pantheon, 1977). Piven and Cloward, *Movements,* p. 26. For a useful recent overview of social movement theory, see Craig Jenkins, "Resource Mobilization Theory and the Study of Social Movements," *Annual Review of Sociology* 9 (1983): 527–53; also Jo Freeman, "On the Origins of Social Movements," in Jo Freeman, ed., *The Social Movements of the Sixties and Seventies* (New York: Longman, 1983), pp. 8–30.

23. Grimké, in Alice Rossi, ed., *The Feminist Papers: From Adams to de Beauvoir* (New York: Columbia University Press, 1973), p. 308; Nicholas Salvatore, *Eugene Debs: Citizen and Socialist* (Urbana: University of Illinois Press, 1981), p. 60; Martin Luther King, Jr., *Why We Can't Wait* (New York: Harper, 1963), p. 99.

24. The story of the General Assembly is taken from Peter Jay Rachleff, "Black, White, and Gray: Working-Class Activism in Richmond, Virginia, 1865–1890" (Ph.D. dissertation, University of Pittsburgh, 1981), pp. 788–91; Mullen's speech, 789–91.

25. Rachleff, ibid., p. 747.

2: Crossing the Jordan

1. Vincent Harding, *There Is a River: The Black Struggle for Freedom in America* (New York: Harcourt, 1981), p. 62.

2. Kardiner and Ovesey quoted in Lawrence W. Levine, *Black Culture and Black Consciousness: Afro-American Folk Thought from Slavery to Freedom* (New York: Oxford, 1977), p. 442. Stanley Elkins, quoted in Herbert G. Gutman, *The Black Family in Slavery and Freedom, 1750–1925* (New York: Pantheon, 1976), p. 306.

3. Levine, *Black Culture,* p. xi; Gutman, *Black Family,* p. 103.

4. Gutman, op. cit., p. 217.

5. George Fredrickson makes this point about family relationships in his review essay, "The Gutman Report," *New York Review of Books,* Sept. 30, 1976, pp. 18–27.

6. Eugene Genovese, *Roll, Jordan, Roll: The World the Slaves Made* (New York: Pantheon, 1972), p. 188.

7. Ibid., p. 236; Levine, *Black Culture*, p. 41; Carrol in Gayraud Wilmore, *Black Religion and Black Radicalism* (Garden City, N.Y.: Doubleday, 1972), p. 65.

8. Wilmore, op. cit., p. 17; Genovese, *Roll, Jordan,* pp. 246–249; Albert J. Raboteau, *Slave Religion: The "Invisible Institution" in the Antebellum South* (New York: Oxford University Press, 1978) has an excellent detailed description of such techniques. See especially chap. 5, "Religious Life in the Slave Community."

9. Wilmore, *Black Religion,* p. 45.

10. Lester quoted in Genovese, *Roll, Jordan,* p. 253; Levine, *Black Culture,* p. 44.

11. Genovese, *Roll, Jordan,* p. 257–58, 199; Wilmore, *Black Religion,* pp. 70–72, 105–6.

12. Wilmore, *Black Religion,* p. 104.

13. Harding, *River,* pp. 45–56.

14. Ibid., pp. 44–45.

15. Wilmore, *Black Religion,* pp. 79–86.

16. *Times* (Charleston, South Carolina), in ibid., p. 83; see also, Harding, *River,* p. 66.

17. Harding, *River,* pp. 66–69.

18. "Walker's Appeal" described in Wilmore, *Black Religion,* pp. 53–60, 75–93; also, Harding, *River,* pp. 86–94.

19. Harding, *River,* p. 102.

20. Gary Nash, *Red, White and Black: The Peoples of Early America* (Englewood Cliffs, N.J.: Prentice-Hall, 1974), p. 192; Harding, *River,* p. 111.

21. Soldier quoted from Eric Foner, "The Hidden History of Emancipation," *New York Review of Books,* Mar. 1, 1984, p. 39.

22. Harding, *River,* pp. 278–79.

23. Ibid., p. 265.

24. Description of Richmond parade from Peter Jay Rachleff, "Black, White, and Gray: Working-Class Activism in Richmond, Virginia, 1865–1890" (Ph.D. dissertation, University of Pittsburgh, 1981), p. 243.

25. Peter J. Rachleff, *Black Labor in the South: Richmond, Virginia, 1865–1890* (Philadelphia: Temple University Press, 1984), pp. 4, 35.

26. Rachleff, "Black, White, and Gray," pp. 18–33; quote from p. 28.

27. Rachleff, *Black Labor,* pp. 13–14.

28. Ibid., pp. 35–37.

29. Ibid., pp. 94–95; also, Rachleff, "Black, White, and Gray," pp. 518–56.

30. Rachleff, *Black Labor,* pp. 81–82.

31. Ibid., pp. 86–108.

32. Ibid., pp. 94–98.

33. Ibid., p. 105.

34. Ibid., pp. 104–8.

35. Mahalia Jackson, "The Strength of the Negro Mother," in Gerda

Lerner, ed., *Black Women in White America: A Documentary History* (New York: Pantheon Books, 1972), pp. 584–85.

36. Levine, *Black Culture*, pp. 138–58; Chase, p. 141; Towne, 141; Levine, 143, 158.

37. Maya Angelou in Levine, p. 154.

38. Anderson and Dorsey quoted in ibid., pp. 185–86.

39. Aldon Morris, *The Origins of the Civil Rights Movement: Black Communities Organizing for Change* (New York: Free Press, 1984), p. 98.

40. On economic changes in the rural South, Anthony Oberschall, *Social Conflict and Social Movements* (Englewood Cliffs, N.J.: Prentice-Hall, 1973), pp. 205–9.

41. Morris, *Origins*, pp. 7–9, 79–80; Oberschall, *Conflict*, pp. 209–11.

42. Oberschall, ibid., pp. 205–7, 216; Lomax quoted 219–20.

43. Stephen B. Oates, *Let the Trumpet Sound: The Life of Martin Luther King, Jr.* (New York: Harper & Row, 1982), pp. 62–63.

44. Ibid., p. 12.

45. Ibid., pp. 19–20.

46. Harvey Cox, *Religion in the Secular City* (New York: Simon & Schuster, 1983), pp. 164, 177.

47. King's theological development and views are discussed in detail in Oates, *Trumpet*, pp. 25–41.

48. Ibid., pp. 57–59; Oberschall, *Conflict*, pp. 126–127.

49. Oates, *Trumpet*, pp. 63–65

50. Nixon quoted in Oates, p. 68; also, on politics of King's election and parallels in other cities, Morris, *Origins*, pp. 43–44.

51. Oates, *Trumpet*, p. 69.

52. King's speech in ibid., p. 71.

53. King's observations in ibid., pp. 72–73.

54. Mayor's comments, old Mother Pollard, black leader's comments, Juliette Morgan's letter, in ibid., pp. 76–77.

55. White judge and racist handbill, in ibid., p. 91.

56. King's observations on his tour in ibid., p. 99.

57. Ibid., pp. 103–4.

58. The creation of SCLC is described in detail in Morris, *Origins*, pp. 82–99. Abernathy quoted, p. 94; Baker quoted, pp. 103–4, 112.

59. Black women's role in the civil rights movement is described in Sara M. Evans, *Personal Politics: The Origins of Women's Liberation in the Civil Rights Movement and the New Left* (New York: Knopf, 1979), pp. 39–41; 51–53. Sherrod quoted pp. 51–52; and Jacqueline Jones, *Labor of Love, Labor of Sorrow: Black Women, Work and the Family from Slavery to the Present* (New York: Basic, 1985), pp. 275–301.

60. Citizenship Education and SCLC's program are described in Morris, *Origins*, pp. 149–57, and 236–37. Morris, p. 49; Cotton, p. 239. For a detailed description of the Highlander program and its origins, see also Carl Tjerandsen, *Education for Citizenship: A Foundation's Experience* (Santa Cruz: Emil Schwarzhaupt Foundation, 1980), pp. 139–98.

61. Janitor quoted in Oates, *Trumpet,* p. 112; research team study described in Frederick Soloman et al., "Civil Rights Activity and Reduction of Crime Among Negroes," *Archives of General Psychiatry* 12 (March 1965): 227–36.

62. *Time* quoted in Oates, *Trumpet,* p. 254.

63. Pat Watters and Reese Cleghorn, *Climbing Jacob's Ladder: The Arrival of Negroes in Southern Politics* (New York: Harcourt, Brace and World, 1967), p. 6.

64. Oates, *Trumpet,* pp. 288, 251.

3: Beyond the Dictates of Prudence

1. Jean Bethke Elstain, "Feminism, Family, and Community," *Dissent* (Fall 1982): 442–49, quotes from pp. 449, 442; Barbara Ehrenreich, "On Feminism, Family, and Community," *Dissent* (Winter 1983): 103–6, quotes from p. 105; Jean Bethke Elstain, "On Feminism, Family and Community," *Dissent* (Winter 1983): 106–9, quote from p. 107.

2. See Linda Kerber, *Women of the Republic: Intellect and Ideology in Revolutionary America* (Chapel Hill: University of North Carolina Press, 1980); Mary Beth Norton, *Liberty's Daughters: The Revolutionary Experience of American Women, 1750–1800* (Boston: Little, Brown, 1980); Laurel Thatcher Ulrich, *Good Wives: Image and Reality in the Lives of Women in Northern New England, 1650–1750* (New York: Knopf, 1982).

3. Sarah Jay to Catharine Livingston, July 16, 1783, quoted in Kerber, *Women of the Republic,* p. 78.

4. Norton, *Liberty's Daughters,* p. 170.

5. Quote from Kerber, *Women of the Republic,* pp. 104–5; see also Norton, *Liberty's Daughters,* p. 187.

6. Edmund S. Morgan, *The Puritan Family: Religious and Domestic Relations in Seventeenth-Century New England,* rev. ed. (New York: Harper Torchbooks, 1966).

7. See Eric J. Hobsbawm, *The Age of Revolution: 1789–1848* (New York: New American Library, 1962).

8. Charles Brockden Brown quoted in Kerber, *Women of the Republic,* p. 121.

9. Quotes from Jean Bethke Elstain, *Public Man, Private Woman: Women in Social and Political Thought* (Princeton: Princeton University Press, 1981), pp. 162, 165; and Jean Jacques Rousseau in Kerber, *Women of the Republic,* p. 26.

10. Alice Rossi, ed., *The Feminist Papers* (New York: Columbia University Press, 1973), pp. 10–11, 13.

11. Paula Baker, "The Domestication of Politics: Women and American Political Society, 1780–1920," *American Historical Review* 89 (June 1984): 628.

12. Suzanne Lebsock, *The Free Women of Petersburg: Status and Culture in a Southern Town, 1784–1860* (New York: Norton, 1984), p. xix; Carol

Gilligan, *In a Different Voice: Psychological Theory and Women's Development* (Cambridge, Mass.: Harvard University Press, 1982).

13. See Nancy Cott, *Bonds of Womanhood: The Woman's Sphere in New England* (New Haven: Yale University Press, 1977); Kerber, *Women of the Republic;* Keith Melder, *Beginnings of Sisterhood: The American Woman's Rights Movement, 1800–1850* (New York: Schocken, 1977); quote from Melder, pp. 33–34.

14. Quote from Cott, *Bonds of Womanhood,* p. 125; on Emma Willard, see Anne Firor Scott, *Making the Invisible Woman Visible* (Urbana: University of Illinois Press, 1984), pp. 64–88; see also Melder, *Beginnings of Sisterhood.*

15. Melder, *Beginnings of Sisterhood,* pp. 36–38, quote from p. 38; Barbara Leslie Epstein, *The Politics of Domesticity: Women, Evangelism and Temperance in Nineteenth Century America* (Middletown, Conn.: Wesleyan University Press, 1981), chap. 2, pp. 45–66; Rossi, ed., *The Feminist Papers,* pp. 54–58.

16. Quote from Mary Ryan, *Cradle of the Middle Class: The Family in Oneida, New York, 1790–1865* (New York: Cambridge University Press, 1981), p. 105.

17. Quote from Ryan, *Cradle of the Middle Class,* pp. 119–20; see also Carroll Smith-Rosenberg, "Beauty, the Beast and the Militant Woman: A Case Study in Sex Roles and Social Stress in Jacksonian America," *American Quarterly* 23 (October 1971): 490–508; Barbara J. Berg, *The Remembered Gate: Origins of American Feminism, the Woman and the City, 1800–1860* (New York: Oxford University Press, 1978).

18. Cott, *Bonds of Womanhood,* p. 154.

19. Child quoted in Melder, *Beginnings of Sisterhood,* p. 43; Mary P. Ryan, *Womanhood in America: From Colonial Times to the Present,* 2d ed. (New York: New Viewpoints, 1979), p. 107.

20. Nancy A. Hewitt, *Women's Activism and Social Change: Rochester, New York, 1822–1872* (Ithaca, N.Y.: Cornell University Press, 1984).

21. Quoted in ibid., p. 93. On Quakers see also Mary Maples Dunn, "Women of Light," in Carol Berkin and Mary Beth Norton, eds., *Women of America: A Documentary History* (Boston: Houghton-Mifflin, 1979), pp. 114–33, and Gerda Lerner, *The Grimké Sisters from South Carolina* (New York: Schocken, 1966), esp. pp. 60–61.

22. "The General Association of Massachusetts (Orthodox) to the Churches under their Care," 1837, in Rossi, ed., *The Feminist Papers,* p. 304.

23. Angelina Grimké, *An Appeal to the Women of the Nominally Free States,* 1st ed. (New York: W. S. Dorr, 1837), quoted in Lerner, *The Grimké Sisters,* p. 161; Sarah Grimké, *Letters on the Equality of the Sexes and the Condition of Women* (Boston, 1838), in Rossi, ed., *The Feminist Papers,* pp. 307–8.

24. See Eleanor Flexner, *Century of Struggle* (New York: Atheneum, 1971); Ellen Carol Dubois, *Feminism and Suffrage: The Emergence of an*

Independent Women's Movement in America, 1848–1860 (Ithaca, N.Y.: Cornell University Press, 1978); Rossi, ed., *The Feminist Papers,* pp. 239–426; Paul and Mari Jo Buhle, eds., *The Concise History of Woman Suffrage* (Urbana: University of Illinois Press, 1978), pp. 89–98.

25. See Buhle and Buhle, eds., *Concise History,* pp. 89–137, and Dubois, *Feminism and Suffrage.*

26. See Ruth Bordin, *Woman and Temperance: The Quest for Power and Liberty, 1873–1900* (Philadelphia: Temple University Press, 1980), p. 94; Mary Earhart, *Frances Willard: From Prayers to Politics* (Chicago: University of Chicago Press, 1944); Frances Willard, *Woman and Temperance: Or the Work and Workers of the Women's Christian Temperance Union,* 6th ed. (Evanston, Ill., 1897); Epstein, *The Politics of Domesticity,* pp. 89–114.

27. See accounts in Epstein, *The Politics of Domesticity,* pp. 95–100; and Bordin, *Woman and Temperance,* pp. 15–33.

28. Quoted in Epstein, *The Politics of Domesticity,* p. 96.

29. Quoted in ibid., p. 111.

30. Quoted in ibid., p. 100.

31. Bordin, *Woman and Temperance,* p. 98.

32. Mari Jo Buhle, *Women and American Socialism, 1870–1920* (Urbana: University of Illinois Press, 1981), p. 57; quotes from Estelle B. Freedman, *Their Sister's Keepers: Women's Prison Reform in America, 1830–1930* (Ann Arbor: University of Michigan Press, 1981), p. 89.

33. Epstein, *The Politics of Domesticity,* pp. 113–16.

34. Willard, *Woman and Temperance,* p. 471.

35. See Bordin, *Woman and Temperance,* Appendix, pp. 163–75, for a summary of studies of WCTU leadership and her own figures on their demographic composition. Unfortunately, she does not do a regional analysis.

36. Quotes from Buhle, *Women and American Socialism,* pp. 84, 89.

37. Ibid., pp. 108, 110–12.

38. Baker, "The Domestication of Politics," p. 632.

39. Quoted in Anne Firor Scott, *Making the Invisible Woman Visible,* p. 115.

40. Jane Addams, *Twenty Years at Hull House,* quoted in Mary P. Ryan, *Womanhood in America: From Colonial Times to the Present,* 2d ed. (New York: New Viewpoints, 1979), p. 136; Scott, *Making the Invisible Woman Visible,* p. 121.

41. Baker, "The Domestication of Politics," p. 637.

42. Quote from Buhle, *Women and American Socialism,* pp. 14–15; see also Judith E. Smith, "Our Own Kind: Family and Community Networks in Providence," *Radical History Review* 17 (Spring 1978): 99–120.

43. Nancy Schrom Dye, *As Equals and As Sisters: Feminism, Unionism, and the Women's Trade Union League of New York* (Columbia: University of Missouri Press, 1980); Robin Jacoby, "Feminism and Class Consciousness in the British and American Women's Trade Union Leagues, 1890–1925,"

in Berenice Carroll, ed., *Liberating Women's History: Theoretical and Critical Essays* (Urbana: University of Illinois Press, 1976); and "The Women's Trade Union League and American Feminism," in Milton Cantor and Bruce Laurie, eds., *Class, Sex and the Woman Worker* (Westport, Conn.: Greenwood Press, 1977); Colette Hyman, "Labor Organizing and Female Institution Building: The Chicago Women's Trade Union League, 1904–1924," in Ruth Milkman, ed., *Women in the Twentieth Century Labor Movement* (Boston: Routledge & Kegan Paul, 1985).

44. Baker, "The Domestication of Politics," p. 645.

45. Ibid., pp. 644–47.

46. Jacqueline Dowd Hall, *Revolt Against Chivalry: Jesse Daniel Ames and the Women's Campaign Against Lynching* (New York: Columbia University Press, 1979).

47. Peggy Dennis, *The Autobiography of an American Communist: A Personal View of Political Life* (Berkeley: Lawrence Hall, 1977); Vera Buch Weisbord, *A Radical Life* (Bloomington: Indiana University Press, 1977); other key female leaders in the "old left" included Elizabeth Gurley Flynn, Dorothy Healey, and Ella Reeve Bloor.

48. See Sara Evans, *Personal Politics: The Roots of Women's Liberation in the Civil Rights Movement and the New Left* (New York: Knopf, 1979), pp. 116–24.

49. Ibid., chap. 1.

50. Ibid.; Jo Freeman, *The Politics of Women's Liberation* (New York: Longman, 1975); Edith Hole and Ellen Levine, *Rebirth of Feminism* (New York: Quadrangle, 1971).

51. Irene Tinker, ed., *Women in Washington: Advocates for Public Policy* (Beverly Hills: Sage Publications, 1983); Sara Evans interview with Mildred Jeffrey, Detroit, Dec. 9, 1982.

52. See Esther Peterson, "The Kennedy Commission," and Catherine East, "Newer Commissions," in Tinker, ed., *Women in Washington,* pp. 21–34, 35–44.

53. See Betty Friedan, *It Changed My Life: Writings on the Women's Movement* (New York: Random House, 1976), pp. 75–86.

54. Richard Wrightman Fox and T. J. Jackson Lears, "Introduction," in Richard Wrightman Fox and T. J. Jackson Lears, eds., *The Culture of Consumption: Critical Essays in American History, 1880–1980* (New York: Pantheon Books, 1983), p. xii.

55. Evans, *Personal Politics,* chaps. 2–4; see also Mary Rothschild, *A Case of Black and White: Northern Volunteers and the Southern Freedom Summers, 1964–1965* (Westport, Conn.: Greenwood Press, 1982); Anne Moody, *Coming of Age in Mississippi* (New York: Dell, 1968); Sally Belfrage, *Freedom Summer* (New York: Viking, 1965); Elizabeth Sutherland, ed., *Letters from Mississippi* (New York: McGraw-Hill, 1965).

56. Evans, *Personal Politics,* chaps. 5–7; see also Wini Breines, *Community and Organization in the New Left: The Great Refusal* (New York: Praeger, 1982); James P. O'Brien, "The Development of a New Left in the

United States, 1960–1965" (Ph.D. dissertation, University of Wisconsin, 1971); Kirkpatrick Sale, *SDS* (New York: Vintage, 1973).

57. See Barrie Thorne, "Girls Who Say Yes to Guys Who Say No: Women in the Draft Resistance Movement," paper presented to the American Sociological Association, New Orleans, 1972.

58. For example, see Shulamith Firestone, *The Dialectic of Sex: The Case for Feminist Revolution* (New York: Morrow, 1970); Kate Millett, *Sexual Politics* (New York: Doubleday, 1970); Robin Morgan, *Sisterhood Is Powerful: An Anthology of Writings from the Women's Liberation Movement* (New York: Vintage, 1970). The large body of feminist theory published since the early 1970s is most accessible in the pages of the numerous journals established to encourage feminist theory and scholarship. These include *Signs, Feminist Studies, Quest, Frontiers, Chrysalis, Sinister Wisdom, Off Our Backs,* to name but a few. Socialist feminists have also frequently written for *Socialist Review.*

59. Del Martin and Phyllis Lyon, *Lesbian Woman* (New York: Bantam Books, 1972); see also articles in *The Furies;* Sidney Abbott and Barbara Love, *Sappho Was a Right-On Woman* (New York: Stein & Day, 1973; "The Lesbian Issue," *motive* 32 (1972). For a more recent discussion see Adrienne Rich, "Compulsory Heterosexuality and Lesbian Existence," *Signs* 5 (Summer 1980): 631–60.

60. Sally Martino Fisher, "Profile," *Social Policy* 11 (November/December 1980): 30. For other groups see Irene Tinker, *Women in Washington.*

61. Harry C. Boyte, *Community Is Possible* (New York: Harper, 1984), chap. 4; interview with Bertha Gilkey, St. Louis, August 1964.

62. See Tinker, *Women in Washington.*

63. L. A. Kauffman, "NOW for Something Completely Different," *Progressive,* March 1984, p. 32.

4: Class and Community

1. Thomas Dublin, *Women at Work: The Transformation of Work and Community in Lowell, Massachusetts, 1826–1860* (New York: Columbia University Press, 1981).

2. Description of changing meaning of "class" from Raymond Williams, *Keywords: A Vocabulary of Culture and Society* (New York: Oxford University Press, 1976), pp. 51–59.

3. Karl Marx and Friedrich Engels, "Communist Manifesto," in Lewis Feuer, ed., *Marx and Engels: Basic Writings on Politics and Philosophy* (Garden City, N.Y.: Doubleday, 1969), pp. 1–41; Karl Marx, *Eighteenth Brumaire of Louis Bonaparte* (New York: International Publishers, 1963), pp. 123–24; Friedrich Engels, *The Housing Question* (Moscow: Progress Publishers, 1970), p. 29.

4. Marx is quoted here from Lucio Colletti, *From Rousseau to Lenin: Studies in Ideology and Society* (New York: Monthly Review Press, 1972), pp. 86–88.

5. Engels, *Housing Question*, p. 29.

6. See, for instance, Sean Wilentz, *Chants Democratic: New York City and the Rise of the American Working Class, 1788–1850* (New York: Oxford University Press, 1984). See also chap. 1, n. 10.

7. Sean Wilentz, "Artisan Republican Festivals and the Rise of Class Conflict," in Michael H. Frisch and Daniel J. Walkowitz, eds., *Working-Class America: Essays on Labor, Community, and American Society* (Urbana: University of Illinois Press, 1983), pp. 37–77; quote from p. 61.

8. Charles Stephenson, "A Gathering of Strangers? Mobility, Social Structure, and Political Participation in the Formation of Nineteenth-Century American Workingclass Culture," in Milton Cantor, ed., *American Workingclass Culture: Explorations in American Labor and Social History* (Westport, Conn.: Greenwood Press, 1979), pp. 31–60.

9. Jonathan Prude, "The Social System of Early New England Textile Mills: A Case Study, 1812–40," in Frisch and Walkowitz, eds., *Working-Class America*, pp. 1–36.

10. John Kasson, *Civilizing the Machine: Technology and Republican Values in America* (New York: Penguin, 1977), p. 76.

11. *Voice of Industry*, Mar. 13, 1846, quoted in Thomas Dublin, "Women, Work, and Protest in the Early Lowell Mills: 'The Oppressing Hand of Avarice Would Enslave Us,' " in Milton Cantor and Bruce Laurie, eds., *Class, Sex, and the Woman Worker* (Westport, Conn.: Greenwood Press, 1977), p. 60.

12. Alan Dawley, *Class and Community: The Industrial Revolution in Lynn* (Cambridge, Mass.: Harvard University Press, 1976), chap. 1, pp. 11–41.

13. Ibid., pp. 56–63, quote from p. 56; *The Awl*, July 24, 1844, quoted in Dawley, p. 2.

14. Quoted in ibid., p. 82.

15. Alonzo Lewis, "Cordwainers' Song," 1860, quoted in Dawley, op. cit., pp. 82–83.

16. Ibid., p. 175–79, quote from p. 177.

17. John T. Cumbler, "Labor, Capital, and Community: The Struggle for Power" in Cantor, ed., *American Workingclass Culture*, p. 150.

18. For earlier views of the Knights of Labor, see Gerald N. Grob, *Workers and Utopia, a Study of Ideological Conflict in the American Labor Movement, 1865–1900* (Chicago: University of Chicago Press, 1961); for more recent views see Leon Fink, *Workingmen's Democracy: The Knights of Labor and American Politics* (Urbana: University of Illinois Press, 1982); quote from Dawley, *Class and Community*, p. 192.

19. Peter Jay Rachleff, "Black, White, and Gray: Working-Class Activism in Richmond, Virginia, 1865–1890" (Ph.D. dissertation, University of Pittsburgh, 1981), provides an exhaustive history of the Knights of Labor in Richmond, Virginia. See also Peter Rachleff, *Black Labor in the South: Richmond, Virginia, 1865–1890* (Philadelphia: Temple University Press, 1984).

20. Sara Evans, "Women at War: The Richmond Bread Riot, April 2, 1863" (paper in author's possession).

21. Rachleff, "Black, White, and Gray," p. 144.

22. Ibid., pp. 149, 334–436.

23. Ibid., pp. 577–648, quotes from pp. 633, 634.

24. Ibid., pp. 189–219; quote from Myra Lockett Avery, *Dixie After the War* (Boston: Houghton Mifflin, 1937), p. 264.

25. Rachleff, "Black, White, and Gray," pp. 218, 304–6.

26. For a fuller discussion of Knights of Labor ideology, see Fink, *Workingmen's Democracy.*

27. Rachleff, "Black, White, and Gray," pp. 783, 781–82.

28. Quote from ibid., p. 782.

29. Quote from ibid., p. 750.

30. Quote from ibid., pp. 894, 895; see also pp. 892–1068 and Fink, *Workingmen's Democracy.*

31. Ira Katznelson, *City Trenches: Urban Politics and the Patterning of Class in the United States* (Chicago: University of Chicago Press, 1981).

32. James Green, *The World of the Worker: Labor in Twentieth-Century America* (New York: Hill & Wang, 1980).

33. Ibid., p. 10; see Cumbler, "Labor, Capital, and Community," in Cantor, ed., *American Workingclass Culture,* pp. 149–66.

34. See Green, *World of the Worker,* pp. 11–19; David Brody, *Steelworkers in America: The Non-Union Era* (New York: Cambridge University Press, 1960); Jeremy Brecher, *Strike!* (San Francisco: Straight Arrow Books, 1972).

35. Green, *World of the Worker,* pp. 28–31.

36. Ladies' Waist Makers' Union, *Souvenir History of the Strike* (New York: Ladies' Waist Makers' Union, 1910), quoted in Meredith Tax, *The Rising of the Women: Feminist Solidarity and Class Conflict, 1880–1917* (New York: Monthly Review Press, 1980), p. 207.

37. Mary Heaton Vorse quoted in Green, *World of the Worker,* p. 163.

38. Ronald Schatz, *The Electrical Workers: A History of Labor at General Electric and Westinghouse* (Urbana: University of Illinois Press, 1983), quoted in Green, op. cit., p. 163; see also Green, chap. 5; David Brody, "The Emergence of Mass Production Unionism," in John Braeman, Robert H. Bremner, and Everett Walters, eds., *Change and Continuity in Twentieth-Century America* (Columbus: Ohio State University Press, 1964), pp. 221–62; Irving Howe and Lewis Coser, *The American Communist Party: A Critical History* (New York: Praeger, 1962); interview by Harry Boyte with Terry Pettus, Seattle, Mar. 14, 1968.

39. Stella Nowicki, "Back of the Yards," in Alice and Staughton Lynd, eds., *Rank and File: Personal Histories by Working Class Organizers* (Princeton: Princeton University Press, 1981), pp. 67–88.

40. David Fink, *The Radical Vision of Saul Alinsky* (Maryknoll, N.Y.: Orbis, 1983), p. 15; Saul D. Alinsky, *Rules for Radicals: A Pragmatic Primer for Realistic Radicals* (New York: Vintage, 1972), p. 67.

41. Fink, *Saul Alinsky*, p. 17.

42. Ibid., pp. 15–18.

43. Quote from John Bodnar, *Immigration and Industrialization: Ethnicity in an American Mill Town*, 1870–1940 (Pittsburgh: University of Pittsburgh Press, 1977), p. 112.

44. Ibid., pp. 150–51.

45. Joshua B. Freeman, "Catholics, Communists, and Republicans: Irish Workers and the Organization of the Transport Workers Union" in Frisch and Walkowitz, eds., *Working-Class America*, p. 265.

46. Ibid., p. 276.

47. Quotes from Studs Terkle, *Hard Times: An Oral History of the Depression* (New York: Pantheon, 1970), pp. 158, 161; Louis Adamic, *My America: 1928–1938* (New York: Harper & Brothers, 1938), quoted in Brecher, *Strike!*, pp. 182–83; see also Sidney Fine, *Sitdown: The General Motors Strike of 1936–37* (Ann Arbor: University of Michigan Press, 1969); Brecher, *Strike!*, pp. 186–203.

48. *With Babies and Banners* was produced by the Women's Labor History Film Project, Washington, D.C., and is distributed by New Day Films, Franklin Lakes, N.J.

49. Christopher Lawrence Tomlins, "The State and the Unions: Federal Labor Relations Policy and the Organized Labor Movement in America, 1935–55" (Ph.D. dissertation, The Johns Hopkins University, 1980).

50. Saul Alinsky quoted in Fink, *Saul Alinsky*, p. 66.

51. Chavez quoted in *Farm Labor Organizing, 1905–1967* (New York: National Advisory Committee on Farm Labor, 1967); see also Boyte, *Backyard Revolution*, pp. 50, 94.

52. Sara Evans interview with Day Piercy, Chicago, July 16, 1981, and June 16, 1983.

53. Ibid.; Sara Evans interview with Ellen Cassidy, Bryn Mawr, Pa., July 11, 1981.

54. Piercy interview; Sara Evans interviews with Darlene Stille, Chicago, July 15, 1981; Ann Ladke, Chicago, Apr. 18, 1983; Beata Welsh, Chicago, July 15, 1981; Heather Booth, Chicago, July 15, 1981. On the sit-in, see Chicago *Tribune*, Feb. 3, 4, 6, 9, 1977.

55. Sara Evans interview with Andrea Gunderson, Chicago, Apr. 17, 1983.

56. Sara Evans interviews with Olga Madar, Detroit, Dec. 10, 1982; Dorothy Haener, Detroit, Jan. 21, 1983; Addie Wyatt, Chicago, June 15, 1983; Joyce Miller, New York City, Feb. 7, 1983. CLUW Papers, ca. 1970–1975; Dorothy Haener Papers; UAW Women's Department Papers; Marjorie Stern Papers, 1967–1975, Wayne State University, Archives of Labor and Urban Affairs, Walter P. Reuther Library, Detroit. *New York Times*, Mar. 25, 1974, p. 27.

57. Joan M. Goodin, "Working Women: The Pros and Cons of Unions," in Tinker, ed., *Women in Washington*, pp. 141–42.

58. Sara Evans interview with Joyce Miller, New York City, Feb. 7, 1983.

5: The People Are Together

1. John Prebble, *Culloden* (New York: Atheneum, 1962), pp. 34–35. John Prebble, *The Highland Clearances* (London: Secker and Warburg, 1963), quote on ancient lands, pp. 21–22; observer of boats, p. 205; Ross, p. 290; Stowe's visit, p. 309.

2. Prebble, *Clearances*, p. 306.

3. Loch quoted in ibid., pp. 112–14.

4. Ross quoted, ibid., p. 309; *Sunny Memories* quoted, pp. 310–11.

5. Description of settlement patterns in Duane Meyer, *The Highland Scots of North Carolina: 1732–1776* (Chapel Hill: University of North Carolina Press, 1957); Moore quoted in Irwin Unger and David Reimers, *The Slavery Experience in the United States* (New York: Holt, 1970), p. 192; Hinton Helper, *Impending Crisis of the South* (New York: Burdick Brothers, 1857), pp. 310–11.

6. Viereck quoted in Walter K. Nugent, *The Tolerant Populists: Kansas Populism and Nativism* (Chicago: University of Chicago Press, 1963), p. 9; Hofstadter quoted in ibid., p. 20. Richard Reeves, "The Ideological Election," *New York Times Magazine*, Feb. 19, 1984, p. 28.

7. Whitman quoted in Richard J. Margolis, "The Two Faces of Populism," *The New Leader*, Apr. 18, 1983, p. 9; Paine quoted in Larzer Ziff, "Landlessness: Melville and the Democratic Hero," *democracy* 1 (July 1981): 136.

8. Simon Weil, *The Need for Roots* (Boston: Beacon, 1955), p. 43.

9. Martin Luther King, Jr., *Why We Can't Wait* (New York: Harper, 1963), p. 99.

10. Jefferson in Vernon Louis Parrington, *Main Currents in American Thought: An Interpretation of American Literature from the Beginnings to 1920* (New York: Harcourt, 1927), vol. 1., p. 347; on corporations, in Ted Howard et al., *Voices of the American Revolution* (New York: Bantam, 1975), p. 154.

11. Clement Eaton, *Mind of the Old South* (Baton Rouge: Louisiana State University Press, 1964), pp. 154, 158.

12. Alfred G. Smith, Jr., *Economic Readjustment of an Old Cotton State: South Carolina, 1820–60* (Columbia: University of South Carolina Press, 1958), pp. 22–25.

13. *Columbus Times* in Kenneth Stampp, *The Peculiar Institution: Slavery in the AnteBellum South* (New York: Vintage, 1956), pp. 425–26; *Wilmington Journal* in Charles Johnson, *Shadow of the Plantation* (Chicago: University of Chicago Press, 1934), p. 103.

14. Harris in C. Vann Woodward, *Tom Watson: Agrarian Rebel* (New York: Oxford University Press, 1963), p. 4; Watson in ibid., p. 6.

15. Memoirs of William F. Boyte, dictated in Charlotte, N.C., 1958 (in author's possession), pp. 5, 6, 19, 20.

16. Calhoun, Grady, and Jones in Woodward, *Watson*, pp. 117, 115, 125.

17. Economic background of mills described in detail in Harry C. Boyte, "The Textile Industry: Keel of Southern Industrialization," *Radical America* 6 (March–April 1972): 4–50; also Jacquelyn Hall, Robert Korstad, and Jim Leloudis, " 'Like a Family': Class, Community and Conflict in the Piedmont Textile Industry, 1880–1980," essay prepared for the Future of American Labor History Conference, Northern Illinois University, Dekalb, Ill., Oct. 10–12, 1984.

18. Albert Moore, *History of Alabama and Her People* (Chicago: American Historical Society, 1927), p. 636; figures on wages from C. Vann Woodward, *Origins of the New South* (Baton Rouge: Louisiana State University Press, 1951), pp. 225–26; Craven and *Christian Advocate* quoted from Liston Pope, *Millhands and Preachers: A Study of Gastonia* (New Haven: Yale University Press, 1942), p. 24; enthusiast was John Speake, quoted from Lois MacDonald, *Southern Mill Hills: A Study of Social and Economic Forces in Certain Mill Villages* (New York: Alex Hillman, 1928), p. 17; Glenn Gilman, *Human Relations in the Industrial Southeast: Study of the Textile Industry* (Chapel Hill: University of North Carolina Press, 1956), p. vi.

19. Hall et al., *Community,* pp. 15–16; W. J. Cash, *The Mind of the South* (New York: Knopf, 1941), p. 353.

20. Bruce Palmer, *Man Over Money: The Southern Populist Critique of American Capitalism* (Chapel Hill: University of North Carolina Press, 1980), p. xiv.

21. Woodward, *Watson,* p. 131; Lawrence Goodwyn, *Democratic Promise: The Populist Movement in America* (New York: Oxford University Press, 1976), p. 28.

22. Ibid., pp. 28, 119.

23. Ibid., pp. 42–43, 46–47.

24. Macune quoted in ibid., p. 90; national campaign, p. 91.

25. Ibid., p. 88.

26. Boyte Memoirs, p. 18; Alliance press and lecture circuit, Goodwyn, *Promise,* p. 175, also chap. 12.

27. Schoolroom quote from Goodwyn, op. cit., p. 3; on lecturers' experiences, see chap. 3; 1892 platform, p. 265.

28. Watson quoted in Woodward, *Watson,* p. 139; Goodwyn, *The Populist Moment: A Short History of the Agrarian Revolt in America* (New York: Oxford University Press, 1978), p. 34.

29. North Carolina allianceman in Palmer, *Man,* pp. 20–21; Watson in Woodward, *Watson,* p. 135.

30. Thompson in Palmer, *Man,* p. 25; Alabama editor in Frederick A. Bode, *Protestantism and the New South: North Carolina Baptists and Methodists in Political Crisis, 1894–1903* (Charlottesville: University of Virginia Press, 1975), pp. 39–41.

31. Lamb in Goodwyn, *Promise,* p. 66.

32. Mari Jo Buhle, *Women and American Socialism: 1870–1920* (Urbana: University of Illinois Press, 1981), pp. 82–83.

33. Julie Roy Jeffrey, "Women in the Southern Farmers Alliance: A Reconsideration of the Role and Status of Women in the Late 19th Century South," *Feminist Studies* 3 (Fall 1975): 75–77.

34. Moore, Brown in ibid., pp. 72–73; Buhle, *Women,* p. 84.

35. Watson in Woodward, *Watson,* p. 208; Nugent, *Tolerant Populists,* pp. 231, 233.

36. Watson in Woodward, *Watson,* p. 220.

37. Watson in Margolis, "Two Sides," p. 9; Alabama *Sentinel* and Corothers, Goodwyn, *Promise,* pp. 284–85.

38. Story of Mississippi Populists in Brad Pigott, "Populist Revival in Mississippi?," *Southern Changes,* January–February 1983, pp. 12–17; Arkansas and Texas, Goodwyn, *Promise,* p. 298.

39. Story of effort to save the Texas Exchange, Goodwyn, pp. 127–39, 170.

40. Ibid., p. 151.

41. Leon Fink, *Workingmen's Democracy: The Knights of Labor and American Politics* (Urbana: University of Illinois Press, 1983), p. 32. See also Buhle, op. cit.

42. Palmer, *Men,* pp. 35–37.

43. On Goodwyn's argument about the "shadow movement," see, for instance, *Promise,* pp. 207–10. Critics of Goodwyn have raised questions about his data on the cooperatives and populism in states like Nebraska, but detailed studies of the populist movement, such as Steven Hahn's fine work on Georgia populists, *The Roots of Southern Populism* (New Haven: Yale University Press, 1982), largely substantiate the argument about populist "movement culture." The most detailed criticism of Goodwyn is found in Stanley B. Parsons et al., "The Role of Cooperatives in the Development of the Movement Culture of Populism," *Journal of American History* 69 (1983): 866–85. See also Martin Ridge, "Populism Redux: John D. Hicks and *The Populist Revolt,*" *Reviews in American History* 13 (March 1985): 142–54. For a discussion of the strike by black sharecroppers, and other issues involved in populist historiography from a Marxist perspective, see James Green, "Populism, Socialism and the Promise of Democracy," *Radical History Review* 24 (Fall 1980): 7–40; and also Green, "Culture, Politics and Workers' Response to Industrialization in the U.S.," *Radical America* 16 (January–April 1982): 101–28; also Barry Goldberg, "A New Look at Labor History," *Social Policy,* Winter 1982, pp. 54–62.

44. Piggott, "Revival," pp. 12–13.

45. Bode, *Protestantism,* quotes pp. 123, 124, 125, 131, 138.

46. On the populist legacy drawn on by the Socialist Party, see James Green, *Grass-Roots Socialism: Radical Movements in the Southwest, 1895–1943* (Baton Rouge: Louisiana State University Press, 1978). Alan Brinkley, *Voices of Protest* (New York: Knopf, 1982).

47. Brinkley, op. cit., p. 166.

48. Hall et al., "Community," pp. 27–28.

6: Free Spaces

1. The story of Melville is from Larzer Ziff, "Landlessness: Melville and the Democratic Hero," *democracy* 1 (July 1981): 130–31.

2. Sheldon Wolin, "What Revolutionary Action Means Today," *democracy* 2 (Fall 1982): 18.

3. Baker Brownell, *The Human Community* (New York: Harper, 1953), pp. 135, 19–20.

4. Arthur Schlesinger, *The Vital Center* (Cambridge, Mass.: Houghton Mifflin, 1949), pp. 4, 51; Marshall Berman, *All That Is Solid Melts into Air: The Experience of Modernity* (New York: Simon & Schuster, 1982), p. 48.

5. Robert A. Nisbet, "The Total Community," in Marvin E. Olsen, ed., *Power in Societies* (New York: Macmillan, 1970), p. 423; Peter Berger, *Facing Up to Modernity: Excursions in Society, Politics and Religion* (New York: Basic, 1977), p. 134.

6. Berger, op. cit., p. 135.

7. Douglas Kellner, "Ideology, Marxism and Advanced Capitalism," *Socialist Review* 42 (1978): 53; John Rawls, *A Theory of Justice* (New York: Oxford University Press, 1972), p. 13.

8. Craig Calhoun, "The Radicalism of Tradition: Community Strength or Venerable Disguise and Borrowed Language?," *The American Journal of Sociology* 88 (March 1983): 898.

9. Quoted in Sara M. Evans, *Personal Politics: The Roots of Women's Liberation in the Civil Rights Movement and the New Left* (New York: Knopf, 1978), p. 125.

10. Lewis Mumford, *The Condition of Man* (New York: Harcourt, 1951), p. 282.

11. Gerda Lerner, *The Majority Finds Its Past: Placing Women in History* (New York: Oxford University Press, 1979), p. xiv.

12. Gilkey story taken from Harry C. Boyte, *Community Is Possible: Repairing America's Roots* (New York: Harper, 1984), pp. 95–113.

13. Sara Evans interviews with leaders and participants in National Congress of Neighborhood Women: Marie Bueno, Brooklyn, N.Y., Apr. 4, 1983; Jan Peterson, Brooklyn, N.Y., Apr. 19, 1983, Jan Kowalsky, Brooklyn, N.Y., Apr. 20, 1983; Alice Quinn, Brooklyn, N.Y., Apr. 20, 1983; Sally Martino Fisher, Brooklyn, N.Y., Apr. 21, 1983; Francine Moccio, Brooklyn, N.Y., Apr. 21, 1983.

14. Harry C. Boyte interview with Ernesto Cortes, San Antonio, Texas, July 3, 1983.

15. COPS impact described in Boyte, *Community,* chap. 5.

16. SFOP described in ibid., chap. 6.

17. Harry C. Boyte interview with Robert Hudak, Des Plaines, Ill., Apr. 27, 1985.

INDEX